YOURS ALWAYS

A Holocaust Love Story

by

Kitty Zilversmit

CDL PRESS
BETHESDA, MARYLAND

Library of Congress Cataloging-in-Publication Data
Zilversmit, Kitty, 1919-
      Yours always : a Holocaust love story / by Kitty Zilversmit.
            p.   cm. — (Occasional publications of the Department of
      Near Eastern Studies and the Program of Jewish Studies, Cornell
      University ; v. 2)
            Includes index.
            ISBN 1-883053-21-8
            1. Zilversmit, Kitty, 1919-.   2. Jews—Persecutions—Netherlands.
      3. Holocaust, Jewish (1939-1945)—Netherlands—Personal narratives.
      4. Zilversmit, Kitty, 1919- —Correspondence.   5.   Zilversmit,
      Donald—Correspondence.   I. Title.   II. Series.
      DS135.N6Z55   1995
      940.53' 18' 09492—dc20   95-46767
                                                                CIP

The male and female figures on the cover have been reproduced with the kind
permission of the artist, Avrum Ashery, from his work *Shalom Bayit*.

ISBN 1-883053-21-8

OCCASIONAL PUBLICATIONS OF THE

DEPARTMENT OF NEAR EASTERN STUDIES

AND THE

PROGRAM OF JEWISH STUDIES

CORNELL UNIVERSITY

Edited by

Ross Brann
and
David I. Owen

Editorial Committee

Ross Brann,
David I. Owen,
David S. Powers,
Gary A. Rendsburg

In loving memory
זכרו לברכה
of those of my immediate family who died in Sobibor

my father
Leopold Lehman Fonteyn,
b. 1876, deported to Sobibor, June 6, 1943

my mother
Gracia Fonteyn-Jessurun Lobo,
b. 1885, deported to Sobibor, June 6, 1943

my sister
Susan,
b. 1917, deported to Sobibor, date unknown

my brothers
Jack Fonteyn,
b. 1924, deported to Sobibor, date unknown
Eduard Fonteyn,
b. 1928, deported to Sobibor, June 6, 1943

and to my brother
Leo Fonteyn,
b. 1922, who survived the horrors of Buchenwald

★★★

and to the memory of
Reverend Ader
and
Reverend and Mrs. Boon
who were instrumental in providing me a sanctuary

EDITOR'S PREFACE

The curriculum of Cornell's Program of Jewish Studies incorporates a wide variety of subjects from the origins of Israel in the ancient Near East, through Biblical, post-Biblical and Medieval, modern Middle East studies to Holocaust and eastern European Jewish civilization. The affiliated faculty represent this diversity of interest and expertise. The Occasional Publication series reflects this diversity and the current volume, a memoir of the Sho'ah (Holocaust) in the Netherlands, represents the first publication in the area of Holocaust Studies.

Kitty Zilversmit, the author of this memoir, is a member of the Cornell community, her husband Don being a professor emeritus of nutritional sciences and biochemistry. Her moving account is symbolic of the unique phenomenon we are witnessing at the present time as the surviving generation of the Sho'ah passes from our midst and attempts to record the unimaginable events that happened a half century ago. Kitty's story, like so many others of her generation, appears late in her life after decades of suppression. We can only begin to appreciate the anguish that the retelling of her experiences created for herself, her husband and her children. Yet, in that retelling, she has not only freed herself of a great burden but has also provided us with the eternal truth that only the eye witness can provide. She adds another perspective—another story—to the few that have been told and the many that never will. She speaks out not only for herself and her lost family but for all those who did nor survive or are otherwise unable to speak for themselves. We are proud to be able to include this testimony in our series as part of the ongoing process of educating our students to the reality of the Sho'ah at a time when forces are attempting the opposite.

We are grateful to a number of people for making the publication of this volume possible—the Drukier Family Fund for Holocaust and Jewish Studies endowed by Ira, Gale, and Jennifer Drukier, for enabling us to continue to support study and research on the Sho'ah and encourage its teaching in our curriculum; Robert Milch for his efficient copy editing; and finally Kitty herself who overcame her fears and enthusiastically joined us in the production of this remarkable work.

David I. Owen
Director, Program of Jewish Studies
June 20, 1995
Ithaca, New York

PROLOGUE

The Liberation—May 5, 1945

It has finally happened! The miracle I've been dreaming about for so many years is really here! Holland—liberated by the Allies! As I watch from my bedroom window, the streets magically fill with people. Flags appear everywhere. Bells ringing—horns blowing—people dancing in the street. We have all suffered so much hardship over the last five years, and now, this long-hoped-for happiness is almost unbearable. We are free. Even on the most weary faces, joy shows through for the first time in years. Where has all this energy been hidden? With so many years of extreme pressure suddenly lifted, the street scene, the radio broadcasts, the news reports—all our responses are simply incredible.

At Vredeveld, the nursing home where I have been in hiding for the past year and a half, the voice of Mr. Boon, the director, is heard over the loudspeaker. He asks that all residents assemble in the main lounge because he has an important announcement to make. As soon as everyone is comfortable, he addresses the group in his usual quiet voice. He begins with congratulations to us on the liberation of our country. Then he makes a special announcement which he says he has been waiting a long time to make.

"In our midst," he begins, "and all through the war, four Jewish girls and four elderly Jewish ladies have been hiding at Vredeveld. And now I am finally able to tell you, and to thank you, because you have all helped to save the lives of these people."

The director's wife, Mrs. Boon, is making a similar announcement to the staff in their living quarters. Now we are introduced by our real names. For the first time in a year and a half people will be calling me by my real name, Kitty Fonteyn!

Mrs. Boon is serving refreshments. Now all the girls who work at Vredeveld are outside dancing in the street. We all join hands in a big circle and dance in celebration of our new freedom.

I too am dancing with my friends and with those I worked with during my underground time at Vredeveld, but I suddenly feel an overwhelming emptiness in the pit of my stomach. Why am I dancing? For me the war is hardly over. Where is my family? My mother and father, my three brothers and my sister? And where is my fiancé, Don? Will I ever be able to find them, even if they have survived the war? I abruptly realize that my own personal war is only just beginning.

I leave the circle of dancing girls, run up to my room, sit on my bed, and cry. I must try to organize my thoughts. Where should I begin? How can I get in touch with the proper authorities? Who can help me locate my family? They must be somewhere, they could not have disappeared from the face of the earth. Could they possibly be in Russia, and not yet have had enough time to contact the right official?

Sitting on my bed, trying to put the pieces together, I am unable to think straight. Will Don come back for me and still want to marry me after so many years? Are we still the same people we were when we said goodbye six years ago, what with all we have each been through?

If only we could pick up the pieces exactly where they were before the war. If only life were still simple and wonderful, as it was back then, when my most difficult problem was my father's strictness or trying to catch Don's eye at the synagogue. All I can do now is wait and see what the future holds, as I lie on my bed, crying, with the painful knowledge that what used to be reality for me now feels like someone else's life in another world . . .

ACKNOWLEDGMENTS

I owe many thanks to my family and friends who supported me while I was writing this book. First of all, to my husband Don, who bailed me out numerous times, even over the phone, when I was stuck on the word processor.

To my daughters—Lee Ann, who changed my handwritten pages into a typed manuscript; the difference was phenomenal; to Susan, who edited painstakingly and was able to make me talk about my experiences all during my writing; to Jo, who asked many questions and who wrote a letter which is part of this book; and to my son-in-law, Bob Karrow, who offered many suggestions and spent many hours constructing the index. I love you all and will never forget your encouragement throughout.

To Le Moyne Farrell who taught me about plot line and structure; to Susan Bryson, for her guidance throughout this process; to Professor Barton Friedman and his wife Sheila, who spent many hours editing my manuscript and improving the style of the text. I thank you very much for your patience and criticism.

To Debby Carmichael, Dorothy Carreiro, Ingrid Covary, Martha Mapes, Ann Pendergrass, Allison Shaw, Bea Stiers and Lynn Wilkes, I am most grateful for all your help.

And last, but not least, to David I. Owen, Professor of Ancient Near Eastern History and Archaeology and Director of the Program of Jewish Studies at Cornell, who expedited the final editing and printing of this book, and to Dr. Mark E. Cohen of CDL Press who took such care in the layout and printing.

TABLE OF CONTENTS

LIST OF FIGURES

THE NETHERLANDS

NORTH SEA

WADDENZEE

TEXEL

AFSLUITDIJK

Delfzijl

GRONINGEN
Groningen

Leeuwarden

FRIESLAND

Westerbork

DRENTE

Den Helder

WIERINGERMEER

Meppel

Schoorl
Alkmaar

NOORD-

Zwolle

OVERIJSEL

Ommen
Almelo

Beverwijk
Ijmuiden

HOLLAND
Zaandam

Hengelo

Haarlem
Amsterdam
Hilversum

Putten
Barneveld

Deventer

Enschede

Leiden
Wassenaar
Scheveningen

Soest
Apeldoorn
Amersfoort

Zutphen

Utrecht

UTRECHT

GELDERLAND

's'Gravenhage

Wageningen

Winterswijk

Delft **ZUID-**
Rotterdam

LEK R.

Arnhem

Schoonhoven

HOLLAND Dordrecht

Nijmegen

MEUSE R.

Heusden

RHINE R.

's'Hertogenbosch

Moerdijk
Vught
Haren
St. Michielsgestel

Walcheren
Middelburg
Vlissingen

ZEELAND

Roosendaal Breda
Bergen op Zoom
Tilburg

**NOORD-
BRABANT**

LIMBURG

Venlo

Eindhoven

Roermond

Maastricht

BELGIUM

GERMANY

MILES

0 5 10   20   30   40   50

From: Werner Warmbrunn, *The Dutch under German Occupation 1940-1945*
(Stanford University Press, 1963)

xv

I

Early Spring, 1937

Going to the Orthodox synagogue on Saturday mornings was one of my regular weekly activities. It would not be accurate to say that I attended solely for the services, however, because that was not the case. It was also a way to meet friends. My mother let me use her seat in the women's gallery upstairs, since she went to the synagogue only on the High Holidays.

Mother's seat, the best in the house, was on the left side of the synagogue. We were separated from the men by diagonal wooden latticework, but were by no means isolated. Although women could not actively participate in the services, we had an excellent view of the downstairs, where the services were conducted. But there was something downstairs I was more interested in than the service.

I knew I was supposed to attend to my prayer book, but my eyes often wandered to a seat downstairs, almost straight across from me. I didn't know who he was, but I had seen him walking along the neighborhood streets a couple of times. I had been struck by his resolute walk, his dark wavy hair and his handsome serious face. Watching in the synagogue, I had also noticed that his eyes were not always focused on his prayer book during the services and would wander up to the women's gallery, where our eyes would meet. When this happened I would blush deeply, but luckily he couldn't see that from such a distance. After the service ended and the men went outside, I could get a closer look at him and we would smile shyly at one another. I didn't know anything about him; the only thing I could be sure of was that he was Jewish. He was always immaculately dressed and one morning wore a navy blue suit, pale blue shirt, and red tie. I thought he looked sharp.

On a Saturday afternoon in April I was housebound with a sprained ankle, which was to keep me inside for several days. Although I was disappointed at first, after thinking it over I didn't really mind too much, since my family had settled me in my favorite chair, set up a little table next to me with my books, and waited on me while I kept my feet elevated. It was a typical Dutch day, rainy and dark. I had a good book to read, a Dutch translation of *Gone with the Wind* by Margaret Mitchell. I felt tranquil and warm inside on this gloomy day. There was something else I felt good about. Not long before I had persuaded my mother to let me sew a dress for myself. I had been sewing doll's clothes for years and logically pointed out to her that there would be no difference except for the dimensions. I knew a basic pattern I could use, and I had all the equipment I needed.

When I first told my mother of my plan, she didn't believe I would be able to do it, but had agreed to let me try. She went to a nearby fabric store and bought a pretty piece of cotton, with a white background and a small print pattern. She had given it to me a couple of weeks before and had said: "I bought you a piece of fabric. See what you can do with it." I had replied, "Mother, it's wonderful, but what if it doesn't work out?" As a matter of fact, she had said that she wouldn't mind—that it would be good practice for me, and if the fabric were ruined, not much would be lost, because she hadn't spent much on it.

With such encouragement, so characteristic of my mother, how could I have gone wrong? I had jumped into my project, using a T-shirt as a pattern for cutting out the fabric, and had improvised by adding pieces of tissue paper here and there to fill in the gaps. I had decided to decorate the neckline and sleeves with gathered white lace. Now my homemade dress was finished. I felt glamorous wearing it even though an experienced eye would have spotted immediately that the garment was not from the finest boutique. I felt incredibly proud of my dress and my accomplishment.

As a matter of fact I was wearing the dress the Saturday afternoon I was confined to the house with a sprained ankle, not that we were expecting any company. It was the weekend of the yearly cancer drive, when volunteers sold buttons to raise money for cancer research. As a courtesy there was always a solicitation held in advance, so that religious Jews, forbidden to carry money on the Sabbath, could purchase their orange buttons and pin them to their coats before the Sabbath. My mother had bought seven cancer buttons the day before, one for each member of the family, and she had placed my button on the table next to me.

The front doorbell rang and one of my younger brothers opened the door. In walked Leni Swelheim, my girlfriend, Joe Wynberg, our cantor-to-be, and, to my surprise, the young man with the serious face, who was introduced as Donald Zilversmit. I couldn't believe my eyes at the sight of him entering our house. Why was he here? Had he come to see me? Although I was delighted to see him, I wondered whether Leni had talked him into accompanying them? Now, at least, I knew his name, Donald Zilversmit; it sounded nice, I thought. For the time being I had to be satisfied that he was here; I would find out the details later.

They said hello, "Shabbat Shalom," and apologized for dropping in on us uninvited. Leni said they had been passing by and she had wanted to see how I was getting along. They promised to stay for only a minute and then go on their way again. Everybody was always welcome in our house. While pouring tea and offering some of her homemade butter cake, mother convinced them to stay and visit for awhile. No one could have refused.

The conversation was lively, and among other things Joe Wynberg told us about how he had come to Utrecht some weeks ago to audition for a position as a cantor. He told us about his good fortune to have been offered the position. My father, who was on the board of directors of the synagogue, had told us the story before, but it was interesting to listen to this energetic young man and relate it from his perspective. When my friends were ready to leave, they apologized for staying so long. Joe Wynberg mentioned how pretty I looked, and I felt proud to tell him that I had made the dress myself. I was seventeen at the time.

Don Zilversmit, the serious young man, was quiet that day. It was his first visit to our home, but I sensed that it would not be his last. I felt certain that something had happened between us that afternoon. Before leaving, Joe Wynberg mentioned that he had been stopped several times by cancer-drive solicitors. It made him feel bad that he couldn't buy an orange button because it was Shabbat. I said: "Why don't you take my button. I assure you, I won't be going anywhere today."

Leni later told me that after they left my house, Don asked Joe to exchange Kitty's button for his.

I don't remember how long my ankle kept me from going out, but Don wasted no time in returning. The next weekend he came to the house to ask how the ankle was healing. Although it was raining, I thought that I could chance a short walk with him. However, we walked for a long time, and it was amazing how well my ankle felt!

It was wonderful to be with him. We had so much to talk about and so much in common. We saw one another the next Shabbat afternoon at Akiva, the Zionist youth organization. Its meetings were educational, with time for socializing and refreshments toward the end. The group sang Israeli songs and, as usual, I was asked to sing the solo to "Eliyahu," a beautifully sensitive song in A-minor, whose haunting melody still lingers in my mind.

When Don walked me home that night after the meeting, he confessed his surprise that not only did I sing, but that the quality of my voice was so fine and pure, a lyric soprano. I was flattered.

Until then I hadn't even known whether Don liked music. He particularly liked Jewish liturgical music, he told me. He went to Rotterdam frequently to spend weekends with his aunt and uncle,

Sara and Maurice Zilversmit, so that he could attend synagogue with them on Shabbat morning and hear Cantor Rokach, who had a magnificent baritone voice.

As the weeks passed and our walks became more and more frequent, rain or shine, we learned a lot about one another.

2

Falling in Love

My birthday was in May, and my mother planned a small party for me. In Holland, birthdays are cause for celebration regardless of age. Of course, I invited Don, my girlfriend Leni, and her boyfriend, Joe. My sister Sue (who was two years older than I) invited her girlfriend Riet Danner, and my three brothers each invited a friend. It was going to be a full house, but that was part of the fun. Even though Don was not really a shy person, by evening he still wasn't quite able to muster up the courage to give me my present. Instead, he asked Leni to give it to me. He had bought a reproduction of "The Bridge" by Vincent van Gogh. He already knew that Vincent was my favorite painter. Needless to say, I was flattered.

I played a lot of music on the piano that night. Don was standing at my right side and didn't want me to stop. I also accompanied Joe Wynberg in two beautiful arias, one from Donizetti's "Elisir d'amore" and the other from "Les Pêcheurs de Perles" by Bizet. I didn't have the sheet music but had heard both arias many times; I transposed them to match his velvety tenor voice and accompanied him without any trouble. It was an intense pleasure to accompany Joe, his voice was beautiful and sensitive. The ensemble sounded as though we had played together for years. For my brothers Leo, Jack, and Eddy, the real party would not begin until later, when refreshments were served. They went into the yard to play with their friends while my sister and I celebrated my birthday with my friends inside. Mother had outdone herself once again. She could produce delicious desserts without apparent work, and this birthday celebration was no exception. She set the table with a bouquet of flowers as a centerpiece. Soon it was time to serve refreshments. As always, mother's specialties were delicious, and everyone enjoyed and appreciated them.

It was getting late. Joe and Leni thanked me for the music and the lovely party. Soon Susan's friend Riet and the boys' friends also left.

Don stopped briefly in the hall while putting on his jacket and said: "I'm going to have a very busy day tomorrow, but I know I'll want to get away from the books for a while after dinner. Would you take a little walk with me around 7:30 or so?"

"I'd like that very much. I'm looking forward to it."

"I enjoyed the evening immensely," Don added. He thanked me, holding my hand briefly before he left. It had been a wonderful evening, and many thoughts of my party and my new friend Don lingered on long after I lay down to go to sleep. Sleep didn't come quickly that night.

★ ★ ★

Don and I continued to see a lot of each other. I really loved to be with my new friend. Getting to know Don and spending all that time with him was special and appealing. His honesty and seriousness quickly showed me that I could always count on him to be truthful and reliable. He was sensible and bright, but above all he had a wonderful sense of humor and we laughed a lot. One day, feeling especially brave during one of our customary walks, I confessed to Don that I was experiencing significant trouble sleeping at night. Not only was that very unusual for me, I explained, but I would often lie awake all night and didn't really seem to need any sleep. Also strange was the fact that I had completely lost my appetite, an equally unusual phenomenon for me.

Don listened with interest to my story because, odd as it sounded, he was experiencing the same symptoms. Don conjectured that these symptoms must signify something. He thought

[7]

they meant he had fallen in love with me and wondered whether the same thing could be happening to me. Being inexperienced in such matters, I couldn't tell him. I really didn't know and honestly was not able to answer his question. I told him I had experienced many puppy-loves, but somehow felt that this was different.

Suddenly Don couldn't stand it anymore. He put his arms around me and said: "Please tell me how you feel about me, I can't take this uncertainty any longer." He told me he was going to Switzerland on a vacation with his parents in a few days and didn't know if he could stand being away from me for four weeks. I knew I had to say something so instinctively I replied: "Don't be so devastated that you are going away. You'll have plenty of time to think about me, and I'll certainly be able to tell you whether I missed you when you return. Maybe this will be a good test for us."

Of course, Don agreed that my reply sounded logical and he thought he could live with it. "I should go away from you and all our questions will sort themselves out."

After he left me that night, I didn't see him again until his return from Switzerland. Well, I missed him more than I could have imagined possible. I must have lost ten pounds, and I was already so skinny to begin with. Here I was shedding all those pounds without even trying! Finally Don returned from vacation, healthy and tanned, and when I looked at him I knew I wanted to be with him from that time forward.

I told mother and father that Don and I had become very close and that we had fallen in love with each other. I can still see my father's face when he said: "And what do you think you know about love when you're barely eighteen years old and have hardly lived? You're still a child!" I was dumbfounded and couldn't think of a reply.

Father wanted to have a talk with Don, because, according to him, our relationship was just ridiculous. I tried to show respect for father's opinion, but privately I thought he was being obnoxious and unreasonable. Don assured me that he was not afraid to talk to my father and he set a date for the event. He would officially ask for my hand in marriage; that was the thing to do. I don't remember how many days passed till Don came to the house, but the memory of that evening will always remain with me. The doorbell rang and there he was. I led him into the living room and then went to fetch my father. When we returned to the living room, father looked at me and said: "Would you please excuse us now."

After approximately fifteen minutes, Don came out. I asked him whether he could stay for awhile and have a cup of tea with us, but he said he had to leave immediately. I got his jacket for him, and when we approached the front door, Don said: "I must talk with you as soon as you can get away from here." I promised him I would.

Don told me later that my father had started the discussion by saying: "Well, young man, how do you plan to make a living to support my daughter? It will be more than six years before you get your Ph.D. By the time you're through with your studies, you may have become tired of my daughter and have found someone else. She'll have lost all those years waiting for you to finish your degree. In all good conscience I am afraid I will have to forbid you to see my daughter again."

Don countered that this demand was unreasonable and he would continue to see me, regardless. My father answered: "If that's the way you feel, I will make it extremely difficult for you to see her. I myself will accompany her to and from activities and meetings at night or wherever else she must go, and if I can't do it myself, I'll send a cab for her."

After Don left the house that night, my father sat down with me. Now it was my turn. At the time, I didn't have a clue as to what the content of father's discussion with Don had been. I had only noticed that Don was in a tremendous hurry to get out of the house. Father started by saying that I would not be allowed to see Don anymore, upon which I promptly responded: "Father, that's impossible. I will continue to see him."

Kitty and Don, Spring 1937

After Don and I had a chance to compare notes, I learned that father had told me the same thing he had told Don—that if he couldn't personally escort me to keep Don away, he would send a taxi for me. Despite my father's warnings, I didn't feel as upset as one might think, and I remember feeling that I simply didn't want to talk about it anymore. After all, what could I have said to contradict my father? Father kept his promise for a few weeks, but must finally have gotten tired of the silly routine he had imposed on us. Meanwhile, little did he know how much laughter he caused when my sister Sue and I were at the Club.

The Club was a Jewish organization Sue and I belonged to. Most of the members were in their teens, some a little older. There were weekly meetings, with an occasional lecture, but in general the meetings were social. Often, when the hired pianist didn't show up, I was asked to play in his place. I always enjoyed playing the piano, and although the "jazz" I played sometimes sounded more like Chopin, the members seemed delighted with it. Even more important, the dancing could continue now that they had found someone to play.

Sue and I were regular participants at the fun gatherings that took place at the Club. We were among the few members who had to comply with a strict curfew. For the Fonteyn girls, Sue and Kitty, the deadline was 11:00 p.m., not really an unreasonable hour for fifty years ago. But now that my father intended to keep Don and me apart—well, that was a different matter indeed. Father walked us to the meetings on several occasions, but for our curfew he ordered a cab.

One evening in particular I will never forget. Everyone was on the dance floor having a grand time when the door opened and the custodian came in. He motioned to signify that he had a message to convey. Everyone stopped dancing just long enough for him to say: "There's a cab here for the Fonteyn girls." This was the first time a cab had ever been sent for us, and nobody had any idea why it was happening now. The same thing occurred the following week, and this time, when the custodian walked in at 11:00 p.m. sharp, the dancing stopped abruptly, and, as though they had all rehearsed it, everyone said in unison: "Time for the Fonteyn girls to go home!"

Don and I continued to see each other regularly. Once we accidentally met my father on the street as Don was walking me home.

I felt no guilt that evening as I sat across from father at the dinner table, and from then on father began to relax the discipline considerably. Slowly Don was accepted into our family, and father and he eventually became good friends. From then on Don would come home with us after services every Friday evening and have Shabbat dinner with the family. On Shabbat morning, he would invariably have lunch with us, and we would spend most of the weekend together.

★ ★ ★

It was an idyllic time for us, but just across the border the news was ominous. Ever since Hitler had become Reich Chancellor in 1933, the situation for the Jews of Germany had been deteriorating. Between 1933 and 1938 they had been systematically denied their civil rights through laws designed to exclude them from mainstream German life. After 1934, Jewish doctors and dentists could no longer treat Gentile patients. Jewish teachers could not teach in public schools, and lawyers had to give up their practices, except for Jewish clients. Jewish newspapers were shut down. Jews who eventually managed to get out of Germany, sometimes with great difficulty, had to leave all their possessions behind and could take only the clothes on their backs and the equivalent of ten dollars in their pockets. Those who remained in Germany were declared second-class citizens.

In March 1938, the German army annexed Austria. After the *Anschluss*, the Jews of Austria lost their civil rights. The Nazis harassed and humiliated them. Jewish homes were looted and seized, and Jews were arrested. It was in Austria that the deportations to labor camps began. In Austria alone, more than forty synagogues were destroyed.

★ ★ ★

In the summer of 1938, as yet untouched by the events in Germany and Austria, Don and I made plans to take a brief vacation together. We came up with a novel idea. We decided to go to Scheveningen, a beach resort on the west coast of the Netherlands, close to The Hague. I would stay at the pension where my parents always stayed, and Don would stay with his aunt and uncle, Sara and Maurice Zilversmit, who were to be in Scheveningen for the summer. Nobody could possibly have any objections, I thought. I told mother in advance about our plan and she didn't object. I don't know, however, whether she ever told father.

Don and I took the train to The Hague and then a tram to Scheveningen. We took long walks on the beach along the ocean, right at the water's edge. We found topics for conversation, from literature to politics, the future of our Jewish people, and, of course, sex. It was exciting to both of us that for the first time in our lives we could actually discuss this with a member of the opposite sex. It gave us a sense of freedom neither of us had ever known before. We felt good about it. It seemed we could talk about anything.

We swam in the ocean and played in the waves, we ran up and down the many steps leading to the concert hall, the Kurhaus, we walked along the Boulevard holding hands; everything was exciting. One day, on the way to the Kurhaus, Don proudly showed me two tickets he had gotten the day before. Arthur Rubinstein was going to perform Tchaikovsky's piano concerto with the Amsterdam Concertgebouw Orchestra. He knew I couldn't possibly object. I had never heard Rubenstein perform on stage.

During the concert, as is often the case even today, I was moved to tears. I was incredibly grateful for the generous hankies Don carried in his pocket, because the tears kept coming. It became a standard joke in the family: "If Kitty didn't cry during a concert, she didn't have a good time." Afterwards I asked Don whether he had enjoyed the concert as much as I did. He said he had enjoyed it very much: Tchaikovsky was his favorite composer, but he had done something besides listening. He explained that he had been intrigued by the gorgeous Venetian crystal chandelier in the concert hall. By using some clever calculations he had figured out how many light bulbs there were on the other side of the chandelier! There must have been thousands of bulbs on it, and I was in awe of Don's ingenuity.

But soon our vacation drew to an end. We concluded our last evening with an Indonesian rice table, always one of the main attractions in Scheveningen. People come from all over the world to this wonderful restaurant to taste its more than fifty dishes. Our week together in Scheveningen had been a memorable vacation, indeed, that we would not easily forget. We had shared a wonderful time and became just that much closer.

★ ★ ★

By the fall of 1938, however, Jews everywhere could not help but be aware of how the world was changing. On the evening of November 9, 1938, and into the early hours of the next day, Nazi storm troopers in Germany attacked and burned two hundred synagogues, destroying seventy-five. Torah scrolls, prayer books, and prayer shawls were thrown in the streets and trampled upon. The windows of Jewish shops were broken. Jewish businesses were looted and destroyed, as were many Jewish homes and schools.

That night came to be called Kristallnacht, the night of shattered glass. It was clearly a prelude to the Holocaust; on that night alone, 30,000 Jews were sent to Dachau, Buchenwald, and Sachsenhausen. It was a night of horror for Jews throughout Germany. That night the Germans lost all pretense of civility. The world was shocked, but in the end did little to help; few countries increased their quotas to absorb more Jewish immigrants.

During these years, many refugees from Germany had crossed the border into Holland and tried to make a living for themselves and their families. Some of them peddled goods from house to house. They built up a clientele, visiting Jewish families to sell their wares. My mother was a regular customer of several of these refugees. They always had lunch at our house. I remember vividly that when we came home from school one noon, Mr. Levine was already sitting down eating his lunch. I can still hear my mother saying, "Poor people; let them have at least a good meal." I am sure mother fed many more.

3

Don

Lisa Zilversmit, my mother-in-law, treated me like a daughter and told me wonderful stories about Don. He had been born in 1919 in Hengelo, a small, quiet town in the eastern part of the Netherlands, near the German border. Lisa's first child, he was delivered at home by Dr. Frank, the family doctor. Forceps were needed, and in the process Lisa was badly torn. With no anesthesia given, the memories of the excruciating pain must have remained vivid for her for years to come. Herman Zilversmit, the anxious new father, pacing the floor downstairs, was called in to see his wife and newborn son. Dr. Frank was a friend of the family, and once he had his first look at Don he exclaimed: "I hate to tell you, but he is not a good-looking baby. He is covered with hair and his head comes to a point." He had not meant to be unkind, but the Dutch are outspoken by nature and not always diplomatic. The new mother was visibly hurt by his rude remarks. She thought her baby was beautiful, like most mothers when they see their baby for the first time and marvel at the wonder of childbirth.

When Don was one and a half years old, his brother Bert was born. Now Lisa had two little ones in diapers, and life would have been very hectic had she not had good help. According to Lisa, Don loved the baby very much. Whenever he cried, Don sat under his little bed and sang, to soothe him. Lisa later admitted that when the boys were little, she often felt incompetent to take care of them—as if she had two left hands, she used to say. Therefore, Don and Bert were often left in the care of their nanny, Mientje.

On weekends the Zilversmit family visited Grandpa and Grandma de Winter. Grandma's eyesight was very poor and she could not longer read. A visit from the grandchildren was a great event for her. Lisa dressed the boys in their all-white linen suits, so they would look especially nice for grandma. One day they came downstairs before Lisa was through getting dressed. The boys, vivacious and naughty as they were, couldn't resist the temptation to walk through a big puddle in front of the house. Don just had to try the puddle with one foot, and as usual Bert copied everything Don did. Before long, having forgotten all about being dressed up and ready to see grandma, both boys were slopping through the puddle. Presently Lisa came downstairs all dressed up, followed by Herman. At the sight of the boys she let out a yelp: "Dear God, look at those children, they've been playing in the mud." They were sent upstairs to Mientje, who soon had the rascals cleaned up.

Even worse, once, on the maid's afternoon off, the two boys carried all the kitchen furniture into the backyard as a prank. When she came home just in time to fix dinner, she found the furniture and everything else outside. The boys were nowhere to be found.

Lisa's parents, Mr. and Mrs. de Winter, were originally from Lith, North Brabant, but had moved to Hengelo. Mr. de Winter, who was born in 1870, and was known to the family as Grandpa de Winter, had a wholesale textile business in den Bosch.

Herman Zilversmit, Don's father, imported and exported meats, both wholesale and retail, all over the world. He also had a retail butcher shop in Hengelo.

A younger brother, Martin Zilversmit, had a meat packing business in Wierden, Overijsel, which imported and exported to firms all over the world. Later they moved to Wassenaar, near The Hague.

★ ★ ★

When Don was old enough, he was eager to start school. Lisa was amazed at the questions he was always asking her, way beyond his years, it seemed. He wanted to know all about the stars and where lightning and thunder came from. Later his questions turned philosophical; after all, he was reading Plato at six. She was convinced that he was very bright. Strangely enough, however, much as he liked to read at home, he did not enjoy school. Nobody could understand it. Was he bored, or was there something wrong with him? Don's third-grade teacher could think of nothing good to tell his anxious mother when she went to school to ask about his progress. "First of all," the teacher began, "his penmanship is atrocious; I can't read his writing." Lisa asked whether the principal would allow Don to print rather than use cursive, but that was against the school rules. There was no way an exception could be made. The teacher reiterated his concerns to Lisa before she left. He was sure Don didn't have the intelligence to go to college. Secondary school was definitely out of the question; why waste a good education on a boy like this?

Although no mother likes to hear that her child is not doing well in school, Lisa took the teacher's criticism in stride. She thought to herself, "A stupid child couldn't possibly ask the questions he asks." He used to ask questions all the time; no, this was not a stupid child.

One day, when Don came home from school, Lisa noticed a trickle of blood on his left ear. Startled by the sight, she asked Don if he had been in a fight. Don started talking, big tears running down his cheeks. The teacher had asked him a question which he could not answer. Angry because he thought Don should have known the answer, the teacher had pulled Don out of his seat by his ear, putting him to shame in front of all the children. When Lisa heard this story, she knew that Don was telling the truth.

Lisa was furious. How could such a thing have happened? What kind of place am I sending my child to? That man is not fit to teach

children and should be fired! Impulsively, she grabbed the phone
. . . but no, she thought, I'd better go to school in the morning.

Early the next morning she was the first person to enter the
school and insisted on seeing the principal. She didn't want to see
the teacher, she went right to the top. She told the principal her
story; he was very sympathetic and apologized, expressing dismay
that anything like this could have happened in his school. He
would immediately speak to the teacher. He assured her that nothing of the sort would ever happen again. Lisa replied that his assur-
ances were unnecessary because Don would not be returning to
school. She would give him a few days to recover from this traumatic experience and then enroll him in a private school.

What a change occurred in Don! "Of course, if he wants to
print, there's no reason on earth why he shouldn't do so," the
teacher at the new school assured Lisa. Encouraged by this teacher,
who obviously loved children, Don developed the most beautiful
printing after a couple of months. Something very remarkable
happened besides. The teacher noticed that Don was unable to see
what was written on the blackboard. Perhaps that was why he had
performed so poorly during his first few years in school. Don's new
teacher called Lisa and told her what she had discovered.

Lisa immediately made an appointment with the ophthalmol-
ogist. The examination confirmed that his eyesight was poor and
he needed glasses. It took only a few days for the glasses to be ready,
and what a difference they made. The next day in school was quite
remarkable for Don. For the first time, he could actually see what
was written on the blackboard! From that day forward Don's
academic life changed dramatically. He would soon be "soaring"
ahead, blossoming into an eager student. Not only did he continue
to read avidly at home, but school became one of his very favorite
places.

★ ★ ★

As a young boy, Don was very close to his aunt and uncle, Sara and Maurice Zilversmit. Maurice was an accountant by profession and lived in Rotterdam. Sara and Maurice didn't have any children but were very fond of Don and Bert. On weekends the boys would often visit Maurice and Sara, and these occasions were filled with many happy memories for Don. He was a child who always asked questions. But he was never quite happy with the answers and was always searching for more. Uncle Maurice was a scholar; his knowledge of Judaism—its history, the Torah, Talmud, and Gemara—was phenomenal. In addition, unlike Don's own parents, Uncle Maurice was very religious. Their conversations were open-ended, and Don was fascinated by Maurice's tales and anecdotes. He and his uncle were forever arguing about science, philosophy, and religion.

One day, Don and Maurice went to the beach together. It was a beautiful sunny day and they had nothing to do but enjoy each other, walk on the sand, and talk. As they strolled they gathered shells, and Maurice stuffed them all into his pockets. On the way home, back to Hengelo, Maurice wanted to prove a point to Don. As the train moved inland, Maurice suddenly opened the window of the compartment and threw the shells out, a few at a time. Puzzled, Don asked: "What are you doing that for?" "Well," Maurice replied in his, soft melodious voice, "someday somebody is going to find those shells and scientists will say that once upon a time the sea reached all the way to here. Doesn't that prove to you that science is not always right?"

Under Maurice's gentle but significant influence Don became very interested in Judaism, its history, people, and religion. Without Don realizing it, his uncle's religious convictions were influencing his own beliefs.

Meantime, Don began to prepare for his Bar Mitzvah. For his parents, Lisa and Herman, becoming Bar Mitzvah was nothing more than the right thing to do for tradition's sake. However, for Don, it had become quite a different matter. Serious as he always was, he couldn't just become Bar Mitzvah for Bar Mitzvah's sake, because he knew that on that day he would become a Jewish man in the true sense of the word, observing all of God's commandments. Don never did anything halfway; for him, his Bar Mitzvah would have to be done with heart and soul.

One day Don decided to have a serious talk with his mother. "Mother, how can I possibly become Bar Mitzvah, read the Torah, do everything I have been taught to do as a Jewish man, if we don't even have a kosher home? I have learned so much from Uncle Maurice; he is such a wise man. Every day now I am studying how to live as a Jew. I feel a terrible conflict within myself; I know that you and father want me to become Bar Mitzvah, but I want it for deeper reasons than you could ever imagine. Let me come to the point: I would like you to make this house a kosher home."

Lisa was very surprised. Never in her wildest dreams would she have expected her son to ask such a thing. Don continued to put pressure on his mother. He wanted to eat from kosher dishes, because how could a good Jew say the blessing over *treife* (non-kosher food)? Lisa knew in her heart that what her son was saying made sense. But she couldn't help thinking that he was becoming a fanatic, that this was going a bit too far! She could not just throw out all her dishes, her silver, her pots and pans, just because her son had a whim. At his age, how serious could he be about all this religion!

But in the weeks that followed, Don insisted that if the dishes were not replaced by new ones, he would no longer eat at home, especially after his Bar Mitzvah. In the end Lisa gave in to Don's demands. She bought two new sets of dishes, one for dairy and one for meat. And as if that were not bad enough, she also had to buy two new sets of kitchen utensils and throw the old ones out. Lisa's cooperation—her Bar Mitzvah gift, as it were—meant more to Don than anything else.

Martin Zilversmit was not a religious man, but for some reason he felt that someone in the Zilversmit family should become a rabbi. Of course, all eyes turned to Don, who was now completely immersed in religion. On occasion, the thought of becoming a rabbi certainly had crossed Don's mind. However, when he was in high school he became fascinated with the sciences. It became apparent that chemistry was his favorite subject, and he decided early in his high school years that he wanted to become a chemist.

Don went through several chemistry sets at home, as he had an insatiable curiosity about chemicals. Lisa and Herman counted themselves lucky that he blew up their garage only once. He began to think seriously about which university he wanted to attend to obtain superior training in chemistry. After finishing high school with honors he decided that the school of his choice was the State University in Utrecht. He enrolled in 1936.

As Don reminisced with me about his past, he noted that it was his decision to attend school in Utrecht that ultimately led us to meet and become friends. I secretly thought how lucky I was that this wonderful young student had chosen my hometown in which to pursue his studies.

4

My Family

My mother was born in Amsterdam. Her ancestors were expelled from Spain about 1492 as a result of the Spanish Inquisition. Some of these refugees, Sephardic Jews, eventually settled in Holland, where they could live as free people. My father's forebears probably came from Eastern Europe and are known as Ashkenazim.

My parents met at a dance in Amsterdam. I remember my father telling me about the first time he saw my mother. She was standing across the room, engaged in conversation with a young man. She had not noticed him looking at her, which he considered lucky, because it meant he could continue to observe her unobtrusively. He liked how she looked. She was five feet three inches tall, with dark brown wavy hair, gray-green eyes, and a beautiful olive-colored complexion. That night, he recalled, she was wearing a beautiful dress and colored stockings. Even her nails were polished, an uncommon custom at the time. Not wasting any time, he walked over and introduced himself. "I am Leopold Fonteyn," he said, a bit apprehensive that she might find him too forward. Her name was Gracia Jessurun Lobo. There was an instant attraction and they danced with one another the rest of the evening. That was the start of their romance!

As they got to know one another, my parents found they could talk about almost anything. My father remembered how shocked he was to find out that Gracia was an atheist. Father was a very religious man, and this drastic difference, he thought, would surely interfere with their having a future together. But he was falling in love, and soon they decided to get married. My mother promised my father that she would learn all about the dietary laws and faithfully observe the Jewish holidays. She would do it because she loved him. They were married in 1915 and settled in Utrecht.

★ ★ ★

Mother was our friend. She was always there for us when we needed her. She was easygoing and loved to laugh and have fun with us. Mother had always been overweight as long as I can remember, presumably because she loved to eat. She could never resist fresh bread and butter. She loved potatoes in any shape or form. Her butter cake was delicious and disappeared almost as fast as it was baked. She did all the cooking because she enjoyed it. She was an excellent organizer and an avid reader. She made many trips to the neighborhood library. She knew the librarians, sometimes telling us that one of them, in anticipation of her next visit, had set aside a couple of her favorite books for her.

Father was very strict with us, and his discipline was taken seriously by the children. He was a devoted husband and was very much in love with my mother even though they had been married for many years. Father was a handsome man of approximately five feet five inches with a tiny little beard, dark wavy hair, and a good complexion. He usually walked fast, with an energetic spring in his step. When he was not away from home, he spent much of his spare time with my brothers. He taught them wood-working and how to use tools safely. Father was a representative for A. W. Sabel & Co., a paint manufacturer and distributer in Zaandam, North Holland. Two brothers, Kees and August Sabel, headed the company. Father's work frequently took him out of town on business. Every Friday, he went to Zaandam to bring his report of the past week's sales to Mr. Sabel.

During the depression father regularly visited his sister, Chell Engelander, and when he did so would always give her a check.

She and her family needed help because they were going through hard times. Her husband, Uncle Ies, was out of work, as were most diamond workers. They had two sons, Leo and Hans. It was a *mitzvah* (good deed) to help others. Even after the depression, father visited his sister weekly. From her house he would go to the kosher cheese store, owned by a woman named Fietje, to buy our family's weekly supply. Then he would stop at the neighborhood candy store to pick up all of mother's favorites. When father came home on Friday afternoon, already in the Shabbat mood, he unpacked all the newly purchased delicacies and put them on the table while the rest of the family stood around, just watching this joyous ceremony and applauding his efforts with our usual comments of approval.

Many of our family activities revolved around the synagogue and the Jewish community. Although mother had a seat reserved for her all through the year, she only attended services on Rosh Hashanah, and then, strictly to please father. She would sit through the service from beginning to end, standing whenever the rest of the congregation stood, but she would not hold a prayer book; no use pretending she could read Hebrew—that would have been against her principles. As a child, I was often embarrassed by the fact that my mother seemed to be the only person at services not holding a prayer book. Later on, as I matured and became wiser, I began to realize that my mother was right to stick with her convictions.

★ ★ ★

SHABBAT

It is Friday afternoon. No matter where I am or what I am doing, I see about getting myself home—either by bike or whatever means of transportation is available, just so long as I can be home before dusk. Shabbat starts early during the winter months, sometimes as early as 3:30 p.m.

When I enter the house, the aroma of chicken soup and other delicacies meets me at the front door. Father and the boys are already dressed for services at the synagogue. Susan and I busy ourselves finishing up little chores before dinner and get dressed before the men come home. Every Friday, Jews are required to drop whatever they have been doing all week and enjoy the privilege of Shabbat, to be free of one's normal routine.

Pretty soon the men will be home for dinner. The dinner table is set with a pretty tablecloth and the good dishes. My mother has already lit the Shabbat candles. Now the front door opens and the whole family is home, ravenously hungry, as always. Father recites the Kiddush blessing over the wine and the silver Kiddush cup is passed around, everybody taking a sip of the wine. The Hamotzi blessing is recited over the bread and now the soup is served, piping hot, and it sets everyone aglow. The dinner consists of several courses which vary from week to week. Dessert will be served later in the evening. Together we sing Shir Hama'alot, the grace after meals.

The dishes are quickly cleared and washed, although sometimes not without an argument about who is to wash and who is to dry; and meanwhile the boys have a chance to run around and get rid of some of their excess energy. The table is set again for dessert, and after we have sampled the homemade cakes, we sing the traditional Friday evening Zemirot. Usually one of the children starts giggling for no apparent reason, and gradually all of us are infected with contagious laughter. Usually mother laughs too, but father doesn't always know what to do. Sometimes he asserts his authority by sending the offender to his or her room. But other times he relaxes and laughs right along with us. At times like this we all feel so good as a family.

Friday evening is spent relaxing, talking, eating, and singing. However, as religious Jews who observe Shabbat we carefully plan ahead to organize everything before Shabbat begins. Since we are not supposed to turn the electric lights on or off after dusk Friday evening, father has installed a Shabbat clock which automatically turns the lights off or on. My mother has to literally "beat the clock" to put everything away before the clock turns off all the lights in the house. There are floating candles in a glass of water and oil, one in each room so we can find our way around. On Shabbat we are not allowed to use the telephone, cook, or even turn on the stove. We have a Shabbat oven, as we call it. It consists of a metal plate with four short legs placed over the gas burners of the stove. The burners are set on low shortly before Shabbat starts, to keep water warm for us so that we can make tea and coffee with extract prepared in advance. We are only allowed to warm up precooked food on top of the metal plate. We are not supposed to ride our bikes or use public transportation; we walk wherever we go. We are not allowed to carry anything, since that is considered work. We can't spend money, cut paper, open letters, or even keep the fire stoked and burning. It was fortunate, therefore, that during the winter we had stoves that use anthracite that burns slowly, keep the house warm, and need little care. Because we are used to living by these rules, I don't miss any of the normal routines we forgo on Shabbat.

On Saturday morning we all walk to the synagogue for services, except mother, who excuses herself. After coming home we eat a traditional fish lunch, always a treat.

★ ★ ★

My parents' first baby was stillborn. It was a painful time, but they consoled one another with thoughts that there would be other babies in the future. Susan was born in 1917. I came along in 1919, Leo in 1922, and Jack in 1924. In 1928, at the age of forty-three, my mother found herself pregnant once again. I am sure this came as quite a surprise to her, although she never let on.

I was nine years old when my baby brother Eddy was born. Early in her pregnancy, mother called the midwife who had been with her for her two previous births. Dora de Vries checked her calendar, but no one had booked any appointments for December. She would arrive at the house a few days before the due date,

Kitty's Parents

December 14, to begin the preparations. Dora was a popular midwife, not only because of her nursing skills, but because she had a wonderful way with the older children. I remember her clearly. She was tall and rather heavy-set but well-proportioned, and always presented herself in a clean white nurse's uniform. She had a round face, a fresh, smooth complexion, and dark, soft eyes. Her hair was pulled straight back, braided and formed into a chignon, low on the nape of her neck. She never married but was clearly the motherly type; children were her business.

Fall came and it was time for us to go back to school. Mother's time for delivery was not so far off now. She had made arrangements to distribute us to various neighbors once labor started. Dora arrived at the house on mother's due date, December 14. One week passed but nothing happened. Dr. Aussems, the obstetrician, advised mother to exercise and walk as much as possible to speed up the process a little. "Somebody is obviously wrong about the due date," he said. While we were in school, Dora and mother would walk downtown, exercising as they called it. "Why not sit down and have a cup of coffee and a pastry?" After all, mother was eating for two. Mother could now eat without guilt but, as always, not without gaining weight.

When the first contractions started, the children were sent to their predetermined places. Dr. Aussems came to the house to deliver the baby. I imagine it was a normal delivery because I never noticed or heard anything to the contrary.

When we were called home, we all ran upstairs to my parents' bedroom. We were met at the door by Dora. We gathered around the bassinet and there was the little one, pink and wrinkled with dark hair, a little boy. We looked in amazement; he was so tiny. We were so excited at seeing the new baby that I don't remember whether we even went to mother's bedside. On the eighth day the circumcision took place at home. Afterwards there was the traditional lunch. The mohel who performed the operation was qualified according to Jewish law, and it was carried out with antiseptic preparations.

★ ★ ★

We were animal lovers from way back. We had a veranda just off our dining room which overlooked a big backyard. There was a terrace in front of the veranda built of flat concrete blocks. The terrace continued on into a rectangular walkway which went around the yard, leaving a wide space in the middle for a flower garden with mother's favorite flowers, a varied selection of dahlias. All the Fonteyn children spent a lot of time playing in the backyard as we grew up.

Like many families, we had several pets and loved them all. My favorite was Moortje, our cat. I adored her shiny jet-black coat and the way she always snuggled up against our feet under the table at mealtimes. I always found it hard to give away the kittens; their prospective homes were inspected and researched as carefully as they would have been had we been working for an adoption agency. There were often disagreements over who was to clean the turtle cage and the goldfish bowl. We also had a big turtle that roamed freely in the flower beds. We fed him fresh lettuce.

When our non-Jewish friends had chicks for Easter, of course we wanted some too. When our chicks began to grow up, we couldn't part with them. Before father was aware of it, he was

The Fonteyn Children
Left to right: *Jack, Kitty, Eddy, Leo, Susan*

appointed to built a coop for the chicks. Then we children had a fabulous idea. We wanted to watch a new generation of chicks grow up from the very beginning. Soft-hearted as mother was, she pleaded with father: "Let the children have their chicks; I can't see anything wrong with it." Before long we had a brood hen, sitting on her eggs. After twenty-one days of waiting, we witnessed the chicks hatch. The eggshells began to crack, the eggs moving slightly in the process. The outside shell was separated slowly but surely as the chicks struggled into the outside world. They looked confused, wet, and tired. They dried off quickly and soon became beautiful, fluffy, pale-yellow creatures. After seven to ten days, they began to show some early white feathers and the yellow fluff started to disappear. They were not quite as cute anymore, but we loved them just the same.

Then our chicks needed more space to exercise, so father and the boys built a chicken run. Not too long after that, they built an official hen-house and the hens began to lay eggs. The standard joke around our place was: "I wonder which came first, the egg or the hen-house?"

It wasn't long before my father and the boys were building again. "When you have animals you have to take care of them," was the family's favorite motto. We gradually accumulated more and more eggs, not yet every day but regularly. Before long mother had fresh eggs to bake in her pound cake and we also had fresh eggs for breakfast. I never got tired of scrambled eggs on a buttered matzo. Our yard was beginning to look like a miniature poultry farm; we had at least twelve hens and one rooster.

When the days grew shorter as winter approached, egg production slowed down. The chickens not only went to sleep earlier but also consumed less food. My father must have been secretly reading the latest literature on raising poultry, because one day he assembled the whole family and announced that he wanted to put an electric light in the chicken coop to extend the waking hours of the birds. That way they would eat more food and produce more eggs. He didn't need to ask what we thought of his plan, because as soon as he proposed the idea we wholeheartedly agreed. After all, we were all poultry experts! After a couple of weeks' work the wiring was ready to be tested. The family assembled in front of the chicken coop and my father threw the switch. We cheered so loudly we were probably heard all over the neighborhood. We were as proud as if we had lit up the Eiffel Tower.

On occasion we would eat one of our chickens without much thought or protest from the children. Father called the shochet, the person authorized to slaughter poultry according to Jewish law. He never came before 9:00 p.m. to ensure that the children were asleep. But once father made a serious mistake. He inadvertently grabbed the wrong chicken in the dark. This particular chicken actually had a name, Zangy (Dutch for "singing"), because her cackle sounded like a melody as she proudly strutted in the chicken run.

The next morning, one of my brothers noticed that Zangy was missing. That evening, when Zangy was carried into the dining room on a large platter and placed on the table, we children put out heads down and refused to eat dinner. We remained sitting with our heads bowed in total silence for the whole meal until dessert was served, at which time we cheered up just enough to eat some of mother's delicious cake.

★ ★ ★

I became interested in music at a very early age. After I outgrew the toddler stage I discovered the piano. It soon became apparent to my parents that the piano would be my favorite toy. My mother often caught me pushing the keys down gently, listening and concentrating with total fascination to the sound of the instrument. Born with the gift of perfect pitch, I began picking out melodies on the piano when I was not yet three years old. I started playing pieces I had heard, with two hands, applying perfect harmony as though someone had carefully taught me. It became a game, to play the same song in different keys, and later on I transposed the National Anthem up and down the keyboard. I composed two different accompaniments to favorite songs I knew.

I vividly remember listening to the Salvation Army band in downtown Utrecht, when we were shopping one day. This was my first experience with a group of live musicians playing various instruments. I remember having a tug of war with my mother when she told me it was time to go home. She persisted in pulling my hand but I wriggled free, unable to get enough of this wonderful music. After that my mother would jokingly bring up the subject of the Salvation Army band, saying: "You would think she was listening to the Concertgebouw Orchestra!"

Soon thereafter, my mother started taking me to concerts. There were weekly "Volks Concerts" in Utrecht, with excellent performing soloists. On one occasion, my mother took me to Amsterdam to hear Rosa Spier, a noted Dutch harpist, who was performing with the Concertgebouw Orchestra. I became infatuated with the harp and wanted to have one of my own. This would have been no small matter, as a harp would have cost several thousand guilders. Luckily my mother was able to convince me that, for now, the piano was a more versatile instrument.

Every year the members of our Jewish children's organization put on a major play as well as some less ambitious productions, such as storytelling and Jewish holiday celebrations. The chairman, Eduard Heymans, was totally devoted to the organization's members and activities. Parents also became involved, helping to make the necessary costumes for the productions. One day, Mr. Heymans approached my mother. He had been wondering whether I would be willing to participate in one of the programs. My mother thought I was a little young for this but told him she would discuss it with me and see how I reacted. Well, it appealed to me the minute mother started to talk about it. It didn't matter what I would do, as long as I could play the piano. I suppose I was a real ham, no inhibitions whatsoever. Oh, how I was to change in later years when I became my own critic!

As it happened, I had improvised a melody to the night-prayers which I said every night before going to sleep. I am sure my mother must have helped me with the lyrics, but in the end I had put it together, accompaniment and all. Therefore the choice was not hard; my mother thought I should perform the night-prayers because I could already do them so well.

There was to be a bed for me on stage just as at home, and I was supposed to say my prayers just as I always did. I had only one important decision to make: which pajamas to wear on stage! I chose to wear pale-green pajamas, which my mother then made for me in anticipation of my debut performance. Finally the night of the big event arrived. We were all dressed up. Susan had on a pretty dress and I was in my pajamas. I was five years old then and very small for my age. I had dark-brown hair, which my mother had arranged into ringlets for the occasion. I had brown eyes and very rosy cheeks. Mother told me in advance that the people in the audience would applaud after I finished singing my night-prayers.

While I lay in my little bed on stage, with my head resting on my right hand, the heavy red-velvet curtain opened and parted in the middle. I vividly recall the people in the hall applauding before my performance. I said to myself: "They're all wrong, because I haven't done anything yet." I sang my prayers without hesitation in a clear, sweet voice. Now there was more applause, and I had to do it all over again. Then I was led to the piano, off to the right side of the stage, and accompanied myself in more night-prayers. By that time, I was sure, everybody was ready to go to sleep. But I was wrong. There was even more applause! Well, it had been a beautiful evening.

★ ★ ★

At our house music was frequently the focus of activity. One would always hear somebody playing or singing. My mother played the piano very well and father had a beautiful baritone voice. He sang in the synagogue's small choir on special occasions. My parents had been opera lovers for as long as I could remember. They had an old-fashioned gramophone with a wide horned speaker and had accumulated many records. On weekends they frequently sat on the living room couch listening to their favorite opera. I can see my father, one arm around my mother's shoulder, the other hand conducting parts of the music he knew so well, talking about the plot and listening, sometimes with misty eyes.

I spent a great deal of my time at the piano and played continuously. In the process, I developed the bad habit of using the soft pedal to mute the sounds, out of fear that I would be chased away from the piano by one of my brothers or even by my sister, Susan. She sometimes came into the living room when I was practicing. I remember in particular how fond she was of the "Peer Gynt Suite" by Grieg. I played the whole suite, "Morgenstimmung (Morning mood)," "Aases Tod (Aases Death)," and finally "Anitras Tanz (Anitra's Dance)." Invariably, Susan would come into the room whenever she heard the beginning of the "Peer Gynt Suite." As she listened her whole demeanor softened. Then she would demand that I play it all over again. At these times there was complete harmony between us. On other occasions, when I accompanied myself on the piano while singing, Susan would pick up a book—any book—open it, and, in front of the entire family, mimic me by mouthing the words as I sang. Being a real actress, she would soon have everyone roaring with laughter and I would invariably run away from the piano, annoyed at the interruption. Susan had started lessons once, but had not continued. None of the boys played the piano. I was the only child in the family to follow in my parents' footsteps where music was concerned.

When I was around six or seven, my parents decided to have me evaluated by several competent musicians. My first visit was with Catharine van Rennes, a composer of songs for both adults and children. She was already quite an elderly lady, very tall, and her hair was thin and gray. She was not very friendly when she spoke to me, and her manner was stern and businesslike, so I didn't like her very much. She had many voice students and was undoubtedly well respected, as evidenced by the fact that she taught voice to Juliana, the Dutch crown princess. I remember her huge studio with the concert grand piano, glossy and beautiful, and encompassed by glorious oriental rugs.

Miss van Rennes started out the audition by playing a song for me: her most famous composition, "Het Zonnelied" ("Song of the Sun"). After that, it was my turn to play and as soon as I sat down at the keyboard, I began to feel comfortable. I sang my songs for which I had made up two different accompaniments. Then she started to play some musical games with me. She played an unfamiliar melody on the piano, stopping after several measures, and asked me to finish it. That was easy. She had me walk along the wall in big circles, adjusting my pace according to the tempo she was playing. She also asked me to transpose my compositions. She tested my ear with my back to the piano. I had to repeat and sing any melody she played. After the audition was over, Miss van Rennes told my parents that I was a gifted child and that she herself had been capable of all these things when she was my age. She suggested that I start taking piano lessons soon, and recommended Dr. Averkamp, the director of the Utrecht Conservatory.

In the interim, my parents had already made arrangements to take me to Julius Roëngen, the director of the Amsterdam Conservatory. Mr. Roëngen was quite elderly, with a mop of gray, untidy hair. He too played some musical games with me, similar to what Catharine van Rennes had done. He listened to my compositions and songs. In contrast to Miss van Rennes, he gave me lots of praise. However, my parents were not allowed in the room with me and therefore I wasn't very happy; in fact, I was near tears. While playing for him, I noticed two people sitting on a couch in an alcove adjoining the room, apparently listening to me. After I was through, my parents were called in. I didn't understand much of the conversation, but I was happy to leave with them. Mr. Roëngen told my parents that I was certainly a gifted child and would have no trouble getting a full scholarship at any conservatory.

Now it was time to see Dr. Averkamp at the Utrecht Conservatory. I liked him immediately and I believe the feeling was mutual. I played many pieces for him. Unfortunately, he said, he couldn't take me as a pupil because he only taught Conservatory students. Once I had learned the basics, however, he would consider taking me on as a private pupil. He recommended one of his favorite graduate students, who he thought would be just the right person to start me off and teach me the basics. Her name was Miss Reizinger.

It was like love at first sight. I adored Miss Reizinger from the very beginning, and she loved me too. I thought she was so beautiful with her blonde, short, curly hair and blue eyes. She had a fresh pinkish complexion and was rather chubby. She wore such pretty dresses and had small, delicate hands. I loved to watch her play the piano. On the coffee table sat a candy dish, and after each lesson, if I did well, I could choose a candy. We always had so much fun during the lessons; she did so many things with me.

There was a lot of ear training with my back to the piano. I had to write down melodies she played for me. She taught me to transpose by sight because I already knew how to transpose by ear. I went through all the basic literature; early beginner books, followed by Clementi and Kuhlau sonatinas, early Bach pieces, Mozart sonatas, and Bach inventions. Each lesson was special, and it was exciting to play such a variety of music. However, my mother questioned how thoroughly I was taught and wondered whether I had really ended up with the right teacher. My mother played the piano well and was a pretty good critic. She thought

Miss Reizinger was much too lenient and could probably not handle a child like me.

One afternoon, before I went to my lesson, mother asked me to play my assignment for her. I was only too happy to sit down and play through everything again. My mother commented that she didn't think Miss Reizinger would be happy with the way I had practiced this week; my pieces were just not polished, nor had I carefully executed the composer's wishes, nor had I bothered to figure out the correct notes in the final chord of my Mozart sonata. I, on the other hand, felt I didn't have to look at the final chords because I could hear them in my head, and I couldn't see what difference it really made. Anyway, I felt I was doing fine, because I invariably came home from each lesson with new assignments. Miss Reizinger always told me I had practiced well and gave me new pieces. Mother later told me that if Miss Reizinger had been able to find a diplomatic way to tell me that I was actually sloppy in my practice, I would gladly have accepted her criticism because I loved her so much.

Then Dr. Averkamp, who was to have been my next teacher, suddenly died. At the time I didn't understand the significance of his death. Because my relationship with Miss Reizinger was so special, mother was fearful that finding me a new teacher might kill my enthusiasm for the piano. However, she was well aware that I was developing sloppy fingering habits under Miss Reizinger's guidance, which would later have to be corrected. Despite her concerns, mother soon found Hans (short for Johanna) Vega, and I changed teachers.

Hans Vega taught part-time at the Amsterdam Conservatory, and the remaining days of the week taught private students at her home in Utrecht. With Hans as teacher I practiced a lot of piano and dreamed of someday going to a conservatory myself. For my fourteenth birthday, mother had all her own Mozart and Beethoven sonatas rebound and gave them to me as a present. It was a beautiful, fingered, Peters edition. I was very touched and have been using the sonatas ever since.

★ ★ ★

PASSOVER

To get ready for Pesach (Passover) at our home, the Jewish spring cleaning, as it is called, is in itself a major operation. Under normal circumstances, every kosher home has two sets of dishes and pots and pans, one for dairy, the other for meat dishes. But for Pesach these dishes cannot be used and are all put away for the week. Instead the Pesach dishes are taken out of their boxes, washed, and put into the freshly cleaned kitchen cabinets. Luckily, the usual glassware and silver can be used for the week of Pesach, after they are treated with boiling water, a process called kashering.

A couple of days before Pesach, matzos in big round boxes are delivered to the house. Mother always carefully plans the lunch on the day of the Seder. All leftover chometz (leavened food) has to be used or thrown out, since the house must be free of leaven during the week of Pesach. Because mother just refuses to throw it out, she invents new and spectacular dishes using these ingredients. She creates the most wondrous casseroles, and consequently, on the last day before Pesach, we end up with a feast of abundance.

When we come home from school for lunch at noon, we all participate in the final search for chometz. In accordance with the old Jewish custom, my mother has just finished hiding little pieces of bread in corners all over the house. The ceremonial search, which becomes a game for the children, takes place in every Orthodox home.

Father leads the procession, holding a lit candle and followed by all the children, through the whole house, all of us looking in every corner for chometz. We have great fun finding all the chometz. We nudge one another, saying, "They call this a clean house?" Someone at the end of the line, usually me, carefully sweeps up all the crumbs.

THE SEDER

We gather around the table, all seven of us, for the Seder. My grandmother, who lives with us, usually goes to bed soon, because she becomes too tired sitting up so long. Everybody has a Haggadah, with a beautifully illustrated Hebrew text. That way we can follow the narrative of the Jews in bondage in Egypt, the story of the ten plagues, and finally the Exodus. The Seder plate is placed in the middle of the table. The essentials for conducting the Seder are a roasted egg, which signifies life; a shankbone, to remind us of the sacrifice of the lamb; bitter herbs, to remind us of the hard time the Israelites went through when they were slaves under the Pharaohs; and finally, charoset, a mixture of ground-up nuts, raisins, apples, and cinnamon, mixed together with wine, to signify the mortar the Israelites used to build heavy stone walls while enslaved.

Father, as head of the household, always conducts the Seder. We hear the story as he tells it every year, about the Exodus from Egypt, where the Jewish people were slaves for forty years under Pharaoh. The youngest of the children asks the traditional Four Questions, starting with, "Why is this night different from all other nights?" The answer, designed to stimulate the child's mind, is always skillfully handled by my father:

"A message came for the Jewish people to leave Egypt at once, and go to Canaan, the Promised Land. They must not have gotten sufficient notice to finish the bread baking. Under the circumstances, they didn't have time to let the bread rise adequately. Instead, out came these awful-looking flat matzos. It must have been a shocking experience, but they couldn't afford to let it bother them; they had more important things to worry about, like packing up their belongings and wrapping up their flat bread, now a total failure. Now you understand why we eat matzos, unleavened bread, for one week when we celebrate Pesach."

That is the way my father tells the story, and every year, when he tells it, we laugh. Between the first and second parts of the Seder, a festive meal is served. It is customary to drink four glasses of wine, two during the first part of the Seder and two during the second part. For the children, my mother boils a mixture of water, raisins, spices, and some wine for flavor. During the second part, we sing the traditional and beautiful Seder songs, my mother often harmonizing, as she can do so artfully. It creates a wonderful feeling of belonging.

Occasionally, during the second half of the Seder, mother dozes off. The delicious meal, the two glasses of wine, and all the work of preparing for this celebration have made her sleepy. We watch her head drop slowly onto her chest and see her wake up all of a sudden, looking surprised to realize that she had, indeed, dozed off. Father invariably stops reading from the Haggadah and makes a brief comment like: "Any good Jewish wife and mother is entitled to doze off during the Seder," praising her for having done a remarkable job. He knows what an ordeal it is for her to sit through the whole Seder. She can't follow the text, whereas we children have all learned to read Hebrew. It will be late tonight before we are in bed, especially for the younger boys, but Pesach comes just once a year.

★ ★ ★

One morning after Passover services something happened which left an indelible impression on me. I was standing outside watching the congregants emerge from the synagogue when Mrs. Tal, the rabbi's wife, came out. I knew her and Rabbi Tal well and had often been invited to their house for Shabbat lunch after services. She walked toward me, shook my hand, and wished me a happy holiday. I was in my early teens. "Did you have a good Seder last night?" Mrs. Tal asked.

"Oh, yes, we had a beautiful Seder." Then the conversation shifted to the luncheon before the Seder.

"I bet," Mrs. Tal said, "that you had an especially nice luncheon yesterday."

"Yes, my mother really outdid herself again."

Now Mrs. Tal's curiosity had been aroused and she asked: "What kind of dishes did your mother fix, Kitty?" I told her about the wonderful matzo ball soup my mother had prepared, when suddenly I saw in Mrs. Tal's face that I must have said something very bad. Her facial expression suddenly changed to total disapproval. She looked down instead of looking me in the eye, as though she didn't know what to say. After a few seconds, she looked at me and said, "Kitty, you couldn't have had matzo ball soup for lunch yesterday."

"Well, of course we did; it was really delicious soup."

Now her face became stern and she seemed very distraught. Then she said: "Kitty, don't you know you are not allowed to eat matzos until the blessing over the matzo has been said during the Seder? Your mother made a mistake."

I sensed that Mrs. Tal was testing my mother because she knew she was not a religious person, and it made me furious. Never in my life had I felt such humiliation. This woman, whom I really liked, had the audacity to tell me that my mother had made a mistake? I felt such hurt for my mother, who had innocently done something wrong simply because she was trying to treat and surprise her family.

I don't know whether my father had noticed the transgression, but if he did, he never said anything and enjoyed the soup as much as we all did. I never had the courage to tell my parents about my conversation with Mrs. Tal.

★ ★ ★

The whole family helped plan and looked forward to celebrating my brother Leo's Bar Mitzvah at the end of October, 1935. Several months in advance, my father had made arrangements with the rabbi to prepare Leo for the part he had to perform during the

Saturday morning service. He had to read the Torah, the Five Books of Moses, in Hebrew of course and with the traditional cantillation. The Bar Mitzvah celebration is generally divided into two parts, religious and social. Leo was not particularly interested in the extra training, nor was he terribly eager to attend services in the synagogue, especially in the winter early in the morning. However, it was exciting to become Bar Mitzvah like all his friends. And what twelve-year-old boy would have the courage to go against his father's authority?

Mother planned the reception, which would take place in the afternoon at home. Kappie Cohen, the kosher baker, assured mother that he would take care of everything and bring his "entourage" to help with the serving. (Mr. Cohen, Kappie's father, employed several young men from Germany in his bakery. He gave them room and board. For the young men, the job meant a reprieve from Nazi propaganda, anti-Semitism, and personal humiliation.) In due time, there would be an advertisement placed in the orthodox paper, *Nieuw Israelitisch Weekblad* (*New Jewish Weekly*), to announce the Bar Mitzvah and to invite friends and family to the service and reception.

While the preparations proceeded, and Leo studied like mad, life went on as usual. My mother and Leo continued their regular shopping trips, with Leo always carrying the packages for her. In all seriousness, she often remarked that he was the most gallant boy she'd ever seen.

Finally October 28 arrived. We all walked to the synagogue, including my mother. This event she couldn't miss. Leo looked terrific in his new navy-blue suit, his first long pants, white shirt, and bow tie; the hat, almost too much for so young a boy, was part of the traditional outfit. When Leo was called to the almemor, the platform from which the Torah was read, his voice from the onset sounded clear and full. It went without a flaw. He was self-assured, showing no trace of nervousness. My parents had reason to be very proud of him, and my father's face glowed throughout.

When we got home from the synagogue we ate a wonderful lunch. Pretty soon the doorbell rang and the first visitors began to arrive. Kappie was a tremendous help and the refreshments were scrumptious. I can still see the enormous wooden boxes of pastries, delivered to the house the day before and carefully stored in the cellar, where it was cool. Leo received many gifts and was spoiled by family and friends.

According to Jewish law, Leo could now be counted as an adult and was qualified to participate in a minyan, the quorum of ten men needed for a prayer service. Well, there was no danger that this was going to happen anytime soon, because right after the Bar Mitzvah all the children came down with chicken pox. We all had light cases except Leo, who was covered from top to bottom. He was miserable, the itching was unbearable, sleeping almost impossible. Some pox became infected, and one left a very distinct mark above his right eye. When he was all better, we teased him that such a handsome boy would have to go through life with such an ugly scar over his eye. I in particular would remember that pockmark many years later.

★ ★ ★

SUKKOT

For the festival of Sukkot (Tabernacles) we have our own sukkah, the temporary outdoor dwelling in which the festival is traditionally observed. The back porch, opening off the kitchen, is turned into a little room just for that week. It makes an ideal sukkah because it has no permanent roof, so one can see the sky as it is supposed to be. With a few boards, my father closes the open spaces which under normal circumstances look out into the backyard. A few wooden slats are nailed on top of the sukkah-to-be, to hold up the straw, which is braided into a roof so that at night we can see the stars shining through it. My father ingeniously makes a cover over the straw roof to protect us from rain. It is operated by a rope and a pulley from a bedroom window overhead. When an unexpected shower surprises us, one of us yells: "It's raining; somebody please run upstairs and let the cover down." The children are in charge of decorating the sukkah. We like to stick flowers and greenery through the braided straw roof and even find some pictures to put on the wall. We have a long narrow table small enough to fit in the sukkah, a narrow uncomfortable bench for the children to sit on, and two chairs for my parents on the opposite side. It is customary to visit with friends in one's sukkah.

★ ★ ★

I cannot close this account of my childhood memories without mentioning Carola Marcus. Several years before the war the synagogue in Utrecht asked its members to volunteer to take in a Jewish child from Germany for several weeks during the summer vacation. One could specify in advance the age and sex of the child one would prefer. My parents, of course, immediately decided we would take a child. A girl, approximately twelve or a little older, would be ideal for our family. Susan and I looked forward with curiosity to meeting her.

It was the summer of 1935, two years after Hitler became Reich Chancellor. The children arrived and here was Carola! She was tall for her fourteen years, with gray eyes and straight blonde hair. We liked her even before we actually met her, because she had been assigned to us, and as children we were so excited to have her. Carola was a darling girl, and we all grew very fond of her. She was obviously from a good family, extremely well behaved and pleasant to have around. She never talked about her family, or about the political situation in Germany. It was best not to talk of what was happening at home, across the border. But she did talk a lot about her brother Bubby; they were apparently very close.

We took her on all our outings, and whenever there was a communication problem, we used the international language, our hands. By the time summer drew to an end, however, all the children were bilingual; no communication problems anymore. It had been a good experience for all of us and we were sorry to see Carola go home. The next summer the program continued, and it was only natural that she would come back to us. But after Carola went home that summer, the program was abruptly stopped and we never heard from her again. It was a real disappointment, since we had looked forward so much to having her with us again. Instead it created an atmosphere of foreboding, because we sensed that something terrible had happened.

★ ★ ★

I thought how lucky we were, to live in Holland. I had never met with even a single incident of anti-Semitism, nor had my family. During the winter months, when Shabbat started as early as 3:30 p.m., someone in school would knock on each classroom door, indicating that it was time for the Jewish children to go home. This was a normal routine that everyone was familiar with, and was taken for granted.

I remember my father coming home once. Someone in the house had turned on the radio. Suddenly we heard the screaming voice of Hitler and wild applause from a hysterical crowd. My father shouted: "Turn off the radio, I won't tolerate that murderer's voice in my house!"

Although we lived uncomfortably close to the German border, my father always said: "Yes, but that's Germany; nothing will happen in Holland, the Dutch simply wouldn't allow it." And so we lived in those oppressive times, each thinking his own thoughts. On the surface calm, occupied with the ordinary daily routine, while a storm was brewing around us.

In retrospect, I can't remember ever having had an "in-depth" conversation with my parents about the situation in Germany. Maybe they thought that the problems were too overwhelming and wanted to protect their children.

★ ★ ★

It was not until the war was over that I learned how our Judaism had affected my prospects as a musician. The Goud family were very close friends and neighbors for many years. Their daughter Lucy was a graduate of the Amsterdam Conservatory; she was a fine pianist and I loved to listen to her play. Lucy, too, never missed a chance to have me play for her. Our music sessions were always very exciting. During a postwar visit to the Gouds I learned that my parents had already decided when I was in my early teens that I would not be allowed to study at a conservatory. As a student and then as a conservatory graduate, I would have been required to concertize on Shabbat, something my parents felt would be totally out of the question. Rabbi Tal had a tremendous influence on the people in his congregation. My father felt great respect for this man and would never have contradicted him. It seems to me now that it must have been the rabbi who convinced my parents that I should not pursue my studies at a conservatory. Even now, the thought surprises me, and I wonder why my parents never talked about it with me.

5

Separation

In 1939 Don's uncle Martin Zilversmit and his wife Janny decided the time had come for them and their two small sons, Ralph and Arthur, to leave Holland. They were not sure whether the move would be permanent, but at least they would take a trip to the United States to see how they liked it over there. They left for the States in the spring of that year. Once there, they literally crisscrossed the country to see where they might like to live. They decided that California had the ideal climate and settled down in San Mateo.

Martin and Janny corresponded often with Don's parents and urged them to emigrate to America. From their vantage point in the United States, they felt they were in a better position to judge the political atmosphere in Europe. They could see that the situation was deteriorating daily. Letters came all the time imploring: "Why is it so hard to decide? We're getting nervous and impatient. Please make up your minds quickly. There is no need to wait. You should pack up and leave as soon as possible."

Don's parents lived in Hengelo, which is in the eastern part of Holland, close to the German border. They were awakened sometimes from their sleep in the middle of the night by refugees ringing the doorbell and asking whether they could please spend the night at their house. Many of these refugees were taken in by relatives, so that they would not become a burden on the Dutch government. But others were not so fortunate. Intimidated by Germany and afraid to give legal status to those refugees not provided for by relatives, the Dutch government built a camp in the province of Drente, close to the German border, to house refugees who had nowhere else to stay. The camp provided only simple barracks but at least it offered shelter for those with no other alternative. That same camp, Westerbork, was later used by the Germans as a transit camp to house Dutch Jews. They were detained in Westerbork until they were put on transports to the east.

Letters from the United States arrived almost every day. Martin and Janny were anxious and couldn't understand why Lisa and Herman Zilversmit seemed unable to make up their minds. There were certainly reasons for concern, but the Zilversmits were so well situated in Holland that they didn't really want to leave. Although there was always the possibility of a German invasion, Holland had remained neutral during the First World War. Many people believed that it would be neutral again in the event of war, and others simply thought that nothing all that serious was going to happen. Further, since much of Holland could be flooded at a moment's notice, many believed that the Germans wouldn't want to bother with so small a country. No one really knew the right course to take.

★ ★ ★

We had enjoyed two wonderful years together when Don told me one evening in the early summer of 1939 that his parents were talking about emigrating to the United States. The political situation didn't look good, and staying in Holland meant taking a risk, they thought. It was so difficult to decide what to do. Don certainly didn't want to leave Holland; it seemed unthinkable for us to separate at this time in our lives, unless I could go with them to the States.

We discussed this problem at great length and ultimately agreed that if the situation was really as dangerous as some people thought it was, and if his parents decided to leave for the States, Don would go with them. If war broke out, at least he would be able to continue his studies over there. And if the situation later stabilized, he could return at that time.

It was hard for Don's family to decide whether to emigrate, but his mother gave the final push by threatening her husband and sons that if they didn't make up their minds soon she would go by herself. She took charge of getting the official documents ready and within six weeks they had their immigration papers in hand. Don's parents expressed an interest in taking me with them, but there wasn't enough time for the two sets of parents to arrive at a final decision about something so momentous. My parents and I talked about it at great length, and in the end agreed that if Don and I still felt the same about each other after one year had passed, they would give me permission to follow him to America. This plan seemed reasonable enough at the time, and we were relieved to put this important decision behind us.

★ ★ ★

Don went to Hengelo to organize his possessions and decide what to take with him to the States. His books would have to be carefully sorted and given away to those who could make good use of them. When Don arrived home there was quite a commotion at the Zilversmit house. Their possessions had been divided into different piles. Items they would need to set up housekeeping would go with them on the boat. The Zilversmits had many valuable antiques which were packed separately and would be shipped to them later. The furniture was not of immediate importance; it would be safe and cared for in storage. It didn't take Don long to go through his possessions: he quickly put the items that were important to him in boxes and labeled them, and then his job was done. He stayed overnight, more to be of moral support to his parents than for any great need he had himself.

Although the Zilversmits were leaving of their own free will, there was an undercurrent of tension and uncertainty that Don was well aware of. The family couldn't help but wonder if emigrating was really the right thing to do and wondered why they were going through all this trouble. Don left for Utrecht the next morning and there had to pack once more. His room in Utrecht had to be vacated. He gave many of his things away, only taking his books and clothes. He had many good friends to say goodbye to but felt confident he would see them again.

For Lisa, Herman, and Bert it didn't take long for the six weeks of organizing to pass. They spent their last night in Holland with Lisa's sister Ans and her husband Max, who lived in Arnhem. They felt such relief to get away from all those boxes and suitcases and to arrive in a familiar, orderly home once again. When August 15 arrived, the day of their departure, I went with them to the port in Rotterdam where the luxurious Statendam of the Holland-America Line was docked.

★ ★ ★

They took the train to Utrecht, where they would change trains and continue to Rotterdam. Since Don and I were both in Utrecht, we were to meet the family at the station. We knew that once they arrived in Utrecht, there would be ample time to visit and say our goodbyes. They still had several hours before they would need to leave for Rotterdam.

As the train came squealing to a stop, Ans and Max disembarked, followed by Lisa, Herman, and Bert. The usual greetings were exchanged. Lisa suggested: "Why don't we go and sit down in the coffee shop where we can talk; we have a lot of time before our departure to Rotterdam." Suddenly Herman realized that his briefcase, holding all his important papers—banknotes, visas, passports, everything—was missing. He tried to remain calm; after all, it couldn't be true! He asked whether anyone else had been holding the briefcase or possibly had put it somewhere.

Mr. Zilversmit was so nervous and upset that he had trouble concentrating and thinking clearly. He thought he must have either lost the briefcase on the train to Utrecht or left it at home.

Since he didn't really remember having it with him, Lisa decisively suggested that somebody had better go back quickly to Arnhem to look for the lost briefcase. Max and Don decided to go, and before we realized it, they were on the train for Arnhem. It would be at least a couple of hours before they were back at the station.

While anxiously waiting for them to return, hopefully with the briefcase, we really said very little. We were too tense to make pleasant conversation over our coffee and weren't sure whether or not to say farewell. After all, without their papers, the Zilversmits could hardly leave the country. When Max and Don arrived in Arnhem, Max called his home and asked the house-keeper to look for the lost briefcase. She took a quick look around and told him that it was safely tucked away in a corner. She called a cab and met the men at the station. Mr. Zilversmit had simply forgotten to take it with him in all the confusion. As Max triumphantly approached us, waving the briefcase over his head, we all breathed a loud, happy sigh of relief. Now the Zilversmits could sail as planned.

I was completely exhausted by the time we arrived at the ship. Now there wasn't even time left to say goodbye. The passengers, however, were allowed to show their cabins and parts of this float-ing palace to those who were seeing them off. Don showed me his quarters, the lounges, and the dining rooms. I was so overcome with the dread of our separation that I only saw the gangplank, heavy red carpets, and lots of bright chandeliers. We consoled one another over and over again; it was only one year, it would pass quickly, we would write everything and often, of course. Those last embraces didn't seem real, and suddenly it was time for visitors to leave the ship.

There was lots of activity on the wharf while the final prepa-rations for sailing were being carried out. The gangplank and mooring ropes were pulled in. The passengers stood on deck as the ship was pulled out of its berth by a tugboat. Ans, Max, and I watched the Statendam move slowly out of the harbor. The

Zilversmits were all on deck. I followed Don with misty eyes until his features began to fade. Slowly we left the wharf, turning around again and again to watch the beautiful ship sail away. Max called me back to reality: "We'll miss the train to Utrecht if we linger too long."

We took a taxi back to the station. We were in no mood for conversation during the train ride back to Utrecht and I am sure Ans and Max were sad, too, with Lisa and Herman gone. I got off in Utrecht. Ans and Max would continue to Arnhem.

My parents were waiting for me at the station. When we got home, my father poured me a big glass of red wine, something he had never done before. The only times he had allowed us to drink wine were on Friday night and Shabbat morning, when the blessing over the wine was recited, and during the Seder on Pesach. Mother beat up a couple of eggs and sugar for me and mixed it with the wine. She didn't know whether I had eaten an evening meal, nor did she ask. At least, she thought, this drink would provide me with some nourishment if I hadn't eaten. We stayed quietly together in the living room for a little while longer; then mother took me to my bedroom, where I silently undressed and fell into bed. I must have fallen asleep almost instantly. I was emotionally exhausted and father's wine did the rest.

I wanted to be busy and keep my mind occupied so that I wouldn't have too much time to think about Don's departure. I felt that a very precious and dear part of me had been taken away. Life would be so different, not having him close, and I would miss him terribly. However, I was determined to fill up all my spare time. The year would pass quickly if I kept busy. No use in pitying myself; I'll do something useful instead, I reasoned.

Since I had always wanted to take a course in fashion-designing, I thought it would be a splendid idea to do so now. I decided to find out whether I could still enroll for the fall semester. Excited at the prospect of doing something completely new, I went to the School for Design the next day and was delighted to hear that there was still room for me. It was perfect timing; the course would take a year and was to start in September. I would finish just before going to the States. I had already signed up for an English-conversational course so that I would be proficient in the language when I set foot in America next August.

Suddenly I wondered how I would be able to do it all; I also had so much piano to practice! Oddly enough, my new feelings of anxiety over my heavy workload seemed to minimize some of the pain I had felt after Don left.

★ ★ ★

September, 1939

The first letters from Don started to arrive in September. The voyage on board the Statendam had been wonderful. The weather was gorgeous and the passengers were constantly spoiled and pampered by the crew. After a luxurious Dutch breakfast in the morning, bouillon was served on deck at 10:30 a.m. and lunch served at noon. There were movies to go to during the day. There was a library on board, two swimming pools, and entertainment at night. Don met interesting people on board and had lots of time to sit on a comfortable deck chair in the sun, reading or just doing nothing. What luxury!

Don described the dinners at night as extraordinary, served with the utmost grace and care, and with an endless variety of food. One evening, when ordering her dinner, Lisa asked the waiter whether he could bring her the same dessert as she had seen the lady at the next table eating. She motioned in the direction very carefully so as not to attract any attention to herself. The waiter informed her that it was not a dessert but a salad. Well, Lisa thought, a salad would be even better than dessert and wanted to try it even more because it looked so beautiful. "Would you please be so kind?" she asked him. Of course, she could have anything she wanted.

The salad was now served, since she had just finished her hors d'oeuvre. But after the first bite of the salad she was puzzled. It looked like whipped cream but it hardly tasted like it; as a matter of fact, it tasted sour. It couldn't be spoiled, not on the Statendam, but it was different from anything she had ever tasted. I could visualize the expression on Lisa's face from Don's descriptive letter. I had seen that expression on Lisa before when she was eating something she didn't care for. It was her first encounter with cottage cheese, something we were not familiar with in Holland.

Life on board ship had been very pleasant, Don wrote, but the voyage was now drawing to an end. When the ship neared the American coast, they saw the Statue of Liberty in all its glory. Because it was the year of the World's Fair, the Zilversmits had decided in advance to stay in New York for a few days of sightseeing. Their first impressions, the encounter with the big city, the expansive World's Fair (an experience in itself), the crowds of people, the noise, were simply overwhelming; it was too much to take in all at once and they felt they would certainly have to come back in the future. They left for Chicago, where they spent five days with friends of Herman's; then on to San Francisco, where Janny and Martin Zilversmit picked them up at the station.

Don and his family stayed with the Zilversmits in San Mateo for a week. The next step was to find a place to live. Since Don was going to attend the University of California in Berkeley, they decided to find housing in that vicinity. September 1, 1939, the day of their arrival in San Francisco, was also the day that Hitler's army marched into Poland.

★ ★ ★

Escaped through the eye of a needle, everyone said, but the opening was so small that they hurt themselves on all sides. The Zilversmits had left Holland just in time. Hitler's policy of aggression was only just beginning. The Zilversmits could count themselves lucky that they'd had the foresight and the means to leave

Holland behind. Of course that didn't mean that the move was not traumatic in the beginning, as Don explained in his first letter from Oakland.

Life in the United States was very difficult for them at first, Don wrote; so much so, he said, that it was a good thing they had only bought one-way tickets. Otherwise, they might have turned around and gone home again, because new problems arose almost daily. Everything was so different: the language, the shopping, nothing delivered to the house as they were used to in Holland. They wanted to do everything themselves rather than with hired help.

Don took the streetcar, a long one-hour trip, to the Berkeley campus, for this was the United States, and the distances were substantial compared to a small country like Holland. The Zilversmits bought a new Buick, and Herman and Bert set out to get their driving licenses.

The family began house-hunting and found an apartment in Oakland, big enough so each of the boys could have his own room. It would do very well for now, they thought. They looked the place over, but wanted to think about it at least overnight before signing the lease. Herman was sure he'd be able to find the apartment again without any trouble because he would immediately recognize the red stone steps leading to the front door. Unfortunately he had not noticed that all the houses had red front steps. Trying to find the apartment the next day became an excruciatingly painful experience. Finally they found their place with the red steps and signed the lease. Lisa said it felt good not to have the responsibility of having a house of their own to start with, and they moved in almost immediately.

★ ★ ★

Don wrote that he missed Utrecht very much. He missed his friends, of course, but above all, he missed me terribly. He missed the wonderful freedom of life on his own that he had experienced while

Kitty after Don Left for U.S. (1939)

at the university in Utrecht; now living at home again he was bound by his parents' rules. Also, it was not easy, at first, to adjust to an American university. Not only was he learning in a different language but the academic system at Berkeley, and presumably in the entire United States, was totally different from what he was accustomed to.

At his new school there were periodic exams and final grades for each course, but in Holland there had been no regular examinations for undergraduate students. The only exams were given at the end of four years, just before graduation. Because of this, Don had no grades demonstrating his academic performance to show the admissions officers. Consequently, they didn't really know where he would fit in. Since he had finished his junior year in Holland, he was placed in the third year. After a few weeks at Berkeley it became much easier, even though he found the new routine of test-taking somewhat repetitive and childish. He wrote that sometimes he felt he was back in high school in Holland.

But there were also many things he liked about college in the United States. The Americans were very different from the Dutch, more friendly and helpful, free and easygoing. He was very impressed by the casual relationship between professors and students. In Holland, professors were in their "ivory tower." The students had virtually no contact with them and were essentially left on their own. It was very refreshing for Don to discover the informal, down-to-earth atmosphere that existed between professors and students. Also, the more relaxed way they dressed was entirely different. In Holland it would have been unthinkable for a professor to give a lecture without wearing a dress shirt and tie. Not here, however; they could dress as they pleased and generally dressed to be comfortable.

Don particularly wrote about an experience with one of his professors that had amused him. One morning he was running up the steps leading to the main entrance of the university when he saw one of his professors. Having become accustomed to the informality in this new academic setting, Don stopped the professor halfway up the steps and asked if he could spare a few minutes. The professor gladly agreed and invited Don to sit down. So they sat down right on the steps where they had met. Don was having a problem with a mathematical equation; he had written down several hypotheses but couldn't come to a reasonable solution to the problem. The professor happened to have a piece of chalk in his pocket and wrote one equation after another on the concrete steps. When he ran out of space on one step, they simply dropped down to the next and continued writing until a solution was found.

Don wrote that he was beginning to feel at home. Lisa and Herman were also adjusting to the new environment and were facing their problems head-on. Although they were not altogether unfamiliar with English, their vocabulary and conversational skills were inadequate. Aware that they had to do something about the language barrier, they enrolled in an evening class in English conversation. Lisa, forty-two, and Herman, fifty-one, found it difficult to be back in school. But there was a pleasant compensation for their efforts. They met another couple in their class who had immigrated from Germany a year earlier. The four of them became the best of friends and soon were regular bridge partners. Felix and Leonore were optometrists and had opened their own business in Oakland, becoming very successful. Don's brother

Bert, who was also working to improve his English, found a job in a supermarket.

★ ★ ★

More letters kept coming from Don. Sometimes the mailman would ring the doorbell on Sunday morning and deliver a fat airmail letter, sometimes two. I blessed the efficiency of the Dutch postal service. I will never know why his letters were delivered on Sunday, because they weren't marked "special delivery." Oh, how I lived for his letters; I missed his unexpected visits, his phone calls, and our walks. I missed everything about him. But I kept very busy. My fashion-design course had started, and so had my English course. I liked my course work very much and was especially pleased that it would have a practical application, which I thought was important. Despite the fact that my courses kept me busy, I continued to practice the piano. The year was passing quickly and I was glad I didn't have time to feel sorry for myself.

★ ★ ★

February, 1940

Another letter from Don. He suggested that I start getting my immigration papers ready in preparation for coming to the United States. He cautioned that the political situation in Europe was deteriorating too fast for comfort. He was convinced that in America they had a much better perspective on the situation than we did in Holland. I decided to let my parents read Don's letter and see how they would react. My father was negative. "Well, you can see that Don has already become Americanized! I think he's exaggerating to the point of being ridiculous; besides, we agreed that you would follow him to the States after one year and not sooner. The bottom line is that I don't think anything is going to happen to us, and you know that many people share my opinion." There was no way that my father would give his approval for me to leave

Holland before the year was over. I tried to reason with him and repeatedly pointed out that Don was honest, sincere, and above all, terribly worried about me. I knew that Don was not just taking advantage of the world situation to get me there as soon as possible. But convincing my father was hopeless, and in the end I resigned myself to the fact that August was not so terribly far off.

6

War!

I was awakened early in the morning by a stream of bright sunlight coming through my bedroom window and a low monotonous hum that I couldn't immediately identify. I quickly got out of bed and found my parents already up. They, too, had heard the strange droning and wondered what it was. I got dressed in a hurry. Mother said that it was probably our air force on maneuvers. It seemed a likely explanation at the time, but as the sounds grew louder we became increasingly apprehensive.

All three of us went outside to find an otherwise beautiful sky blackened with literally hundreds of little spots. The droning continued. The horrifying realization struck each of us at the same time: they were German airplanes! We went inside and turned on the radio. To our dismay the broadcast confirmed our fears:

At three o'clock that morning, Nazi troops had started across the Dutch border. German planes had bombed Dutch airfields and dropped paratroopers on strategic locations.

A few hours later, the German ambassador delivered a declaration in the name of his government, stating that German troops had entered the Netherlands to protect Dutch neutrality against an imminent Allied invasion aimed at the Ruhr Valley.

He advised the Dutch government not to offer pointless resistance, but rather to place the country under the Reich's protection. Only then would Germany guarantee the continuation of the monarchy and the independence of the Netherlands.

The Dutch government rejected the German allegations and declared that the country would resist. England and France were asked for military aid. Later that day, Queen Wilhelmina issued a proclamation repudiating the German invasion and branding it a breach of international law and decency. We knew there was nothing we could do. We sat stunned, and listened helplessly to one horrid broadcast after another.

Soon after the invasion, it became apparent that the German advance was overwhelmingly successful. On the first day of the attack, the Luftwaffe had succeeded in destroying most of Holland's military planes and German paratroopers had secured a number of airfields around The Hague and Rotterdam. Furthermore, it became increasingly clear that the invaders were planning to capture the Queen.

With our military power lessening, the Dutch cabinet recommended that Queen Wilhelmina seek safety for herself and her family. The commander-in-chief of the Dutch forces, General H. G. Winkelman, said that he could no longer be responsible for her safety. On May 12, Crown Princess Juliana, her children, and Prince Bernhard left for England on a British destroyer. Prince Bernhard returned immediately to join the Dutch troops fighting in Zeeland.

On May 13, the Queen boarded a destroyer. Her cabinet was to follow the next day. Upon her arrival in London the Queen released a statement explaining her reasons for fleeing the Netherlands. She said that she had come to England to protect the interests of her country and to retain her freedom of action, which she would have lost had she fallen into German hands. She also wanted to safeguard the independence of the Dutch East Indies (present-day Indonesia).

We were utterly shocked when we heard the news that the Queen and her family had fled to England. We had such mixed emotions. We were relieved that the royal family were spared any personal injustice at the hands of the Germans, yet simultaneously outraged and shattered that our future was now hopeless. The war had only just begun, but was already lost.

By Tuesday, May 14, the military situation had deteriorated seriously. The Germans cut Holland off from Belgium and established themselves solidly near Rotterdam. They threatened to bomb all of the Netherlands' big cities, starting with Rotterdam.

General Winkelman, the highest Dutch authority after the Queen and
her cabinet had left, tried to negotiate a surrender to avoid the bombing
of Rotterdam. But the negotiations dragged on beyond the German
deadline. The German officers in charge of the surrender negotiations
tried to call off the attack, but were unable to notify one air squadron.
As a result, on the afternoon of May 14, at approximately 1:30 p.m.,
Rotterdam's harbor and downtown area were bombed. Nine hundred
people were killed and thousands more injured or made homeless. That
same afternoon, General Winkelman announced that the nation's military forces would capitulate, and all did surrender except for the Dutch
marines, who kept fighting on in Zeeland.[1]

Even they could not keep going, and it finally ended on May 19.
So ended a five-day war that was to begin five years of deprivation
and despair.

When Holland surrendered, most of the Dutch people hardly
had time to comprehend what had happened. We had not been
prepared to fight a war against an army that had such superior
weapons and numbers. Once the news began to sink in, one might
have expected sighs of relief, at least because there would be no
more loss of innocent life. But most recognized that our misery
was only just now beginning.

★ ★ ★

May 15, 1940

There had been no fighting in Utrecht and, except for our awareness of much air activity, we hardly knew there was a war going
on. Three blocks away from our house was a railroad station, now
an emergency Red Cross shelter. A couple of days earlier my sister
Susan and I had offered our services, but we were not allowed
inside and had gone home. After that we just sat in our living room,
looking at one another, wondering what to do next.

---

1. Much of the preceding material has been taken nearly verbatim from Werner
Warmbrunn, *The Dutch Under German Occupation, 1940-1945*, Stanford: Stanford University
Press, pp. 7-8.

A terrible cloud of gloom began to settle over our home. Mother seemed to have stopped functioning altogether. She just sat in her chair hour after hour, staring into space, her face drawn and pale. Father and the three boys busied themselves with chores around the house; although Leo may have been old enough to understand how serious things were, Eddy and Jack couldn't have had any idea. Our living room had two big bay windows facing the street. Under them were wide wooden shelves which formed two little round window seats. Susan stationed herself on one of them and sat there for hours, looking out toward the end of the street as though she was expecting somebody to come around the corner.

I fixed dinner that night. I didn't know if anybody would eat anything, but I thought we might as well try to go on as normally as possible; the boys would certainly need their dinners. I didn't notice whether anyone actually ate, or was just going through the motions, pretending everything was normal. Later, after everyone had retired for the night, I overheard a conversation between my parents that I would never be able to shake from my memory. My room was next to their bedroom. Mother often left their door open just a crack, an old habit dating back to when we were small children. On the night of May 15, too, the door was ajar. I was falling asleep when I was awakened by quiet but urgent talking emanating from my parents' room. As the minutes passed the talking became increasingly louder until I suddenly realized that mother was actually moaning. I heard her words, but did not really comprehend her meaning: "Let's turn on the gas, please, and get it over with." Suddenly awareness dawned and I found myself sitting straight up and alert in bed. I knew I couldn't let myself miss any of their conversation. I felt such a strange mixture of guilt for intruding on their privacy and terror at the harsh reality my mother's pleading conveyed. But above all, I felt an overwhelming curiosity. I had to keep listening.

It was quiet for a while. But then, out of the night's stillness, new moaning arose . . . terrible, desperate, horrifying outcries. Father tried to reason with her. "No, we can't do that to our children and ourselves; we must have confidence that God will help." It was quiet again, then new sighs of desperation began. I found it hard to imagine that mother was actually contemplating the suicide of her entire family.

I knew that my mother was grief-stricken, but I also knew that she was rational and that her fears were overwhelmingly real. Mother had always been an avid reader and had talked with many refugees who had fled to Holland; she was so afraid of what the future might hold for the Jews of Holland. It was just a matter of time. Events in Germany between 1933 and 1939 had been well documented and were no secret.

After what I had just heard it was impossible for me to go back to sleep. I had to stay up and listen the rest of the night. Even though I was sure mother wanted to do what she felt was best for the family, I was afraid for my life! Her words of despair left me so upset and teary that there was no chance I could get any rest and I remained wide-awake till morning. Finally it grew light outside, and soon I would be able to get up and get dressed. I knew I would never tell mother and father what I had overheard during the night.

I was shocked by my mother's appearance in the morning; she had aged visibly, and for the first time I noticed deep lines around her mouth and chin. But life has a way of going on, even under the most grim of circumstances. Eventually mother, too, found the courage to keep going. I suppose she listened to father, and although she didn't believe in God as he did, she wanted to hope that the future might still be worth living for.

Now there were German soldiers regularly marching through our streets. They were always singing German marching songs, and the sound of their hob-nailed boots would reach our ears long before they came into view. It was nauseating to see these men in our streets, where they had not been invited and were not welcome. Their very presence was threatening.

We later learned that many Jewish people committed suicide during that night of May 15, especially German refugees. They had come to Holland to escape persecution. They felt unable to face the ordeal of life under the Nazis a second time.

* * *

All communication between Don and me had stopped because of the war, but Don had been keeping a diary since 1935 and continued with it in the United States.

Don's Diary: *May 25, 1940*

Much has happened and many things have changed since a few weeks ago. After a relatively quiet beginning, the war has finally exploded in its full and destructive power. On May 10, the Nazi troops marched into Holland, Belgium, and Luxembourg. This is now behind us and we can expect an abundance of satanic cruelty to come.

Holland is no more, Belgium almost no more. A destructive, devastating rain of bombs converted these countries into ashes. Many have perished, fled, or succumbed because of total exhaustion. Who will still be alive, and even those whose bodies are still functioning, how will they live under this barbaric regime? Yes, once again, the Jews are the losers. They are the losers against the power of the Germans and the injustice which they inflict on the Jews. Fortunately we are no match for these bandits and are of a different mentality. But with all that, the facts are very depressing. No sign of life have we received so far. How is Kitty? Could she have managed to flee from the hands of those murderers? I am almost afraid to hope.

How are our other relatives and friends? The mail is at a standstill; all communications are broken, all is silent. All this turns our relief and happiness at being here into grief, and worse, into feelings of despair. We can't do anything but wait and witness how people murder one another. To think about it doesn't help, it will make the situation even more hopeless. Who will win? Who knows what the future holds? Ultimately justice must prevail.

But we human beings don't live forever! We have only a short time on this earth and try to live that time as pleasantly as possible. We had made plans, had made friends, and now, everything gone, crumbled to pieces, destroyed. Our future up in smoke, our friends taken away from us; how can one go on after such a tragedy? The ground under our feet is like quicksand; and how long before we are completely caught in it? Why do innocent people have to suffer so much? Why is it that so many good people are deprived of the opportunity to build a better world? We grow up and educate ourselves. We adapt to situations and become wiser. Generation after generation is born, each learning from the other's accomplishments only to see that life becomes more complicated with a huge question mark; why?

June 20, 1940

Dear Kitty,

Because I have not been able to write to you all these weeks (the American authorities advised against it), I feel compelled to let you hear from me and write a few words. Yes, to hear; because I am convinced that you will hear them if you are still alive. You know what I wish for you and what I think; words are not necessary for us. This week Aunt Anne, Uncle Max, and John are coming here. You probably don't know it, but they were able to flee on May 14 from IJmuiden in the hold of a lime ship. They arrived safely in England at the White Cliffs of Dover and are now on their way to California. Although I am very happy for them, I feel, even more, how terrible it is for you (and therefore for me) that you are still in Holland. The thought that harm may come to you or that someone may try to hurt you makes me desperate; I try to put these thoughts, as much as possible, out of my mind.

July 10, 1940

Dear Kitty,

Six thousand miles from here lies the place where I first saw the world, where I grew up and lived until just yesterday it seems. I am so far away from where I found love and understanding. So very far away and shut off from Kitty, from her caresses, advice, and help.

Unsure about the future and perplexed over the past, while the present is racing on into chaos. It is in this frame of mind that I will come of age; twenty-one years old. This birthday, I am sure, will be atypically unpleasant and confused.

★ ★ ★

July, 1940

At first not much changed after the occupation of Holland. The Germans were on their best behavior, secretly hoping that in the end they would win over the Dutch people—something they never accomplished. Nonetheless, they made it illegal to listen to radio broadcasts from outside the occupied territory. The restriction did not deter many from listening to the BBC. Mother would say: "We can live with rules like that, as long as they let us stay together."

It had become quite clear that my personal dream was now completely destroyed. There was no way I could follow Don to the United States as we had planned when he left last August. During my more pessimistic moods, I had more than once taken the big world atlas out of the bookcase to see whether there was some way, not immediately obvious, to travel to the United States—possibly through Russia. But Holland's borders were closed, and the uncertainty and danger of traveling such a distance alone quickly brought me back to my senses. Don and I would have to see this problem through together—but apart—the best we knew how. After all, I was with my family; there was simply no other way.

No more letters came from Don. All communication had been broken off. In addition, I began to fear that I might not be permitted to finish my course in fashion designing. But nothing like that happened. I finished on time and got an A in the course. At least I had that under my belt.

I carefully put away the course materials and accessories accumulated during the school year into a big box, including numerous paper dress designs one-quarter the original size, and favorite dresses or suits, picked out of fashion magazines, used for practice. I was now able to draft any pattern out of a fashion magazine. I packed up my textbooks on the history of textiles and a sampler, twenty feet long, made out of black wool fabric, containing all my art work requirements: fancy designs made with elongated beads, sequins, appliqué, braids, and batiks, in addition to a collection of tailored pockets and buttonholes.

Life went on as normally as could be expected under the circumstances. We experienced none of the hardships which befell the Austrian Jews when the Nazis invaded that country in 1938, enforcing the Nuremberg Laws, which took away all their civil rights. Mother seemed to recover from the initial shock she felt when Holland was first occupied and appeared to be functioning normally; on the surface, life was as before. I was now spending a lot of time with mother. At my request, she let her domestic help go and I did the daily chores. We had somebody come in once a week just to do the heavy cleaning. That was enough outside assistance, so mother paid me for my help.

I got up early each morning, did my work quickly, and had plenty of time to practice the piano in the afternoon. I was still taking private lessons from Hans Vega at her home when she was not teaching at the Amsterdam Conservatory. Not only was she a marvelous teacher, she was a very special person. She made me work hard; my repertoire was quite demanding, and my lessons a source of delight.

★ ★ ★

Don's Diary: *August 19, 1940*

Fortunately I received several letters from Kitty this week. Some were sent by Clipper and others by boat, the last one dated July 29. Of course, they had all been opened and marked by the censor, but in any case it was at least a sign of life; what a relief! The idea that our letters are going to be opened impedes one in writing one's thoughts and feelings without inhibition. Hopefully, this evil will be of short duration and we'll be able to communicate verbally in the not-too-distant future.

Don's Diary: *August 25, 1940*

It is a good feeling to know that after a relatively lazy three months of vacation, which is nearly over now, it's back to college again. My schedule is just about in order. I was a bit dubious about two classes, electricity and photochemistry, the first one much easier but less instructive. I have tried to tell myself that if I were to choose this unit, I would have a better chance of getting a good grade which later could help me with a fellowship or a job. However, the thought of doing this, like so many other students, who take easy subjects in order to get good grades, would mean, in the end, that I was fooling myself. That made me decide to choose the more difficult courses for which I will have to work a little harder.

A change in my program occurred which perhaps is worth recording. My counselor advised me to take three units of mechanical engineering. It is completely out of my field, but I yielded to the practical side of the question after he made it very clear to me that I should not count too much on a university job and that I was really not prepared to go into industry without at least some engineering. I concurred with his reasoning and, assuming that he was talking from experience, decided for the first time to listen to the voice of technology, which the world prefers to hear over the voice of science. It was a concession I had to make because, under the given circumstances, my chosen course of study would have been too much of a gamble.

This week the third semester starts at Berkeley, and it is also the beginning of my second year in the United States and everything that is connected with that. Of course I have to acknowledge that many of the plans we made with so much cautiousness and reasonableness have not materialized because of factors completely out of our hands caused by the world situation. The conflict we had last year over Kitty's coming to the United States, the meeting with her parents (we thought we had solved all those things so well), now seems completely unimportant.

The complications and turmoil in the world have changed things to an extent that we could never have predicted with our limited vision. That gives me hope that the future may also work out differently than things look at the moment. I know very well that there is no logic in this philosophy, but we have to sacrifice something to keep a beautiful thought alive. Still, it would not be wise to count too much on miracles. Under the present circumstances, Kitty and I could easily become alienated from one another. Now, of course, we love each other endlessly, but after years of separation, would we still resemble the Kitty and Don of 1939? Sometimes life is reasonable, sometimes a gamble, and under the circumstances we must be content to take it as it is presented to us.

December 21, 1940

I have just written Kitty my weekly letter, and as if it isn't bad enough that she is so far away, one cannot even write in detail because of the censor. Our contact this way does not become any stronger. Without her, I live only half a life or less. The only thing I can do is to lose myself in my studies and the artificial world I have built for myself. With the real world and the people around me I have little contact; that's the way I want it. Something has been taken away from me, something very dear and lovely. You have been taken away from me, Kitty, and my heart tightens with fear when I think that I won't be able to get you back before it is too late. You know how much you mean to me; how will I ever live a normal life without you? To have to do without your sweet face, your fine voice and warm eyes is a terrible test: a tragedy. Never again write that it may be a long time before I see you again. At least let my hope for our reunion stay alive; if you kill it, it means that you kill me.

December 29, 1940

Last night I was at the Goldbergs' for a Hanukkah celebration, and I realized (and have since become much more aware of) the following: The more knowledge one accumulates, the more complex things become and therefore much harder to understand. It seems that only a relatively stupid person can say that he understands something completely. I don't know exactly why this thought flared up in my mind again last night, but I was, and still am, very perplexed at how a simple question asked by a child could be answered with so much bombast and roundabout talk before the question was understood. I think that after every five words I could have asked a question and then could have discussed it for hours without introducing subtleties. The answer took several minutes, was full of spiritual and mystical thought, and, as far as I'm concerned, was absolutely no answer at all, but at best a complication of the question that was asked. However, I was surprised that the little boy seemed to understand it, at least in part. I should try to keep my attention on this subject for a while to see whether greater knowledge, in general, brings with it more doubt and less understanding.

Physics and mathematics, so simple and easily explained in high school, gave me a feeling of complete understanding without mystery. Now I experience something quite different. Greater knowledge of facts and deeper penetration into a theory—to abstract an idea—makes for confusion. Nothing "checks" anymore. We work with probabilities, not certainties.

★ ★ ★

By 1941 life began to change under the occupation. Everyone over the age of fifteen was now required to carry an identity card. The Nazis began to eliminate Jews from public life:

Although a seemingly petty annoyance, Jewish volunteers in the air-raid protection service were dismissed. It was now also forbidden to perform ritual slaughter, an element so critical for the Jewish dietary laws. The Nazis began separating Jews from non-Jews by excluding Jews from recreational facilities, such as restaurants and hotels. A special registration for Jews was held in January, and 140,000 complied with the law.

In February, the Jewish Council (Joodsche Raad or Judenrat) came into existence. Its purpose was to function as intermediary between the Germans and the Jewish population. The two main leaders of the Jewish Council were Mr. Abraham Asscher, a prominent Amsterdam business-man who had been active in the Liberal Party, and Professor David Cohen, who taught ancient history at the Municipal University of Amsterdam. Professor Cohen was the chairman of a committee which had been assisting German refugees since 1933. Both men were essen-tially humanists and philanthropists who readily accepted the responsi-bility of serving as chairmen of the Council in the hope that they might be able to help Dutch Jewry in a time of crisis.

In addition, the German High Commissioner ordered all Jewish businesses to register on a special list and German administrators were appointed to run them. Procedures were established for the compulsory sale of all such enterprises by March 1941. Agricultural property too had to be registered, and the sale of these properties was only a matter of time. Although physical persecution of the Jews had not yet started at this early stage, future deportations were foreshadowed by two mass arrests in Amsterdam. The first was in February 1941 in retribution for self-defense action taken by Amsterdam Jews; approximately 400 young Jews were arrested and sent to Mauthausen in Austria. The mass arrest was a reprisal for the planting of a time bomb in Amsterdam; another 220 young men, most German refugees, were picked up and taken to Mauthausen.[2]

It is impossible to forget the first round-up of Jews, called a *razzia*, or "raid." Needless to say, there was real panic. One had to be constantly on the alert not to be in the wrong place at the wrong time, because you could be picked up in a flash. German military trucks, or *overval wagens*, would race through the streets, coming to an abrupt stop. Heavily armed men would jump off and block streets or even whole areas, while more armed men patrolled the area. Any Jew in the cordoned-off area was caught and thrown into a truck—just taken away.

One day, Kappy Cohen, the baker's son, didn't make his usual delivery. We wondered where he could be. We found out the next day that Kappy had gone to Amsterdam to spend the weekend with friends. He had been captured by the Nazis in a *razzia* and sent to Mauthausen, one of 220 young men. There, we know now, they were subjected to inhumanly heavy labor in the stone quarries, treated with great cruelty, and finally starved to death. Kappie's tragedy brought the nightmare still closer to home. It somehow felt much more chilling for someone I knew to have been captured and deported. Any semblance of peace of mind was now completely

---

2. Most of the preceding material has been taken from Werner Warmbrunn, *The Dutch Under German Occupation, 1940-1945*, Stanford: Stanford University Press, pp. 63-65.

gone; one never knew what would happen next. It was best not to be outside, but there was no real safety even at home. As a result of the special registration the previous February, there were now lists of Jews. The Nazis were very meticulous and systematic about picking people up from their houses. One's home became a prison, and deportation by the Nazis continuously threatened.

At least, I thought, the winter was drawing to an end and the days were getting longer, with more daylight to look forward to. Because of the required blackout, the nights were eerie—deadly quiet and bleak, unless there was a full moon. During those long dark nights, every noise from the outside sent adrenaline shooting through my system. The Nazi murderers were everywhere, and we no longer had any rights.

But in spite of everything, spring came suddenly in all its glory, and as always we watched the bulbs develop and burst into gorgeous flowers, a wonder of nature, and we wondered what the future would hold for us.

★ ★ ★

In June 1941 the German army invaded Russia. When the news came, we were devastated and shocked. The Germans, it seemed, were so strong and well organized that they could no longer be stopped. Nevertheless we tried to carry on with life as normally as we could. My father was still working but eventually had to retire. Mother seemed well; the boys were in school, occupied with homework and just being boys. My sister Susan had a job that could actually be called ideal under the circumstances. The State Hospital in Utrecht was operating a kosher diet kitchen, and she was the assistant to the head dietician. Many Jewish patients from surrounding smaller cities and villages went to the hospital in Utrecht for treatment in order to take advantage of the kosher kitchen. On weekends, when the dietician had her day off, Sue frequently asked me to come and assist her in the kitchen. I gladly accepted; I liked the atmosphere at the hospital, and I liked learning about special diets. On occasion, I was sent to the ward when a patient had a special request or sometimes just for a social call.

Soon it would be time for me to look for a job also; I had been talking about it with mother. It would not be easy to find something that was not only safe but in a Jewish setting. How much longer would Jews be allowed to work among non-Jews? Mother had been a nurse before she married father, and she suggested that I think about going into nursing. Being in an all-Jewish hospital could, under the circumstances, be the safest place for me.

The Nederlands Israelitisch Ziekenhuis (Netherlands Jewish Hospital; NIZ for short) in Amsterdam had approximately 500 beds. It was the biggest of the three Jewish hospitals in Amsterdam. If I were accepted into its nursing program, I would get training on the job, live in the dormitory, and earn a small salary. I knew that the war would not be over tomorrow and would probably last a long time. In the interim, maybe I could become a registered nurse, an achievement that would certainly have many practical benefits for me.

A few days later, while shopping, I met Jetty Vromen. I had known her for years. She and her sister Sophy had grown up in the Jewish orphanage in Utrecht, having lost their mother when they were both quite young. Jetty asked me about my plans, since she knew I couldn't go to the United States now to join Don, as planned. She mentioned that she had just accepted a job at Wertheim House, an institution for chronically ill mental patients. She had really wanted to enter the training program at NIZ, but they were not accepting any new applications just now; instead she had put her name on the waiting list. There was no formal training at Wertheim House, but work experience there might help me to get accepted when an opening occurred for new student nurses at NIZ. Jetty suggested that I go to both institutions and at least put my name on the waiting lists.

I discussed all this with my parents, carefully considering every aspect of such a move, and soon decided to apply for a job at Wertheim House. I took the train to Amsterdam the next day. I had no trouble finding Wertheim House; when I got to Wertheim Park, it was right across the street. Luck was with me that day; the head nurse, Miss Levy, was in and was able to see me. I told her how the war had interfered with my plans to go to the United States to be with my fiancé and that I was looking for a job. I also told her about my conversation with Jetty Vromen only the day before. Miss Levy said she could use a new person but not until September. She told me what my work would consist of; it was only practical nursing. After I had worked there for a couple of months, I would be on night duty every fourteen days for one week. I would earn thirty guilders a month with one day a week off. I accepted the job without hesitation and was excited about the prospect of starting work in September.

Not wanting to waste any time I called the hospital and asked to speak with Dr. Kroonenberg, the director and head physician, who did all the hiring. He was not in, so an appointment was set up. When I returned to the hospital on the designated day, Dr. Kroonenberg, a soft-spoken, reserved man, interviewed me. He asked my reasons for going into nursing and wanted to know what kind of work I had done in the past. I answered all his questions and told him I would be starting work at Wertheim House on September 1st. He confirmed that working at Wertheim House was a good idea, but said he wouldn't be able to place me until March of 1942, when the new classes would start.

I was put on the waiting list and told I would be notified when the time came to start training. He sent me to Nurse Zwanenburg, the head nurse, who would tell me what I would need and where to order my uniforms. Nurse Zwanenburg was a middle-aged woman, friendly but businesslike and efficient, and she gave me all the information I needed. I ordered the uniforms immediately because

I knew I could also wear them at Wertheim House. Now there was much work to do in preparation for my move to Amsterdam.

★ ★ ★

Don's Diary: *March 30, 1941*

Now that I have written a letter to Kitty, maybe it would be a good idea to write a few words in my diary. Not that there is much worth mentioning. What in this life is good? Which goals are important, what ultimate truth are we seeking? The movie we saw tonight revived the old questions, and just as in former years, they have not been answered. In all these years I haven't learned very much except what to do with certain chemicals to get a certain result. I seem to be back in the days of doubt and dismay. Days of total skepticism mixed with a serious longing for ideals; only everything seems to be worse and the future is darker. How is everything? Well, it's quite simple. When everything turns out to be a disappointment, isn't that a reason to be discouraged? Everything, you ask? Yes, everything. Are you not satisfied with all your successes in school? Are you not happy that you have escaped the hand of dictators and cannibals, out of the trap of a destructive war? Yes, I admit that "everything" may be a little exaggerated, but much has gone against me although I have tried to prepare myself for it.

At the university it goes so-so if you don't take into consideration that I am not making much progress with my research. But what is it all for? What are all those A's good for? You say that I can continue with my studies . . . no, I am a Jew. You say that now, like all the others whose grades are much lower, I can get an assistantship somewhere . . . no, little or no chance . . . too many Jews. You say that now I could get a job because the country is concentrating on defensive measures for the war? Oh, no, I'm not an American and I am a Jew. All this would not be so terrible if there weren't someone on almost every street corner distributing leaflets for the "noble democracies" where everyone is equal. And that is only the beginning. There is so much more I could lament if I were willing to give up sleep for it. Kitty, the only person who can give me courage, is so endlessly far away, and chances that she will be here within a reasonable time are slim; to keep hoping for that, one would have to be a real optimist.

What good is all this? I wonder, if people could put their happiness and disappointments on a scale, would not most have more of the latter than the former? Why do we accept this? Why is there no protest against this cruel destiny, a future full of shadows; is it all necessary? Did we develop from monkeys only to feel our suffering more strongly, to suffer more of some ingeniously-thought-out ailment? Is development only a way to refine the methods of torture? Is God a way out? Does religion bring deliverance? Can science set us free, or is everything doomed already before we are born? What is good and what is bad? Why is one thing better than another? Are we better than animals led by their instincts? Something seems to be wrong. We people are peculiar. We believe too much of what we and our neighbors say. We see order where chaos reigns; we are naive. Maybe everything we believe and think of as holy is but a shadow, a figment contrived by the imagination to confuse us. Of course, we can't live without certain rules of order and communication, but they should be for our comfort and not for our enslavement, if one looks at it critically.

We are all so prejudiced that we have already decided in advance to exclude our neighbor. We are still too much animal and don't know how to shed that. The road to understanding is long and hard, since misunderstanding generally prevails. Our ideals will be of no use until we understand one another better. Certainly language should be more clear. Instead of propaganda we will have to find ways of communicating; instead of debate, a process of understanding. We should not throw empty words to our fellow men at religious services and raise them to holiness. We will have to change our law codes so that, instead of slavery, man's happiness becomes the first priority.

But alas, look around and see what's happening. Men take up arms, one against the other. One fights for Democracy and against Nazism, for freedom and against the oppressor. What is Democracy if it is worth fighting for? What is it? Is it to destroy Nazism? Is it Hitler? No! Is it the Germans? No. Is it Europe? No. What is it? And this is only one aspect. Men fight for freedom and expose themselves to the greatest suppressor of all time—propaganda. Whether it be English, German, or American propaganda, it kills initiative and takes away the freedom to think. It confuses the masses. It is not surprising that the common man, listening to the radio, hearing many opinions about one subject, is more confused now than before. It is not surprising that he would welcome a system under which he could live easier, through which he would be told how to live, what to do, and what not to do. Is this the beginning of Fascism?

We fight, but don't know for what, because if we did know, we wouldn't fight. But all this doesn't help very much; it only shows that we cannot take things lightly during these terrible times. The future is dark and not worth living for. Will mankind ever see better times again? It looks as though we hold it in our own hands and it is not God who decides. If we want to change things, let us begin from the ground up, let us build on new foundations.

April 13, 1941

The first two days of Passover have gone, and just as last year, I was invited to a Seder at the Fass's home. Since I still don't feel much like studying, I should write a few words in my diary. This time I will start with some news; no politics tonight.

I don't remember whether I wrote about an application I sent off for an assistantship at the University of Minnesota. A polite but negative letter was the only result. I also sent an application to the University of Iowa, from which I have not received a reply. Since I did not hear by April 1, it means I was not accepted. Both jobs fell through. However, this week something different happened, and I feel as though any diversion comes as a sort of relief in the routine of daily life. I was told that the physiology department was looking for a chemist to work in a laboratory and do research with artificial radioactive materials to study their effect on metabolism in cancer patients. I quickly went over to find out about the job. I knew everything was okay immediately because they didn't pay any attention to the race or descent of the applicant and my grades were very good in every respect.

So I'll start my research in June with Dr. I. Chaikoff, M.D., Ph.D., professor in the department of physiology. I will earn fifty dollars per month for which I don't have to give any time outside my work for my Ph.D. It even looks a little "too profitable," and if I like the work, it could offer a good opportunity for progress. At least I cannot complain that I am not getting a rounded education.

In Utrecht special organic chemistry, in Berkeley physical chemistry and now physiology. It looks a little bit like I'll be a jack of all trades. Anyway, "what he has learned cannot be taken away from him," and as otherwise it would have been the end of my studies, this job doesn't look so bad after all, although it is true that I never showed much respect for such unscientific fields. Who knows, it won't all be that bleak, and I may even like it. It is at least as good as a job in industry or the army. Let's conclude that I was lucky in the end.

Besides my studies there are unfortunately still other things that occupy my mind. The Pesach holidays are now over and left me in a better frame of mind. The services I attended in the synagogue played their part in getting me to long for a Jewish life. If Kitty had been here, I certainly wouldn't have waited long to get married. Not that I feel so religious anymore. Coming to the United States has played an important part in turning me into a skeptic, but there is something in the Jewish religion that attracts me a lot. The pull to the Orient? To look at everything realistically makes everything appear very bad and sad. My belief in an Almighty God has diminished a lot, my ideals about helping mankind are gone, my hope for a happy life in the near future is thwarted. The will to live and life's purpose escape me. The why and for what, how and when—that's what is missing. The order is gone and the regularity has vanished. Inner peace has been replaced by unrest, and happiness by worry. Who can still believe in a world that is good when everything is confusion and murder, unreliability and theft? Who can still feel secure when the sword threatens from all sides?

What good are ideals for a better world and a happier life, with progress in medicine and peace, when one bomb can destroy that which all doctors together cannot save? Can one find rest when one lives for headlines and slogans? Can one listen to the honey-sweet, hypocritical words of the spiritual leaders of a world of crime and obstruction? Can we keep hoping when constantly disappointed? For two thousand years, Jews have repeated, *Leshanah haba birushalayim,* "Next year in Jerusalem." Is human patience never exhausted, are we more patient even than God? Interestingly, we have such strong convictions in our routine daily lives, we know so well what's "good" and what's "bad," but in our deepest being, we are confused about every existing principle. There are hypocrites and profiteers who will say anything so long as they and their followers benefit from it; the "pure of heart and mind" look for that support and their tantalizing words.

And now I will go to sleep in order to wake up in the morning with renewed courage and a fresh mind. I will have forgotten most of this and will be able to dive into full life, as do all the other creatures of habit around me. I will observe the rules and conventions of society and soothe my conscience with beautiful words and old fables. I will probably no longer think about all the people who couldn't sleep last night because of bombs, fire, and violence, and those who were unable to sleep because of hunger, or those who were not allowed to close their eyes unless forever. Like everyone else, I will keep my small concerns in my heart and perhaps speak some kindly untruths so as to see some happy faces around me that will make me forget all this sorrow and misery a little. It will be good not to have any time to think about wretchedness and stand by hopelessly, not knowing what to do.

May 10, 1941

One thing comes more and more to the foreground which scares me very much. It has become increasingly hard for me to look at the world as I see it today and bring it into harmony with the classical personal God handed down to us from primeval times. If my thinking continues along these lines, there may be difficulties ahead. How would Kitty react, and what would her attitude be if she knew how much I have changed since I left her? Everything is still in the beginning stages, but any upcoming event may easily swing the balance to the other side. Maybe everything will come out quite differently and any change only be for the better.

June 1, 1941

Shavuot is over, and on both days I went to the Conservative synagogue close to the house, primarily because the cantor has a much better voice than in the one I usually go to. The content of the sermon was of very low caliber. It was some kind of businesslike set-up at best, to advertise certain social events. It didn't say anything new, and personally I attach little value to the interpretation of old sayings in the light of 1941, as we call it. The superficiality was too apparent in every word, and the meaning the sermon was meant to offer failed to appear, although the speaker zealously took pains to choose words that would evoke certain emotions.

More and more I abhor the language of clergymen whose "mouths drip with honey." If they believe it themselves, then at least they are honest and innocent, but sometimes, besides advertising their innocence, they are also dishonest. Of course, it is easier to win people over with a joke than with logic, and this brings its own danger and confusion. And so our clergymen, preaching from the pulpit, do not attempt to teach facts but instead call up strong language and empty, sentimental words, awakening the animal instincts in people. God cannot stand firmly in the world with such defenders and such vendors of spiritual merchandise, not now or ever.

October 3, 1941

It's been some time since I last wrote in my diary. My work in physiology has been going on for several months now and seems to have had a considerable influence on my thought world. If nothing else, it has sharpened my critical sense and brought it to the fore-ground. I must admit that I am often a serious skeptic filled with distrust for the ideas that others speak of so confidently. Scientifically speaking, the work in physiology is very confusing and I am afraid that I will end up on the same road others have taken, that of inac-curacy and being disorganized in thought and speech. The only defense is perhaps some exaggerated disbelief that continually forces me to think and talk as precisely as possible. Of course that doesn't encourage animated conversation, but I'm afraid that if I let myself be so swept away by religion that I am unable to see the prudent steps taken in science, I will have lost my last value in this life. Don't think that this attitude does not have a cost in deprivation, but on the other hand, it is enormously satisfying to see a problem clear and full as well as in detail. My Orthodox religion was, of course, one of the first sacrifices. It was absolutely impossible for me to combine science and religion. This change from one extreme to the other happened quite suddenly; I actually never went through a transitional state. No, it was a splash out of the idealism of Orthodoxy into noth-ingness, somewhat bleak but refreshing.

Another important thing happened last week. Bert and I refused to join the Dutch forces in England because we wish to become American citizens.

7

Wertheim House

September 1, 1941

When I arrived at Wertheim House in the early afternoon, the head nurse, Miss Levy, met me at the door. After some polite small talk she took me upstairs and showed me to my room. She said that there was no hurry but she would show me the layout of the building after I had unpacked my suitcase.

Wertheim House had around eighty beds, most of them occupied. The patients were all males, chronic schizophrenics and manic depressives. They ranged in age from teenagers to octogenarians.

None of the patients was violent, but the hospital population was a sad group of adults who needed constant care. Some did nothing all day but stare into space. Others looked through magazines, turning pages continuously. Some sat and rocked back and forth without letup, while others performed little jobs in the house. Some helped in the kitchen, some were engaged in doing handicrafts. They all had to be watched and cared for; some had to be bathed, dressed, and fed. Several patients were able to make their beds and were expected to do so.

There were three registered nurses, including the head nurse, and eight practical nurses, as well as a few people hired to do the heavy work around the place. My job consisted of practical nursing only. I worked hard, and in the first week especially, I was very tired. Soon I became accustomed to this busy life and started to enjoy it. I became friends with one of the registered nurses and enjoyed talking with her. She had gotten her training at the Apeldoornse Bos, an institution in Apeldoorn for the mentally ill. She had been at Wertheim House a couple of years.

In retrospect my job was rather monotonous. There was no training and consequently no course work, but there were other compensations. Luckily there was a piano, and I practiced in my spare time. The meals were fun, and I had a chance to get to know the other girls. The staff ate in the dining room, a very pretty room, as was the rest of Wertheim House, a beautiful mansion. Usually Miss Levy would come in after we were seated and have her meal with us. The food was very good, quite starchy but tasty, and I was ravenously hungry around the clock. The conversation was generally interesting, and I soon began to feel at home.

The hospital gave me one day a week off, which was just enough time to catch up on important personal responsibilities, such as shopping, visiting friends, and going home, of course. I had remained in touch with Sara and Maurice Zilversmit, Don's aunt and uncle. They lived in Rotterdam and had a summer home in Noordwijk aan Zee. I was always amazed that I could manage to visit them in Rotterdam in one day and appreciated the Dutch railroad network, one of the most efficient systems in the world.

In the late fall of 1941 Don's aunt and uncle invited me to come to Noordwijk on my next day off. "Even if it gets cold we can still have a good visit," Aunt Sara wrote. As I made my way up the S-shaped walkway leading to the front door of the house, I marveled at their huge and immaculate yard. I admired the beautifully manicured front lawn as I waited for the door to open.

Aunt Sara was a bright, refined woman. She and Uncle Maurice had both been born in Holland. They had met in Amsterdam, fallen in love, and in 1914 decided to marry. They planned to visit friends in Palestine for their honeymoon. Little did the newlyweds know that World War I was about to break out. They were forced to remain in Palestine for the duration. Aunt Sara became director of an orphanage, while Maurice worked in a bank. They finally went home in 1918 after the war. Upon their return to Holland,

Maurice started his studies and became an accountant. Maurice and Sara were exceptionally intelligent and had a lot in common. They were Zionists and devoted much of their spare time to the Zionist cause. Their ideals were admirable.

It was nice to see Don's aunt and uncle again. They looked well and enjoyed living so close to the beach. They asked how I was doing at Wertheim House and how long it would be before I began my training at NIZ. I couldn't have been there more than a half-hour, and Aunt Sara was just carrying in a tray of coffee, when I noticed a car stop and park in the street right in front of their house. I saw an immaculately dressed man in a German uniform get out of the car and walk up their path.

I wondered what he was doing there. At first I assumed that he was lost and wanted to use the telephone, but it didn't take me long to realize that something was seriously wrong. When Uncle Maurice saw the car he turned ashen gray and his chest started fiercely heaving. He was paralyzed with fear. As the man made his way up the walk toward the house, Maurice rose from his chair and began pacing back and forth. He had only a few seconds before he would have to face his visitor, and I watched him swiftly control his breathing. Remarkably, he appeared perfectly composed and in control of his emotions. Never in my life had I witnessed such self-control.

Maurice opened the door. The German officer entered the house and Maurice offered him a seat. Aunt Sara said to me: "We'll go to another room so the men can talk." Once in the den we looked at one another, not speaking. Finally Sara simply said: "He has been here before." I didn't feel I could say anything to help. Her look conveyed such deep concern, and neither of us was in the mood for trying to cover our fear and distress with small talk.

I thought about Uncle Maurice in the other room. Because he was fluent in German, I knew he was able to communicate with the officer. This fact gave me a small shred of faith to hold on to. Maybe Maurice's intelligence and refinement would convey itself to the German. And maybe the officer was one of those rare Germans who was not a Nazi. With a little luck maybe these ingredients would blend together and protect Maurice. I hoped with all my heart that no harm would come to him.

But no, I told myself, I'm just fantasizing. He may arrest all three of us. I pushed these pessimistic thoughts out of my mind before they had time to flourish and destroy any vestige of hope I still felt.

After what seemed like an eternity the man left. Maurice came in to the room. He walked over to a chair and sat on its edge, as rigid and straight as a statue, his eyes glassy, staring ahead into space. He neither moved nor spoke one word to us.

I knew that I should leave. I knew they had to talk and be together. I too had lost the ability to make small talk. On my way back to Wertheim House, I had time to do some thinking. I knew that Maurice had taken charge of Martin and Janny Zilversmit's finances and legal affairs after they left for the United States in 1938. After Herman and Lies left for the States in 1939, Maurice had also begun to look after their affairs. Since Maurice was the only one of the Zilversmit brothers left in Holland, he felt a responsibility to look after their interests, especially since he was a CPA by profession. There was also property to look after. In the meantime, the Zilversmits in the United States had repeatedly urged Sara and Maurice to pack up and come to America while it was still possible for them to leave; Lisa and Herman had made it abundantly clear that their lives were more important than material possessions. But Maurice's sense of responsibility kept him and Sara in Holland.

The chance that Maurice could have been arrested right on the spot that afternoon was very real. He must have thought about the possibility of arrest; being taken to the police station, possibly to be tortured, and to undergo interrogation about why the other Zilversmits had left Holland. It had been a very frightening incident.

I made it safely back to Wertheim House. It felt good to return there. The next day it would be back to work as though nothing had happened.

I had now been in Wertheim House long enough to ask for two days off so I could go home for a weekend. I was looking forward to spending more than one day with my family. Mother didn't like me to travel because "one never knew what danger I might run into." But she felt that if I had to travel, I should come home for a weekend instead of one day, since that would make it worth taking the chance. Using one day from the preceding week and the first day of the following week, I left on Friday afternoon. I took the train to Utrecht and the bus to the Oosterstraat, where we lived. When I first came around the bend on our street, everything felt strange, as though I had been away on a long vacation. "Well, I haven't been home for a long time."

I walked faster as I approached the house, carrying my weekend bag. I didn't have to ring the doorbell because the door opened instantaneously, as if by magic; mother had been watching for me. I thought she looked radiant. She told me that I had put on too much weight, that my face had filled out too much. We laughed, because now I was the one who was getting too fat instead of her.

The boys were funny, they wanted to know all about the *gekken* (Dutch for "crazies"), by which they meant the patients at Wertheim House. They kept at it and wanted to know everything. I couldn't put them off till later, so I sat down with them and answered all their questions, until they were satisfied. But Jack couldn't believe that there wasn't more; "You're just getting tired of talking to us, that's all." I tried to convince them that I had nothing else interesting to report, but then I thought of one more story. I made the boys promise to think about the patients as very sick, pathetic human beings. They promised they would! Then they all came a little closer to really get a good listen. Only then would I start.

"At twelve noon, a warm lunch is served at Wertheim House. In order to alert the patients, a bell rings for approximately fifteen seconds. At the sound of the bell, from every corner of the building, all the patients, even the little old men, make their way, as fast as their legs can carry them, to the dining room. They find their seats at long tables, maybe twenty or more to a table. Then it begins. A salt-shaker is passed from one to another and everybody pours a little heap of salt in the middle of his plate. Of course this happens before any food is in sight; nobody even knows if the food will need any extra salt—but never mind that. Everybody, without exception, participates in this ritual."

The boys laughed uproariously. We all had a good laugh. It was so good to see my brothers again.

Then Susan came home. She looked thinner, I thought, but beautiful as always. Finally father returned home from work. As I kissed him I felt so happy to be with all of them again. We talked a little longer until it was time for the men to get ready to go to the synagogue for Friday evening Shabbat services. Now the women could really talk while we were getting the evening meal ready. It was wonderful to be home and one of the family again, and I realized how very much I missed them.

I had always enjoyed the traditional way Shabbat was celebrated at our house, with blessings over the wine and food before and after dinner, then the singing of the Zemirot with the whole family, mother always harmonizing, something she was very good at, and later, coffee and dessert.

I told them about my visit to the Zilversmits in Noordwijk and how the German officer had come to see Maurice while I was there. Immediately my mother said: "You see, you have to be so careful; we don't know what will happen anymore from one minute to the next. I was right when I told you not to travel unless you really have to." Now I was sorry that I had even mentioned the incident; after all, she had enough to worry about with all the children.

My parents couldn't stop talking about the German invasion of Russia on June 22. Its phenomenal success had made a horrifying impression on everybody. It seemed as though the Nazis couldn't be stopped anymore. We talked about the more recent hardships and inconveniences. Our radios had been confiscated during the summer. Starting in June, every Jew had to have his identification papers stamped with a big black J. Now everyone, Jew and Gentile, had to carry an I.D. card all the time. "We can live with all these regulations as long as they leave us together," mother was still saying.

The next morning I went to the synagogue with my father and the three boys. I saw many of my friends. But Don's seat downstairs was conspicuously empty. Of course I had expected that, but still it struck me, almost as though I had thought he would be there. Later in the day, I had time to visit my best friend, Leni Swelheim, to catch up on everything, good or bad, that had happened during my absence.

Sunday afternoon it was time to return to Amsterdam. It had been such a good visit. I hated to go. We kissed each other good-bye, and as I thanked them for their kindness, my mother said: "Yes, yes, you will be home in plenty of time before dark; please, please be careful." A lot of love and fear was conveyed in this simple message. Then I was out the door and on my way.

On the train back to Amsterdam I relished thoughts of my weekend visit. It had been great to see my family again. Many happy memories flooded my mind on that dreamy ride back. In my reverie I thought of my family's annual vacation and wondered when we would enjoy such pleasures again.

The highlight of the summer for the whole family comes when we take our yearly trip to Scheveningen, our favorite beach resort, close to The Hague. Grandma does not join us but remains at home. We always stay at the same place, Pension Hartog, at the Gevers-dynootweg, one block from the beach. It is convenient to take the train to The Hague and the tram to Scheveningen; it stops at the Geversdynootweg, almost right in front of our pension.

We get settled quickly and freshen up a bit before going to the beach; we have to see whether everything is still the same. Then back to our pension to relax for awhile before dinner. The big table in front of the dining room's bay window, facing the street, is always reserved for the Fonteyn family. The food, its preparation supervised by Mrs. Hartog, is always delicious. We are easy guests, and the sea air gives us all tremendous appetites.

The Kurhaus and Boulevard are located opposite a beautiful white beach which is lined with little gift shops and outdoor cafes. Tables hide under big umbrellas, where we eat the Dutch petit-fours, the pastries, and waffles filled with whipped cream, accompanied by chocolate milk.

The Scheveningen pier is the real attraction for us. A jetty, stretching from the sandy beach far out into the North Sea, about a quarter of a mile long and sixty-five feet wide, has benches on each side to sit on. The pier is brightly painted, with interesting designs. We have great fun watching the fishermen catch their fish, especially the big fish at the end of the pier, or watching the ocean steamers go by. There is always lots of foot traffic on the pier. It is always entertaining to sit down quietly for awhile and watch the people promenading. At the end of the pier stands the giant Rotunda, a building for concerts, cabarets, or any other entertainment scheduled, including special children's shows with clowns and acrobats. We love it all. Mother makes sure that she has plenty of dubbeltjes (dimes) in her pocketbook, because she expects frequent trips to the restroom. Restrooms are never free in Holland.

We spend a lot of time on the beach. Old-fashioned cane beach chairs are always available for daily rental. We spend hours building sand castles with tunnels long enough to reach just to the ocean's edge, where the castle will fill up with sea water and slowly be washed away by the waves.

It is obvious to me that father, in particular, gets a lot of enjoyment out of these vacations because he knows how much my mother enjoys them. Father will jokingly ask mother what she is planning to cook for dinner that night when we are vacationing in Scheveningen, and it is such a treat for her not to have any responsibility for running the family for awhile; vacation provides a wonderful change from the normal daily routine.

But all good things must come to an end, and when the week is over we inevitably take the train back to Utrecht, tired and happy, ready to tackle life's responsibilities again. The children enjoy the railroad station, the puffing locomotive, and the ride back home.

As I let my thoughts wander to those happy times, I thought that my future was eroding away just as those sand castles had done; only now it was real and frightening and with no pleasure attached.

★ ★ ★

I had been working at Wertheim House for some time and was now ready to go on night duty. Except for having to get used to reversing days and nights, I thought night duty would be fun. I would certainly have more time to myself. Upstairs, at the end of the corridor where the nurses' quarters were located, was one bedroom reserved for the night-duty nurse. It was not hard to sleep there during the day because the room was so isolated and out of the way. Off duty at 7:00 a.m., breakfast at 7:30 a.m., and back on duty at 11:00 p.m. I could eat dinner at 6:00 p.m. with everybody else and looked forward each day to my big block of time. I thought it was a pretty good deal. The first night on duty I had little to do except to make rounds once every hour. I carefully inspected each bed to make sure that the patients were sleeping comfortably.

I had discussed my interest in psychiatry with Miss Levy, and she had given me some textbooks on abnormal psychology. It was so quiet during the night that I had plenty of time to read, in addition to my regular duties and keeping watch. The subject of psychology fascinated me. One night, while I was reading on duty, sometime long past midnight, Miss Levy stopped at my desk and gave me two airmail letters. She had taken them out of the mailbox during the afternoon and had forgotten to give them to me. She'd had a busy day and had just finished writing some letters herself when she remembered mine.

They were two fat letters from Don, with the word "censored" in big red letters; they had clearly been opened. I thought it was a miracle that any mail at all would arrive from the United States; it was sometime after December 7, after the attack on Pearl Harbor by the Japanese; America was now officially at war with Germany.

These two letters were to be the first and last letters I received from Don while at Wertheim House. There was nothing in them about Pearl Harbor, since they had been written long before it had occurred.

Although the letters were old, reading them made me feel deliciously close to him. I was overjoyed to read Don's loving and interesting accounts of his work at the university, his family, everything. I read them over and over, now leaning back in my chair.

I began to reflect on how much my life had changed since Don had left. I took his letters in my hands once more, as though holding a precious possession. And I was overcome by a wave of intense gratitude. I felt sincerely happy that Don was not in Holland, although I couldn't begin to describe how much I missed him. At least I didn't have to worry about him; he was safely in the United States. The sound of a siren outside quickly brought me back to reality, to the real world I was living in.

★ ★ ★

The unexpected Japanese attack on Pearl Harbor took place on December 7, 1941. A large part of the American Pacific Fleet was destroyed. Eighteen ships sank to the bottom of the sea and a large number of airplanes went up in flames. Many planes on the ground were put out of commission. Now the United States would be at war irrevocably on the side of the Allies.

Don's Diary: *March 7, 1942*

Soldier Zilversmit 579, 3rd section; arrived in Stratford, Canada, on Friday, February 27. I arrived just as Princess Juliana was about to depart. She had spent all day with the soldiers in the barracks and was about to say goodbye to the men who were boarding the ship for England. These men were ready for active service; they had finished their training and were going to war.

Shortly after Pearl Harbor was attacked, I called the army recruiting office in San Francisco to find out whether Bert and I could join the American forces. We were refused because we were not American citizens and were referred to the Princess Irene Brigade in Canada.[1] From then on, events moved very fast. Bert left a few weeks ago for Stratford, Ontario. I had some work to finish up at the university before I could leave and arrived in Stratford on February 27, 1942.

Don in Canadian-Dutch Army
Princess Irene Brigade

1. Formed by the Dutch government-in-exile and named after Queen Wilhelmina's second daughter, the Princess Irene Brigade was made up of soldiers who escaped from Holland after the German invasion and expatriate Dutchmen from all over the world. Part of the brigade was organized and trained in Canada and served with the Canadian Army.

At Wertheim House, I continued on night duty intermittently. Sometimes, as I sat at my desk I marveled at the beauty of the old mansion, so well kept up inside as well as outside. Coming through the huge double doors, one entered the massive main lobby some thirty or forty feet long.

The lobby floor was white marble, and in the middle, centered on a red woolen rug, were a desk and chair, facing a wide sweeping staircase which led to the second floor. There was a telephone on the desk and an electric bell connected to Miss Levy's bedroom upstairs, in case of an emergency.

I couldn't help but marvel at the beauty and shape of this elegant staircase. It had deep steps and low risers, and was at least eight feet wide. About twenty steps up was a landing, and then the stairs continued on up to the second floor. The woodwork of the staircase as well as the window sills and the doors in the main lobby were polished to a high-gloss reddish-brown.

Wertheim House was originally the home of a family named Wertheimer. Mr. Wertheimer was a wealthy Jewish philanthropist. His family dated back to the early *Hofjuden*, or court Jews, like the Rothschilds. The family had donated Wertheim House to the city of Amsterdam for the less fortunate.

One night, while sitting at my night-duty desk reading, I suddenly noticed out of the corner of my eye that someone was coming down the stairs. No, it couldn't be Simon, but upon looking again I saw that it really was him. He was coming down the middle of the staircase, slightly swaying as though sleepwalking. His silly grin focused on me, exposing his toothless mouth. His white nightshirt, too long and too wide for him, was floating around his body as he slowly approached. He looked like a ghost out of a fairy tale. I couldn't help feeling frightened.

Thinking fast, I remembered the bell I was to use in an emergency. In a flash I knew I had to push the button. Then I got up quickly and walked toward him. I wanted to catch him before he came all the way downstairs. I grabbed his arm firmly and said:

"Come on Simon, let's go back to bed." Halfway up the stairs, Miss Levy met us in her red peignoir. I will never forget the sight of her and what a relief it was to get help so quickly. "Let me take him upstairs for you," she offered.

Suddenly my knees buckled under me as though I had been attacked by a furious dog. I sat down in my chair and soon nurse Levy came down to stay with me for a few minutes. She was sorry it had happened and hoped the incident had not disturbed me too much. She had given Simon a sedative and was sure he'd sleep through the night. He'd probably had a bad dream, she said. She offered to stay downstairs a little longer but I assured her that I was all right. Soon it was time to make rounds again. Upstairs I found everything in order and Simon sleeping peacefully.

A few weeks later I received a letter from NIZ. I was accepted at the hospital to start training on March 1, 1942. I stayed at Wertheim House till the end of February, and had no further scares from the patients.

8

The Nederlands Israelitisch Ziekenhuis

I liked my training and work at the Netherlands Jewish Hospital almost from the very beginning. The building itself, on the Keizersgracht in Amsterdam, was very old and unattractive. Its front entrance consisted of a wide stone-covered archway, just broad enough for two cars to pass through side by side. It also provided emergency access for ambulances since there was no other entrance. Everyone, including visitors, doctors, and nurses used the stone arch to enter the hospital.

Directly upon entering, to the left, were the living quarters of the doctors in residence. A small oblong plaque to the right of the entrance unobtrusively displayed: "Nederlands Israelitisch Ziekenhuis." Although the sign was small, the NIZ was an impressive complex of buildings with approximately 500 beds. Another sign above the stone arch read "Het Zusterhuis." This referred to the nurses's dormitories; some rooms faced the street, while others looked out over the canal on the Keizersgracht.

At the hospital I felt as though I had entered a city in itself, totally self-contained, that had everything and made me feel very protected. I was assigned to a room with three other student nurses on the fourth floor. The rooms were furnished with a desk and one closet for each person. The beds were very comfortable. There were two washbasins in each room, and shower and bath were shared with others down the hall; some rooms even had adjoining bathrooms.

Every student nurse began with a basic course in practical nursing. We learned how to position a bedpan and to take vital signs, such as temperature, pulse, and blood pressure. We also performed regular chores, such as cutting nails and giving enemas, sponge baths, or alcohol rubs.

Nurse Zwanenburg, the head nurse, led the class. Sometimes we practiced putting bandages on each other. In addition, for the first-year nurses theory consisted of two subjects, anatomy and histology, both taught by Dr. Kroonenberg, the director of internal medicine. No time was wasted getting me involved with training, as it started immediately after I began working at the hospital. The practical nursing class took only four weeks; it was easy and fun. However, the work itself was physically hard, and some time passed before I got used to it. If I once thought that working at Wertheim House had been hard. Work at NIZ seemed even harder.

At first nurse trainees were only allowed to work the day shift. After a few weeks we were assigned the late shift, 12:00 noon till 9:00 p.m. with lunch at 12:00, and work starting at 1:00 p.m. I liked the late shift very much. I had a lot of time to myself working that way, and never felt the need to sleep late in the morning as some nurses did. I took advantage of the morning hours to study and play the piano, and I sometimes did some shopping. Being on this schedule, I would often find myself too tired to do anything after 9:00 p.m. I usually socialized a little and sometimes just went to bed early to get extra sleep.

After a few months I was put on the night shift in the women's surgical ward. I was already accustomed to working nights from Wertheim House. Except for "lights on," which had to be answered, and other regular jobs during night duty, it was generally quiet, and usually there was time to sit down and read a little. If there were new patients to admit during the night, however, I would be kept very busy.

Nurse Stern, head nurse of women's surgery, was an arrogant, cold woman. She wore an expression of indifference, and to make matters worse she was very cross-eyed. I never quite knew whether she was looking at me or at someone else; only when she addressed me by my name, "Nurse Fonteyn," could I really be sure that she meant me!

Women's surgery was an exciting ward in which to begin on-the-job training. I would soon be able to attend operations, and ultimately I would have to attend at least sixteen operations during the course of my training to complete my course work. I awaited being called to attend surgery with a curious sense of anticipation. I was always fascinated when I sat down to meals with upper class-mates and listened to their conversation. It became apparent that I had much to learn.

One day, Nurse Stern met me in the hall. She told me about an emergency appendicitis case just admitted to the hospital and asked if I would like to observe the surgery. I felt like putting my arms around Nurse Stern even though I knew that she would not welcome the idea. I was so excited that she had finally asked me to go to surgery that I readily accepted her invitation.

In spite of the fact that I would be given a sterile gown before entering the operating room, Nurse Stern told me to go to my room, put on a clean uniform, and be back in fifteen minutes. I ran upstairs to the dorm and returned just as the patient was being wheeled into the operating room.

The whole procedure took only twenty minutes, including the anesthesia. The patient was given ether. I was disappointed because I was not able to see much of the patient's body; everything was covered with sterile sheets, and less than six inches was exposed within which the surgeon made the incision. Once the incision was made there was only a little blood visible, and what could be seen was quickly picked up with a cotton swab. The surgeon, Dr. Herschel, was dexterous and obviously had done the procedure many times before. Everything happened so matter-of-factly that I was almost disappointed, thinking: "Is this all there is?"

When I returned to the ward, the other nurse trainees asked: "Did you faint?" Still feeling a little bewildered from what I had just experienced, I reassured them that I had felt fine throughout the operation. I knew that it was important that I had the fortitude to observe surgery without buckling under. I was on my way to accumulating the requirements for my first year of training at the hospital. It was an important beginning for me.

Don's Diary: *March 7, 1942*

Life in the army after one week. Good food, not much work. The soldiers and officers are very nice. We're not getting much training, only some military drill and learning how to handle a rifle. I hope that we will soon leave for our wartime destination. My request to join the Medical Corps seems to have been approved by the captain. He thought that they could use me as such very well. The news from Holland is terrible, and for that reason alone it is unbearable to sit at such a distance and know that other people are deprived of their freedom, powerless to do anything. Suddenly it seems not to make any difference in which army we fight. The most important thing now is to destroy the totalitarian forces at all costs.

★ ★ ★

It was the spring of 1942. I worked very hard and was busy all the time. I was working the night shift now and spent a lot of time on my feet. "When this shift is over," I thought, "I would really like to go home for a couple of days."

But the month of May had not started out very well. Jews were now required to wear the Star of David in public. While working at Wertheim House I had gone home several times uneventfully. But it seemed unwise to travel by train with the Star of David pinned on my coat. Therefore I decided there would be no more trips to Utrecht; we would just have to stay in touch by mail. My parents fully agreed. I certainly didn't want to wear that conspicuous yellow star on my chest; it simply was not worth the risk. Consequently, I found myself confined to the hospital grounds most of the time. A trip to the mailbox at the Keizersgracht became my longest foray outside. As time progressed I decided that even that was an unnecessary risk. I could just as well mail my letters from inside the hospital and not be exposed to the danger of being picked up on the street.

Inside the hospital things were changing also. Jewish institutions were no longer allowed to

Kitty in Nurse's Uniform (1942)
Part of the Star of David is visible.

employ non-Jews to help out on Shabbat. We had been relying on this help up to that point to perform jobs like lighting stoves, turning on lights, and answering telephones. Now even observant Jews would have to light the stoves, turn on the lights, and warm up food for the patients on Shabbat.

Upon learning of the new rule, my friend Anneke Levi, another student nurse who worked in my division, said: "Kitty, I can do those things for you on Shabbat; I've never observed Jewish law and it doesn't mean anything to me." I thought about Anneke's offer for a moment and realized that would be just ridiculous. How could I let another Jewish girl light the stove for me or answer the phone? Of course I couldn't accept her offer. I was sure there was an exception to this Jewish law, and that a Jew, in an emergency, was allowed to do anything for another human being under special circumstances. Certainly our current situation could be defined as working under an emergency. From then on I started doing everything myself on Shabbat, and I had no qualms about it whatsoever. However, I couldn't help but think how much things had changed and how insecure my life had become. I thought about how Shabbat was always celebrated in my family and I became quite sentimental and homesick. Those secure and happy days, it seemed, were gone forever.

Jews were now forced to resign from all non-Jewish employment. For the patients in the wards, things were also changing. It often became apparent during visiting hours, when spouses, sons, or daughters, did not appear at their usual time, that they would not be visiting anymore. Visiting hours now became sad realizations for some patients that family members had either been picked up from their homes or arrested elsewhere and sent to Westerbork. Usually there were no messages from the absent loved ones and no letters—not even a postcard. If one was lucky, a neighbor would send a message. The mood at the hospital became depressing, and a cloud of gloom and uncertainty hung over everybody's head.

It was not unusual for the German authorities to come to the hospital at night with lists of certain nurses, doctors, even patients. Usually trucks were waiting outside to take them away to be deported without prior warning. I tried not to dwell on the misery that enveloped us. When I was off duty, there was always studying to be done. The main lounge downstairs was a nice place to sit and relax, listen to the radio, or just talk to someone. There was a very good upright piano in the lounge, which the staff used often. Several of the nurses were very talented. Two girls in particular often made music together. One played the piano extremely well and the other had a very nice soprano voice.

Often, when they were practicing and learning new songs, I sneaked in during their rehearsals and began to memorize the literature for voice by listening carefully. I became familiar with many lieder and arias, ranging from Bach and Handel to Richard Strauss. Before too long I started to accompany some of the other nurses, and later on I began to sing my newly learned repertoire, accompanying my own soprano voice. Playing and singing was a wonderful diversion, and I was happy to learn so many wonderful new songs.

Roosje van Coevorden was a new student nurse who came to work at the hospital. She had a lovely trained mezzo-soprano voice and brought with her a completely new and different repertoire of arias and semi-classical songs from musicals. This opened up a new and previously unexplored world of music for me. I always loved the beautiful way she sang "Het Jagerslied." Roosje and I became good friends, and I was soon her most steady accompanist.

Roosje had a brother, Solly, who played the saxophone very well. I once tried to accompany him, but that was not as easy as I had thought. I had never played a duet with a saxophone player before. I was intrigued by the warm alluring sound of the instrument, another new experience. Solly was actually a medical student, but since Jews were no longer allowed to attend medical school, he was working at the NIZ as a male nurse. Many people had to put their careers on hold during the Nazi occupation. One would take on any job just to stay out of danger and out of the hands of the Germans.

Johnny van Coevorden was the older brother of Roosje and Solly. He was a fine surgeon who worked at the hospital and played the piano with exquisite skill. Johnny was never aware how many times I stood beneath his open window, near the wide stone-covered arch of the hospital's entrance, just listening to him play the piano. He had developed a superb technique, and I was particularly fascinated by his beautiful interpretation of the G-minor Chopin Ballade. Furthermore, as busy as the hospital surgeons were kept, Johnny still found time to take piano lessons. That simply amazed me.

One evening, while practicing my newly acquired repertoire in the lounge, I was totally absorbed in my music. Suddenly I heard people applauding during a brief pause to rearrange my music. During my practice period, the lounge had filled up with people. I turned around to view the audience. Among the faces I recognized Dr. Kroonenberg, the head physician, and his wife sitting on a couch some distance behind me. Somewhat embarrassed I got up to leave, but then there was more applause and I was asked to continue.

As I became more involved in the social life of the hospital I became aware of the constant activity there. There were so many nice and interesting people. Lex Kroonenberg was the second son of Dr. and Mrs. Kroonenberg. He had been an engineering student at the university before the war. Now he was employed at the hospital in the power plant, in charge of heating the hospital and maintaining the hot water supply. He was a strikingly handsome young man who always wore a red kerchief around his neck. I am sure he was vain and knew that the hanky was becoming on him. His face was often black with coal dust which really added to his looks as a maintenance man. But he could play the violin with flair and specialized in a kind of light music somewhere between Dixieland and country music. The oldest son of Dr. and Mrs. Kroonenberg was doing his internship at the hospital. He was a tall, very serious-looking young man. The youngest son, Kees, worked as a nurse at the hospital.

Entertainment for the patients was taken care of by Ies Cohen. I knew him from Utrecht, where he had lived all his life. I ran into him in the hospital one day and asked what he was doing there. "Oh, you don't know," was his reply, "I'm the new man in charge of entertainment for the patients." He had come to the hospital and asked for a job—any kind of job. He had even offered to work as a volunteer. Needless to say he got the job; how could such generosity be refused! The hospital gave him room and board, and I wouldn't have been surprised to find out he was getting a stipend besides. Every day at certain hours he provided programs that were piped through the hospital intercom into the patients' wards and private rooms. He was really very good at this and seemed to enjoy working with all the sound equipment, which he apparently knew a lot about. He developed a variety of programs. The hospital owned a fine collection of records, classical as well as popular music, which he had at his disposal. Other times he would coordinate live entertainment, and sometimes he engaged speakers to present talks on different topics.

Once Ies asked me to put on a program. I actually ended up doing two separate programs, one an all-piano program with Bach, Chopin, and Debussy, and the other an all-vocal program. In the latter I sang mostly lieder, and later in the program I sang some *chazones*, liturgical and traditional melodies used at synagogue services. I knew that the patients would particularly enjoy the *chazones*.

★ ★ ★

There was never an idle moment at the hospital; the place was always buzzing with good things like music and camaraderie and a variety of sad things because of the general situation of uncertainty under German rule. Everybody worked hard, and we were often short of staff. Patients and staff alike seemed to disappear without notice. Ever since the special registration in January, 1941, people who were genuinely afraid were going into hiding whenever there was a chance.

I was approached a couple of times by a man I often saw in the hospital. I didn't know who he was or why he was in there so often. He started talking to me one day and said: "I have a place for you to go underground if you want to." I was so surprised at this unexpected confrontation that I didn't know how to respond. But a couple of weeks later the same man told me again that he had been serious and would help me to go into hiding if I would let him. I was better prepared this time and asked where he would take me. He responded: "It would be too dangerous to give away any of the details now." I promptly told him that I was not interested unless he could tell me more about it. So I kept working, concentrating on my studies at night and playing the piano whenever I had time.

One day about thirty women were admitted to the hospital with scarlet fever. With so many new admissions, all the staff worked themselves silly. This particular group of patients were all artists, painters, poets, writers, and musicians who had been brought to the hospital from a castle in Barneveld where they had been temporarily detained before being sent on to Westerbork. They were a mixture of fine, fascinating people. All seemed highly educated and from cultured backgrounds. I really enjoyed talking with them. Through many of the conversations I had with them about music and the vast literature of lieder, I became acquainted with some beautiful songs written by Hugo Wolff. Interestingly, these people didn't appear sick at all, and although they were treated as infectious patients I felt certain they were in the hospital to prevent their deportation. They all held special papers. Unfortunately in September, 1943, they were sent to Westerbork, and in 1944 (I would later learn) the "Barnevelders" were deported to Theresienstadt, the showplace of Hitler's concentration camps, from which few people eventually returned.

On June 26, 1942, the Zentralstelle ("Central Office"), the German agency in charge of deportation, informed the Jewish Council that the Reich had decided to send Dutch Jews to work in Germany under police protection. This announcement caused great consternation, especially since the first group of Jews was to leave before the middle of the summer of 1942. In the meantime Het Apeldoornse Bos, an institution for the mentally ill in Apeldoorn, had been vacated. The patients had all been taken away in trucks and sent to Germany. Somewhat later the patients at Wertheim House were also taken to Germany. At the time we didn't know that they would all immediately be killed. In preparation for the deportations in the summer of 1942, the security police issued a series of decrees aimed to further isolate the Jews. They had to hand in their bicycles and were simultaneously forbidden to use public transportation. A special curfew from 8:00 p.m. to 6:00 a.m. was established. Jews had to do their shopping at special hours during the day. To make matters worse, they were no longer allowed to use telephones.

The Zentralstelle selected Jews for deportation based on files originally furnished by the Bureau of Population Records and based on a special Jewish census conducted in 1941 at the Reich's request. With the curfew in effect, as well as the specially created files, it became dangerous for Jews to be in their own homes at night, and they were not allowed outside on the streets either. The Germans knew exactly where to find people they wanted to arrest. Home became a prison. Because of the blackout, everything was pitch-black. Every truck or noise outside would shoot adrenaline through one's system. The murderers were everywhere and were pulling our families apart and destroying us. People were now regularly picked up from their homes. It was hard to get a good night's sleep. This was not a conducive environment for studying either. Consequently, it was hard for me to concentrate on my studies, and even harder to keep a cool head.

I often thought about my father, who had so desperately tried to console mother on the night, two years earlier, when Holland had fallen to the Germans. "We must have faith," he said, "and God will help." But the help we all needed so desperately was just not there. Who could we turn to?

During this period Jews were ordered to deposit their money in blocked accounts at certain banks managed by German officials. No withdrawals were permitted from these accounts except for small monthly allowances to meet bare necessities. Jews were also forced to register their properties. The Germans demanded that employers discharge Jews from their jobs and prohibited Jews from certain professions altogether.[1]

---

1. Much of the above has been taken from Werner Warmbrunn, *The Dutch Under German Occupation, 1940-1945*, Stanford: Stanford University Press, 1963 p. 65.

All of this, combined with the knowledge that the Germans had developed a systematic plan for rounding up Jews, made it impossible to think or plan; one developed a sense of numbness to protect one's sanity. I stayed in the hospital almost all the time now; it was the only place I felt 'relatively' safe.

Around this time, the hospital was again invaded by Germans. They came in the afternoon and parked their trucks outside the entrance. I didn't hear the trucks and was unaware at first that anything unusual was happening. I don't know how the word spread, but suddenly Solly came rushing down the hall and said: "Come on, quick."

"What's going on?" I asked. It was obvious that he had been looking for me.

"I'll tell you later; hurry." As we turned a corner, he opened a door and closed it behind us. We went down a flight of stairs. I had never seen this part of the hospital before. We kept walking in what seemed like a huge subterranean stone vault until we caught up with several more people. Then, there was another door, which Solly opened quickly. We all went inside. We were approximately twelve people.

"The Germans are in the hospital again, and we'll try to sit this one out in the cellar until the coast is clear," Solly said. Sometime later we heard the motors of the trucks being started and we knew we could safely come out. The memory of incidents like this one sends shivers down my spine even now as I write these words. I felt such gratitude toward Solly. Had he not specially looked for me, I might have walked right into the Germans' hands. How differently my life could have turned out had he not helped me hide from the Nazis that day.

After an incident like this, we naturally wanted to catch our breath and relax for a change. We would sometimes make fried potatoes when on rare occasions somebody was able to find some extra potatoes and, above all, some oil, a very precious commodity during those times of scarcity. Somebody would always produce a hot-plate for us to use. The potatoes were sliced paper thin and fried in that precious oil until golden brown on both sides. Solly stood patiently bent over the hot-plate, turning the slices one at a time.

Whenever we had a special treat like that we felt it had to be accompanied by a drink. What could be better than ersatz-tea tablets; they colored the hot water in no time and gave the illusion of tea. And was there any "taste," you might ask? No, nothing— no taste at all. We had a special potato-fry in honor of Solly's parents when they came to visit their three children at the hospital. It felt good to have friends and it took away some of the pain of being away from Don and my family.

One morning, when I woke up, I noticed that I was very dizzy. I tried to get up but the room was spinning. One of my roommates called the infirmary and I was transferred to the nurses' sickroom. There were several nurses in the hospital suffering from the same symptoms. Dr. Kroonenberg didn't know what it was but thought it could be a virus. He prescribed complete bed rest, and I was put on Luminal (a mild barbiturate) three times a day. As it turned out, the dizziness subsided very slowly. I was actually in bed for fourteen days before I could get up and go back to work. The rest did me a lot of good. In retrospect, I wondered if the dizziness was just brought on by tension and the total misery that enveloped me. I would not have been surprised if Dr. Kroonenberg had thought the same.

★ ★ ★

The Hollandsche Schouwburg came into being in 1941. It was meant to be an exclusively Jewish theater, for Jews only. Since the Nazi authorities had forbidden the Jewish populace to attend any other form of public entertainment, the Hollandsche Schouwburg became the center of Jewish cultural expression, where famous Jewish artists performed solely for Jewish audiences.

Ironically, the Germans started using the Schouwburg as a detention center during *razzias*, as a place to keep Jews until they could be transported to Westerbork. Overcrowding soon became a significant problem inside the theater. Some people would be detained only a day or two; others as long as a week. There was no privacy, no place to wash up or change clothes, no beds to rest on; just rows of seats. For families with small children and especially for the elderly, the hardship must have been indescribable.

July 15, 1942

It was a terribly sad day for the Jews of Amsterdam when the first transport left for Westerbork. A feeling of hopelessness took over and preoccupied my mind. We were surrounded by criminals. There was fear, panic, and anxiety. What would become of the people who were deported? Was there nothing anyone could do to stop these brutal crimes; was there no justice at all?

My parents and my two youngest brothers, Jack and Eddy, were still in Utrecht, living in the same house. Susan, my older sister, had married Herman de Leeuw, and together they had gone into hiding. I had no contact with them because it was safer for me not to know where they were. Leo, my oldest brother, was active in the underground, and although I had not seen him for a long time, my parents had contact with him.

At the beginning of 1943, my parents were forced to leave their home and move to Amsterdam. Before they left Utrecht, however, they made provisions for Jack to go into hiding. I am sure they were relieved to have found a place where Jack would be safe. My parents took Eddy with them to Amsterdam. He was then fourteen years old.

The Germans called this forced moving "resettlement." It was all part of their vicious plan. At that time, Holland's remaining Jews had to "resettle" in Amsterdam. Deportation and control would be easy once the Germans had them all centralized in one place. By pure coincidence, my parents found an apartment on the Keizersgracht, just on the other side of the bridge, less than one and a half blocks from the hospital. We were now practically next door to one another and counted ourselves lucky that, at least, we could visit one another. I often went to see them in the morning before my shift started, or likewise after my shift was over for the day.

One day I took it upon myself to write a letter to Mr. Sabel, my father's boss. I asked him to come and see me at the hospital. I had been thinking about this for some time and knew I could not postpone it any longer. It seemed the right thing to do.

Some days later I was surprised when Mr. Sabel indeed came to see me. I suppose I had not really expected him to come. Mr. Sabel's first response to me was that I had done something very dangerous by writing to him and asking him to come to the hospital. By doing this I had endangered both of our lives. "I had no choice," I said, and asked him to help my parents go underground because he was the only one I could turn to. He was not very friendly and said he didn't think he could do anything to help them. He left soon thereafter, but not before I told him that I was absolutely counting on his help.

I never told my parents that I had spoken to Mr. Sabel about helping them. I am sure they would have been angry with me, and I didn't want to risk that; they had enough to worry about. However, my parents later told me that even if Mr. Sabel had offered to help them go into hiding, they would have refused, for if they were subsequently found or betrayed, there was a chance that he too would be arrested. My parents didn't want to take that risk. The Germans kept up a fear campaign by announcing that all Jews found in hiding would be deported to Germany with an **S** for *Strafwürdige Jude* ("Jewish criminal") on their identity papers. They would incur extra-heavy punishments. Anyone guilty of complicity, especially those caught for the most serious crime, hiding a Jew, would be deported along with them. My father felt great loyalty toward Mr. Sabel and would not do anything to put him in any kind of danger in light of the German threats. My parents said they were prepared to go to Germany if they were called to leave. They were still young and in very good health; they felt they could work and survive the war.

Several weeks after my parents were resettled in Amsterdam, they had a visitor from Utrecht. He told them that Jack had been picked up by the German police shortly after he went into hiding. Nevertheless, someone had been coming to my parents each week to pick up the check for his room and board; in fact, had been there just a couple of days before.

Later, I found out that Mr. Sabel had been very active in the underground. Then I began to understand his attitude during his visit to the hospital. He had indeed offered my parents a chance to go into hiding; he had found a separate place for each of them. But my parents refused to be separated and declined his offer. How naive they were to leave their fate in the hands of the Germans.

★ ★ ★

I took my final exam for the year and became a second-year student nurse. I could now give injections and help with dispensing medication. We were constantly short-staffed and my feet were often sore and swollen. There were no shoes to be gotten except sandals with wooden soles and fake leather straps that cut harshly into the feet. They made the long hours seem even longer.

I had been working in pediatrics for some time and liked it very much. I loved the children; the babies were precious. Sometimes I had a feeling that some of the children were not there because they were sick, but just in hiding. I will never know.

While working in pediatrics I see my first baby die. He was brought in with pneumonia, at four weeks old. Rumor had it that he was the child of a German soldier and a girl member of the National Socialist Party, a Dutch Nazi sympathizer. I was to watch him carefully, I was told. When I couldn't feel his pulse, I suddenly felt my heart skip a beat and quickly ran to the head nurse. She came immediately to check him, and confirmed that he had died.

It made an indelible impression on me. He was a beautiful baby with a round little face, a victim of circumstances.

★ ★ ★

Early June, 1943

Almost every day, after my day shift was over, I went to my parents' apartment for an afternoon visit. It was a time for us to be together and share the latest news, even though most of the time the news was not good. At least we lived close to one another, and for that we considered ourselves lucky.

On June 6, when I arrived for one of our daily visits, I could see by the expressions on their faces that something was wrong. That was when they broke the news to me. My parents had been notified by the Jewish Council to report for deportation the next day. My mother's voice was a monotone, her attitude fatalistic, as if she had been expecting it to happen any day. She seemed convinced that it was just a matter of time for all of us.

"Take only your most practical and warmest clothes when your time for deportation comes," my mother advised. I was struck by the thought that despite all of her worries she still had the presence of mind to remind me to take my woolen slacks.

She gave me all the cash they had in the house. Then we just sat, looking at one another silently. There was so much I wanted to say but didn't know how. I felt panic-stricken. I wanted so much to console them, to say something, but didn't know how. I felt it was hypocritical to say something like "Well, when you come back," or whatever other untruth I could have dreamed up. We all knew they were going to an unspeakable place from where they might never return. What possible conversation could have made us feel better?

I knew we were all victims at the mercy of murderers, but I didn't want to think about what the outcome of deportation would be. Maybe we all knew the truth deep down but lacked the courage to put our thoughts into words. I had never before experienced a feeling of such complete powerlessness. My family were in one of the last transports to be sent to the East. Meanwhile, I had heard many rumors, and the real horror came through from time to time. Yet I really didn't want to believe there could actually be death camps.

Mother was right when she said: "We are healthy and strong and can work." In another time and place, away from this insanity, that would have been the case. And so we could only try to hope that we would survive our ordeal and eventually be reunited as a family. Words seemed so futile at a time like this. Finally we kissed each other goodbye, mother, father, and poor little Eddy—only fourteen years old.

I stumbled down the stairs, running all the way back to the hospital. My heart was pounding, and I was choking to hold down the tears.

Finally, in the hospital I broke down and cried hysterically. I was hardly aware of who gave me a sedative, and I took it without protest.

★ ★ ★

When my parents, my sister and her husband, and my two brothers were deported to Germany, I asked myself many questions. This useless agony! What had any of them done to have to undergo such horror?

My mother had always been so afraid to be deported. The safety and happiness of her family was the most important thing in her life. To be pulled out of her safe environment where she had lived for many years and raised her children, to be uprooted and put on a transport was an unthinkable thought. Happiness had been replaced by fear, and insecurity and anxiety had become a way of life.

Before the war Holland had been a paradise on earth. The land of plenty . . . now it had been plundered empty by the underworld that ruled the Netherlands and was bent on destroying all hope of a future.

I remembered how my father had refused to let me go to the United States to join Don's family. Don had suggested in a letter that I should get my official papers ready to come to America because the political situation in Holland was rapidly deteriorating. I had been so disappointed, actually angry with my father, because I thought he was stubborn and showed no understanding of Don and my situation. Just three months later, Holland had been invaded by the Germans and it became impossible to leave. Then I came to realize that it would have been even worse for me had my parents given me permission to leave. I would not have had any real contact with them because of the censor. Wouldn't that have been a terrible tragedy too? It would have been worse!

Had I been allowed to go to America with Don, our happiness would have been overshadowed by terrible uncertainty about my family. No, I needed to be with my parents in Holland where I belonged. Just being there was the right thing, for the moral support we all needed so badly. At the time I didn't know that they were going to be deported to Sobibor in Poland. Maybe it was better that way.

Despite my personal crisis, life in the hospital went on. My parents' deportation left a deep void in my life. It was the uncertainty that made it so hard to take. I didn't know what would happen to them. Once they were gone, I never heard a word from them. I tried to push all this sadness out of my mind as best I could, but that was not easy to do. Human tragedies were playing themselves out in the hospital all the time, with deportations happening left and right. The hospital became a very depressing place. Our world was being destroyed right before our very eyes.

Because of my loneliness, and no more regular visits in the afternoon with my family, it seemed even more important to help patients in the wards with extra-kind deeds. I often did this in my spare time and even on my days off-duty. Sometimes I would sit down and talk with someone for just a few minutes or fluff up a pillow. Other times I might get a clean glass of water, mail a letter, or just give a friendly pat on the shoulder. These small acts were easy to do, yet they meant so much to some of the patients.

I will never forget a Mrs. Van Gelder who was brought in on a Thursday. Tests were done on Friday and the biopsy confirmed what we had all been afraid of—Mrs. Van Gelder had cancer. The surgery for a mastectomy was scheduled for Saturday morning. (This emergency surgery on Shabbat was an example of how Jewish law permitted the Sabbath to be violated in special circumstances.) Mrs. van Gelder was very apprehensive and cried a lot; the whole situation was very painful for all of us. Mr. van Gelder came to the hospital on Friday night to say the Kiddush, the blessing over the wine. Hearing him recite the prayer was an emotional experience. They were undoubtedly very religious people. There were many tears. Under normal circumstances it would have been traumatic enough to have a mastectomy. Now one could only imagine what it would mean to be deported after barely having had time to recuperate from such major surgery. I don't know how this case ended, but it was one of the innumerable daily tragedies.

9
Army Life

Don's Diary: October 26, 1942

We have been in Wolverhampton, England, for about three weeks now. Many things have happened even though I didn't write in my diary. I was given four months study leave to go back to the university in Berkeley. During that time, I worked on my Ph.D. thesis on radioactive tracers. I can't imagine having had a better time ever. Not only did I have a lot of luck in the lab, but my evenings out were fantastic.

One month after I left California, I returned to Stratford for more military training, and now we are waiting to go to the front. The training is more intensive here. This afternoon I even won a medal for Bren-gun shooting. However, the social life is terrible; the women ugly, dirty, and unbearable. At night in this blackout, it's not hard to pick up a female, but that is not for me. I miss Kitty here much more than I did when I was in California. Probably not having enough to do gives me more time to worry. I hope to stick to my plan to write in this book regularly from now on. However, it is difficult because there is always someone nearby either shouting or at least talking loud, or who simply has to tell me a very important story. It is very difficult to forget Oakland. Life with Kitty in Oakland seems a faraway paradise. Let's try to be optimistic and hope that the war will be over in three years.

Oh, boy, now there is too much noise around here, entirely too much to concentrate. I should polish my shoes now, and there are socks I still have to wash. Yes, you learn everything. What a world, how happy we are!!

November 15, 1942

The most important thing for me was a conversation with Professor de Boer, a scientist who works in a lab in London and is also in the army, about being transferred to a laboratory in London. I believe he was impressed with me, especially after he received a telegram from Dr. Chaikoff stating that I had done important work for the war effort. Who knows how long it will take, what with the red tape and all; these things usually take a long time. It would be wonderful to work in a laboratory in London for awhile so I won't forget all my chemistry under the circumstances.

During the last three days on leave from London, I went to the theater to see plays. I attend cultural events regularly now and it does a lot for my education; a really refreshing experience after the demoralizing atmosphere of camp life.

Of the people I have met I also have pleasant memories. Fientje Levy, a girl I went out with a few times, is quite a change after the whores in Wolverhampton, a clean, nice, intelligent girl with "prewar standards." I hope that I can keep up the connection for the duration of the war and don't believe that I will be doing any injustice to anyone that way.

I also met a Dutch sailor who provided me with a lot of entertainment during a delay in London. He was an awkward sort of guy, an honest, typical Dutch boy but with a lot of experience. In the camp everything is still the same. I long ago abandoned trying to understand most of the guys. The best principle here is to establish the facts, possibly classify them, and after that, "to keep on breathing." As Dr. Chaikoff used to say—"dogs eat feces." In other words, there is little purpose in trying to discuss moral problems, since no one in camp wants to be bothered with such topics anyway. It is sometimes difficult not to start thinking that one is abnormal when one does not participate in all the "pleasures" almost everybody else in this environment adores. But I can get used to that. It is undoubtedly true that serving in the army is not one of the worst things one can do, but it is an entirely different way of living.

It is 7:00 p.m., and for some time I've been the only one in the barracks. Because I can't see any joy in going out tonight, I have taken over the orderly duty in the sickroom for a friend. Saturday night is the traditional time for "Jan soldier" to go out, and therefore it is the only evening that I can have to myself without interruption. It is really a relief not to have to listen to all the chatter of my fellow soldiers. You can almost be yourself on a night like this, if not for the sergeant coming in several times during the evening to make sure the orderly man on duty is really at his post. The more I hear and listen to the blathering of my superiors, the more I become disillusioned with this life and hope that it won't be long before the second front is opened, so that we can begin to do our job. Not that I feel that I am already such a good soldier, but the monotony and complete purposelessness of this life is getting to me. Also, I have not heard anything about being transferred to London. I am not optimistic, because of all the red tape connected with such a change, that it will ever materialize. The complete disorganization of commands and counter-commands that we hear from our officers, with each one thinking that he's giving the right orders, is confusing, to say the least. As for the military theory we have to learn as soldiers, we are not allowed to ask any questions. The answers cannot be typed up for "security" reasons; perhaps the commander may be embarrassed if he has not remembered the exact sequence in the text. When the commander asks questions, they have to be answered completely mechanically as they appear in the textbook. If all this weren't so terribly tragic, it would be the most hilarious comedy I have ever seen.

Most of our days here are completely purposeless as far as winning the war is concerned. A typical statement of the sergeant's during maneuvers is: "As long as the exercise goes well, the rest will follow by itself." It's almost impossible to conceptualize greater nonsense. Otherwise there is little news to tell about camp life. The food is usually good, taking the circumstances into consideration. The barracks are less desirable but still bearable. Except that when it gets very cold during the winter, especially at night, and when the stove is out, the concrete floors give off a lot of dampness. The beds are good and the straw mattresses really quite comfortable, but there are no sheets or pillowcases. In addition, the storage space provided by our lockers is much too small. When you open your locker, the entire contents usually plunge to the floor. The washrooms are simple; the closest is about 50 yards away and has no warm water. Mirrors are nowhere to be found. The toilets are generally clean, but there is almost never any toilet paper. For warm water and a shower, we have to walk ten minutes. There is a cold-water tap nearby, and if you're not too fussy, you can use it to rinse yourself off, or something like it.

As for the soldier's recreation, that's a different matter, entirely taken care of. There is a nice hall where one can attend movies, shows, and concerts two to four times a week, but a homelike atmosphere is nowhere to be found on the base. The five days last week that I spent in the hospital as a patient reminded me somewhat of being at home. There are plenty of whores; one can find them anywhere and especially in the pubs or bars. In general it looks as if the level of morals and aesthetics of the English girls is a lot lower than that of American girls. Personally, I am very much aware how much I miss Kitty here; much more than I did in the United States. It looks like it is getting worse by the day.

Of course I miss my parents, but to long for your girl, with whom you can live in complete harmony, is a companionship much greater. It is easy to see that contact with a nice girl would improve my situation considerably, and because of that, I think that I will keep in touch with the girls I met in London, who, although they are not my ideal, are nevertheless far above the average. To be able to meet nice families here in the neighborhood where I can pay a visit once in a while would also be very satisfying, much more than going to the movies or to the dance floor. In general I get along very well with my fellow soldiers, but it's true that so far I haven't found anyone I consider a close friend except Harry.[1]

1. Harry Davidson, Don's friend, was also born in Holland. They enlisted and trained together in Canada.

Hopefully, I will soon be transferred to London where I can work in a laboratory. It would be very refreshing to be with people not in the army. Well, I must keep my chin up and have confidence in the future.

December 18, 1942

I was off duty for forty-eight hours. A couple of wonderful days away from heavy exercise and studying military theory, which seems like an endless waste of time. It is Saturday night and I am again taking over for a friend as orderly. It is nice and quiet in the barracks. Most of the men are in town, either dancing or seeking amusement in a whorehouse.

Last week, for the first time, the twelve-mile march carrying full pack was really too much for me, and three days later I could still feel its effects. I have an appointment for Monday to be checked by the doctor. On the one hand, it is satisfying to know that you can be part of the war effort and actively work for the invasion; that is the purpose of it all. On the other hand, it may be that I will be partly rejected and use my capabilities part-time as a chemist working in a laboratory. I am sure that the Allies would profit from that much more in the long run. If I am transferred to London, the danger for me would be less, but I am not sure that is a plus.

I am still convinced that life without Kitty would have little value for me. If I don't find her again, I would rather die in action and at least save a bullet or shrapnel from harming someone else. If Kitty is still alive, it would be terrible for her to find me wounded or dead. It is amazing what a tremendous role Kitty still plays in my life. I haven't seen her in nearly three and a half years, but in my mind I see her so clearly, as though I had said goodbye to her yesterday. Her face, her figure and voice are all as clear to me as they were three or four years ago. Maybe she looks quite different now. Maybe her character has changed too, but what I love is the Kitty of three years ago, the little girl who would come in the afternoon at 1:00 p.m., running upstairs at Schroeder van der Kolk Straat, to leave again after a kiss and a caress. I would hear her whistle and would run to the door, sometimes not quickly enough for her, when I was in the middle of a calculation, and there she was. I can describe the little gray coat she had knitted herself, stitch by stitch. And then at night, those walks, hours on end around the block in the Oosterstraat, where she lived, again and again, and once more for the last time, the parting and good-night kiss in the vestibule of her house, where her father's bike was parked, and that sometimes took hours also. Oh, what a time it was, and how I long to have her back. Little Kit, I miss you so terribly, no one can understand it. I feel so lost and alone and out of place here in these unsociable barracks with all these soldiers around me. I want to be alone so much, alone with you, alone just the two of us, somewhere far away, far from all civilization and war, far from every human being. And then—no, you don't have to talk to me but only look at me with your gorgeous eyes and sit still, while my fingers search through your hair and try to discover where all this loveliness comes from. You are my only hope. I will always love you. I hope you are convinced of that. If so, it might make these terrible times easier for you, too. Maybe you are thinking about me at this very moment. We are not so far apart anymore, only you don't know it, and maybe it's better that way. I have a feeling that you will always be mine, whatever happens, and that I will always be yours.

Now I feel very excited and depressed, and my breathing is uneven. Sometimes I hate it here. It's a good thing that this land is surrounded on all sides by water, otherwise I would surely run away. The system here is morally and emotionally suffocating. The attitude of our officers is often unbearable, and it is hard to be civil under such circumstances. The commands are usually more like snarls or snubs, like "Hey, you over there," as though you didn't have a name; it goes straight to your bone marrow!

It is a sad state of affairs that these yokels can insult you whenever they feel like it, and you have to swallow it like a piece of cake. I'll never get used to that, and a good thing, too. It's enough to give one an inferiority complex. Luckily I am not always in such a mood. Usually I don't pay much attention to all the screaming. I hope tomorrow will be better.

January 6, 1943

Tonight I am in the canteen and I want to write just a few words. The New Year started with a reorganization. I am now in the sixth platoon of the Third Fighting Unit. When the Dutch in the US, Canada, South Africa etc. were recruited they were initially organized in 3 fighting units. In January 1943 the structure was reorganized. The infantry and artillery became a Brigade. The "Fighting unit" was probably equivalent to a battalion or company. A platoon was the next subdivision. On May 31, 1944 I was transferred to Brigade Headquarters with the other ambulance drivers in the Brigade[2] and was appointed platoon truck driver.

The canteen is very busy tonight, as it usually is. Because of a shortage of chairs, some of the men are sitting on beer crates. The conversation is about the usual soldiers' topics. Some of the men, like myself, are trying to write, but that is almost impossible because of all the noise and the many interruptions. Maybe I'll socialize tonight and wait till my next orderly duty to do my writing.

January 26, 1943

Sunday night I was invited to Gerda's house. It was a wonderful evening with just a few friends. Her parents are very nice. She is from a good family and is a good person like Kitty. She is very entertaining and intelligent. That is exactly what makes a friendship like this so difficult. To know a nice girl like Gerda could possibly involve me in a unpleasant situation. How can I analyze a problem like this accurately? The fact is that for the last three and a half years, I have not gone out with girls because I always think about Kitty as my future wife. If Kitty were here, this problem would not exist, but because of this abstinence, I must admit that I am now much more susceptible to the influence of nice girls than when I was working in the lab. The energy that I am now unable to give to my research is searching for an outlet outside of my life here in camp. The coziness and satisfaction that one experiences within a family circle are many. I have

2. See Chapter 15.

been especially aware of that during my days off in London. However, I am too serious to flirt with a girl just for the fun of it. Gerda is the kind of girl one seldom meets. I could easily be caught in my own net if I should try to play with her. In the event I get Kitty back, I would forever be sorry if that were to have happened. Besides, I am sure that my old love would be much stronger than my feelings for my new friend. And as if these problems were not serious enough, there is always that nagging doubt: will I ever get Kitty back? What if the worst has happened and she's no longer alive?

Now wait a minute, who can digest all these problems at once? Why can't I, like everybody else, try to look at things from the lighter side and let things ride for awhile? Why is my intellect so limited as not to be able to solve such a problem? These things undoubtedly occur hundreds of times and no one else seems to have any problem with it. Maybe I have been involved too much and too long with "cause and effect," and thus am unable, even in my everyday life, to act upon a problem without being able to see all future consequences. Have I become addicted to science, as others are to liquor and drugs?

March 16, 1943

It's been quite a while since I last wrote in my diary. The reason must have been that I didn't feel like doing anything at all. I often intended to do some writing at night or some reading, but then the incentive would always leave me at that exact moment. It was really much easier to go to the canteen and sit and talk with some of my friends. There were some important things going on in the camp at the time, but somehow I couldn't become interested in any of them. There was total apathy, and it was not only I who felt that way, for the atmosphere of mild depression seemed to be shared by many of the soldiers. Of course, there were bright spots, like spending a furlough in London. At those times I felt human again.

On one of my furloughs, I spent a couple of days at the library of the Royal Society of Medicine in London to find out whether there was a material reason why so many soldiers suffer from listlessness and depression, which some say is because so-called "anti-sex" drugs are put in our food. After two days of searching I must say that

I could find no proof that the army has used anaphrodisiacs. For now, I've concluded that our physical condition is psychological in origin, just from being in the army and this environment, and has nothing to do with the food we eat.

I spent the weekend with Leslie Mirkin and his wife Suzy (relatives of Harry Davidson), and their extraordinary hospitality always reawakens my confidence in mankind. Nonetheless, the weekend turned out to be a disappointment. For the first time in my life I went out with some friends and had too many beers. I was very sorry, also, that my friend Harry will be leaving soon, and it made me very sad. Another friend suddenly fell seriously ill and was in the hospital. The week went slowly, and when Saturday came I had no money nor the ambition to go out; besides, I had a terrible cold and could hear my chest squeak with each breath.

Because I have been somewhat short of breath lately, I decided to quit smoking. It will not be easy, but is necessary, to prove to myself that I still have control over my desires. The next night I felt better and decided to go to the Jewish Club with Bert and Stokvis. Fred Stokvis is a lawyer by profession and also joined the brigade in Canada. Harry was to come later after he was through visiting the sick patients. It was Harry's farewell party. There was a good lecture on Esperanto, but I found it hard to concentrate. Gerda also came, and I danced with her. The conversation was rather heavy, and Gerda was evidently shocked at my open confession and defense of my agnostic ideas and attitudes. Then came the moments of Harry's goodbye. Gerda turned as white as a sheet when he said: "I may never see you again."

Later in the evening I walked Gerda home and told her that the time would come for all of us to leave, and that I hoped the fighting would start soon. I didn't have much to live for, not only with the uncertainty about Kitty, which was always present, but also because my scientific career would surely be destroyed because of the years of interruption. However, Gerda defended life, inspired by an abundance of energy and a compulsion to live. She told me about her own disappointments but also her happier times. She actually made me feel much encouraged, which I needed at that moment. I apologized for having talked so much about myself that night. In any case, it did me a lot of good to talk about the things that were so important to me. Today, I feel like a different person. I feel energetic again and look at the future with not nearly as much pessimism as I did last week. I can laugh again and participate with the others when there is something to do. I am confident that my inner resources will help sustain me in times of trouble.

May 9, 1943

After Wolverhampton we left for Dalton, Lancashire where the Dutch troops joined up with Scottish troops for further training. We left with a column of over one hundred trucks and motorcycles. The camp is located in hilly terrain. The food is very good, but not always sufficient. Therefore we eat a warm meal at 5:00 p.m. and a later supper at 7:00 p.m. The duties of the men in our platoon differ. Some of us are chauffeurs, who do a lot of driving; others do light infantry duty, and some have jobs like cooking, tailoring, shoe-repair, etc. A little harbor called Barrow, and Walney Island, are on the ocean. The beach consists of large stones, no sand.

June 23, 1943

Now we have moved again, the conditions less pleasant than at the previous camp. I must say that Dalton really grew on me after a few days. It's true that the barracks were very small and dusty, but that didn't matter too much. The infantry drill left us with less pleasant memories. We had exercises three times a day and it seemed as if our unit was worked harder than any of the other units. I myself had a great time as I was often out with the ambulance in the beautiful countryside. I spent many nice weekends in Blackpool, Windermere, and Morecambe. The weather was usually good but there was much rain. The Jewish families in Barrow provided me with pleasant entertainment in their homes. Now we sleep six men to a tent. I am very lucky to have such nice tent companions. It is not bad here, except for the cold-water showers, and that we have nowhere to go to, not even a canteen. There is so much rain. The vehicles sink incredibly deep into the mud and I have to drive through it. Everybody becomes terribly dirty and then we live worse than animals. We go to bed early because there is nowhere to go. It's healthy and it saves money for the weekend and days off duty. Once again I spent last weekend with Suzy and Leslie Mirkin; theirs has become my second home.

July 12, 1943

Yesterday was my twenty-fourth birthday and was celebrated with an intimate circle of six people. When I think about last year I realize how often my circumstances have changed. A wonderful time in California, then less pleasant weeks in Canada, and terrible weather on the boat on the crossing to England. The purposeless but not altogether unpleasant life in Wolverhampton, the conservative but healthy life in Dalton, and now in the woods of Ashridge. We've been lucky with the weather, and life in the tents is actually not as bad as I would have expected it to be, except that there are vermin in our blankets and clothes, but this we have gotten used to and they no longer bother us. The ever present scabies, too, have become less and less bothersome. Even the cold showers are not so bad anymore, and a hot shower once a week seems like pure bliss. It is only the purposelessness of this life we lead, now and in Wolverhampton, that always comes creeping slowly back. In Dalton, fortunately, there was much to do.

We are beginning to realize that a second front is probably not going to happen this year. We can't even train adequately here. What is all this discomfort really for? It almost seems like teasing inflicted on us by the high command. Not likely, I suppose. However, we don't get our cigarette rations on time, they lose a lot of our laundry, and the whole organization seems to be in chaos. The exercises we are doing turn out to be big flops. All the enthusiasm seems to have disappeared, even among the officers. There is talk about disagreements here and there. We're dropping down to the level of disorganization that existed in Wolverhampton. The Dutch Army is preparing for its winter hibernation. All our training this summer seems to have been for nothing. We have failed again, it seems. Will the day ever come when we go across with full confidence, or are we going to reorganize this winter just to train again, and then slumber again for an even more demoralizing winter?

July 30, 1943

Dear Kitty,

This week I received a Red Cross letter from you after not having heard anything for one year. What relief and happiness was wrapped up in that simple little message. It arrived at an inconvenient time. I had just come back from the hospital with the ambulance and had to be ready in three minutes for brigade maneuvers. But I couldn't keep myself from reading your letter first. I am sure you wouldn't be angry with me for having read your letter first instead of getting my equipment. Had they caught me I would have been in trouble, but it was worth the risk. I know now that at least a couple of months ago you were still healthy and well, and that knowledge provides a tremendous boost.

Suddenly I didn't feel like going out on a date I had made. My need for female company amazingly left me. The following week I went to London and made up my mind not to go out. However, I had to look up Lily because I had promised I would. Her mother was seriously ill. They are people without any money and consequently no help. Lily wanted to go to the movies, and I thought that under the circumstances I couldn't refuse her. I am sure you would understand.

Then suddenly I realized that you probably can't go out at all, and although that was not what we had agreed to do when we parted in 1939, it made me feel like a weakling. Why did I feel such a need to go out with a girl? Why couldn't I be satisfied just to think about you, always, just as you think about me? Sometimes I feel like a heel, and hope that you too have had a chance to kiss another boy goodnight. Afterwards I think with aversion how meaningless such a kiss really is if tender feelings and love are not present. I have felt that way every time I kissed a girl, and although it hasn't happened too often, I feel badly about it now because it was devoid of any meaning in comparison to how I feel with you. I think that is the reason why

Yours Always

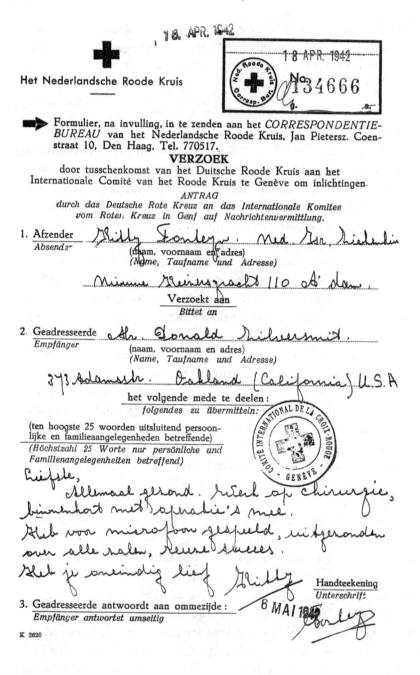

18. APR. 1942

Het Nederlandsche Roode Kruis

[stamp] 1 8 APR 1942
Ned. Roode Kruis
Corresp. Bur.
N⁰ 134666

➤ Formulier, na invulling, in te zenden aan het *CORRESPONDENTIE-BUREAU* van het Nederlandsche Roode Kruis, Jan Pietersz. Coenstraat 10, Den Haag, Tel. 770517.

VERZOEK

door tusschenkomst van het Duitsche Roode Kruis aan het Internationale Comité van het Roode Kruis te Genève om inlichtingen.

ANTRAG

durch das Deutsche Rote Kreuz an das Internationale Komitee vom Roten Kreuz in Genf auf Nachrichtenvermittlung.

1. Afzender / *Absender*

(naam, voornaam en adres)
(Name, Taufname und Adresse)

Verzoekt aan / *Bittet an*

2. Geadresseerde / *Empfänger*

(naam, voornaam en adres)
(Name, Taufname und Adresse)

het volgende mede te deelen: / *folgendes zu übermitteln:*

(ten hoogste 25 woorden uitsluitend persoonlijke en familieaangelegenheden betreffende)
(Höchstzahl 25 Worte nur persönliche und Familienangelegenheiten betreffend)

Handteekening / *Unterschrift*

6 MAI 19..

3. Geadresseerde antwoordt aan ommezijde: / *Empfänger antwortet umseitig*

K 2620

Red Cross Letter – Kitty to Don

[128]

I hate Lilian so much now. It is probably completely out of proportion, but nonetheless, she was the first girl who seduced me to kiss anyone else but you. She awakened certain instincts I thought I had safely under control. I was ashamed of myself and didn't know how to proceed. I met Lily and kissed her too, because I thought I had turned the wrong path and didn't know whether I would ever see you again. They were empty and dry kisses without any feelings except perhaps of lost hope.

Now everything is different. I have you back, my darling; at least I know that you are alive and are thinking of me, although I never had any doubts about you. We are just about together again, and I don't need anyone for the time we will still be apart. I hope that it won't be too much longer, as if the war were only for you and me, for the two of us.

Last week I visited Suzy and Leslie, and we had a long conversation about you. They are always so nice to me. They think that you are the ideal girl for me, imagine that!! But they told me in all seriousness: "Never let your wife read your diary with your most intimate thoughts and experiences"; that would not be right, they thought. I didn't believe them then, and I don't believe it now. I don't believe that you would be so narrow-minded as not to understand that a man, even your man, sometimes needs someone else besides the company of his fellow soldiers and the harsh commands of his superior officers. I believe that the girl I marry will understand me sufficiently to see that such insignificant incidents can't have any serious consequences for the future and our lives together, Darling Kitty, I think that I will never be able to keep anything secret from you, nor would I want to. And I know you feel the same. No, they can't be right; I love you so much, and I know that you would do anything necessary for me.

August 8, 1943

Another Red Cross letter from Kitty. This one sounded even more hopeful than the last, especially because she is taking piano lessons again. I think that is a good sign, and I hope it's not idle optimism! I answered her last letter immediately; I'll answer this one next week. My friend Baart received a letter from his wife. She wants a divorce. He seemed down yesterday, but already last night and today he was having a lot of fun with some girls in the canteen. For some people it must be easy to forget sorrow.

The political news is very good. In Russia everything is going very well. Who knows? Maybe we'll still make it to Holland this year. What a joy it will be to hear Kitty's voice again! I almost cannot imagine such happiness, and I am always afraid that something may go wrong for one of us. Therefore I try to have few illusions, although that too is often difficult.

Now I had better stop, dear Kit. I always think about you and long for you and hope that it won't be too much longer before we are together again. Don't let it be so very long!

10

The Appendectomy

n early September, 1943, the Germans again invaded the hospital. This time it was different. They told the director, Dr. Kroonenberg, in advance that they would deport eighty nurses as well as some doctors and certain patients. They came prepared with lists.

The administration was given one week to vacate the hospital; the remaining staff and patients were to move to the Joodsche Invalide ("Jewish Invalid"), previously a rest home for the elderly. The administration could do nothing to prevent the Nazis from taking over the hospital. The plan was destined to become a reality; it was only a matter of time. But the hospital administration had negotiated one concession; the Germans had given permission for emergency cases scheduled for surgery that morning to proceed.

Upstairs in the dorm I was just leaving my room when I saw Johnny van Coevorden coming toward me in the hallway. It seemed a strange place for him to be, since this was the nurses' quarters. As he drew near he began talking.

"Eighty nurses are going to be deported this morning and we don't know who is to leave with the transport," he said. "I've gotten permission from the German authorities to proceed with several emergency surgeries scheduled for this morning. They promised that these patients will be left behind and will not be deported today. If you want to avoid deportation, I will give you a mock operation this morning." I agreed immediately.

"I'll expect you in the operating room in one hour," Johnny said. I nodded yes.

I was given a general anesthetic, a small incision, and three stitches. Johnny performed a mock appendectomy on me. When I woke up and the anesthesia began to wear off, I found myself in a room I didn't recognize. It must have been on the canal side, the front of the building. I could hear a tremendous commotion outside. I heard truck motors running, doors slamming, people screaming, and Nazi commandos sharply yelling orders in German.

I was lying in bed while my colleagues were being taken away. At that moment I felt sick with guilt, hearing all the confusion outside, knowing that I was safe while my friends and peers were being sent to an unknown nightmare. Then the trucks drove off and it was quiet again. I learned later that the Germans had, indeed, taken eighty nurses and many patients. I was told that I would be allowed to get up the next day, possibly even that night. On the third day the stitches were removed.

When Johnny offered to give me a mock operation, I had no idea that it was actually Solly who had urged him to perform the surgery on me. Solly never mentioned to me that he was my true benefactor. I bought Johnny a beautiful fruit basket accompanied by a note thanking him for his extraordinary deed.

In retrospect it seems like a small gesture to have sent Johnny a basket of fruit with a note of thanks. I wanted to do something for him but didn't know what. I felt so bewildered by his unusual help. What could I possibly have done to repay him?

A few more days and we moved into the Jewish nursing home. Since it had been a home for the elderly, there were many private rooms. These were now converted to basic wards and some into infirmaries or whatever else was needed to make the makeshift hospital work as well as possible.

Solly and I had become good friends. He always seemed to be protecting me, and I hoped that he would continue to do so. He was cheerful and his good disposition was exactly what I needed. Solly was well aware of my relationship with Don. He knew that we had been going together since 1937 and were very much in love. I had certainly talked about Don often enough, even to the point that I may have hurt him. He knew that nothing serious could ever come of our friendship.

I once told Solly that Don used to read to me out loud. I would listen while he sat beside me on a couch with his arm around my shoulder, and I enjoyed that so much. I really missed him so. "Well," Solly responded, "I can read also." He went out and brought back a little book about Greek mythology. We settled somewhere on a sofa, Solly with his arm around my shoulder, just as Don used to do, and he started to read aloud. After he finished reading he asked whether I had liked it. I said that I had indeed liked the story very much, but still—it was just not the same. I know that I hurt him then, although I never wanted to hurt him.

I remember, once when we were in the courtyard of the hospital where several nurses had congregated, that Solly said to one of them, "Oh, you have such beautiful little hips," laughing and making fun while he said it. I thought to myself, I can just imagine Don saying that to a girl. Solly was very flirtatious, and I wondered if a man like him would really be satisfied with only one woman. It also crossed my mind that in a last-resort emergency situation, there would always be a chance that we would have to go into hiding together (it could have been arranged without my knowledge) in order to save our lives. The idea scared me more than I can express. Nevertheless, although my attitude toward Solly may appear contradictory, I liked him very much, and I was very grateful that we could be friends.

But as these things often go, Solly had started to grow very fond of me, and one evening he told me so. I should have had the courage to break off the relationship completely, but I was too cowardly to do that. We were constantly thrown together and worked in very close proximity. Besides, it was so comforting to have someone to lean on. After all, I was all alone and my whole family had been deported. Don was abroad. We were living under terribly stressful conditions, with nothing but destruction around

us, and one had to go on as well as possible under the circumstances, or so I rationalized. It was 1943, I told myself, and we were
all victims of circumstances; it wasn't Solly's or my fault, just one
of those things. I sometimes tried to stay out of his way, but working at the same hospital and often even in the same department,
it just was not always that easy to do.

It was the end of August 1943. I will always remember the night
well. After dinner, I was approached by someone who worked at
the hospital. He said: "Solly has just been picked up by the Sicher-
heitspolizei," the branch of the police in charge of deportation.
He handed over Solly's pen, pencil, and watch, and asked me to
save them for him. Solly also needed a good pair of work shoes,
he said, and he gave me his shoe size. I spread the word that I
needed a pair of shoes quickly. Someone steered me in the right
direction and I found a near-perfect pair of second-hand shoes and
sent them off to Westerbork two days after Solly's arrest. This incident shook me considerably. Would there never be an end to all
this misery? I was stunned. Even though I knew that Jews were
being picked up all the time, it was still shocking to learn that Solly
was now gone.

II

Going into Hiding

I was just about to leave my day shift when another nurse told me that there was a man in the lobby who wanted to talk with me. I went downstairs, where a tall, slender man rose as I approached. He was wearing a light beige raincoat and had a head full of blond curly hair.

"Are you Nurse Fonteyn?" he asked.

"Yes, I am. And you must be the person who wants to see me."

He spoke in a low voice. "Yes. I want you to know that some of your friends have sent me to talk with you about going into hiding."

My heart skipped a beat.

He continued: "They told me you are still working at this hospital. If you are interested in going underground, the time to do so is now. I know a safe place where you can stay."

As he spoke I stared at him in disbelief and thought to myself, "Who is this man?"

Despite my thoughts, my response was calm: "Yes, I'm interested. But you must understand I'm also scared. How do I know your proposal is genuine? Naturally, I want to get away from here and I realize there isn't much time left. I have received other offers, but each time I decided to decline because there was so much secrecy surrounding the proposition. I didn't feel comfortable putting my safety in a stranger's hands without knowing more about where and with whom I was going."

I moved a little closer to him: "You know, I have a fiancé in the United States and want more than anything to be reunited with him after the war. But if you can't give me some details about this undertaking, I'll certainly not be able to accept your offer. I need to know some facts, such as where you plan to take me, and I also need to know something about you. Otherwise, the whole thing is just too dangerous."

"I've heard about girls who accepted similar offers only to fall into the wrong hands. They were seriously abused and, in the end, deported to Germany anyway, sometimes pregnant. If that is the alternative, I would prefer being sent directly to Germany. After all, I am strong and in excellent health. I could work in a camp."

The tall, slender man gave me a long, thoughtful look and said: "I understand your fear and believe it is justified." He then pulled several letters out of his pocket and handed them to me.

Surprisingly, each letter was addressed to me. They had been written by nurses with whom I had undergone training at NIZ, and I immediately recognized the handwriting. I read the first one:

Dear Kitty,

This man has helped me find a safe place underground. You can trust him. He is a decent man and you can take his word at face value. Don't wait too much longer, because you are one of only a few who are still working, and one more day may just be too long to wait.

Sincerely,
Jo Staal

The other letters had a similar tone and were all written by girls I knew.

What a relief it was to have friends vouch for this stranger who had promised to help me hide from the Nazis. When I had finished reading I looked him right in the eye. He stared silently as I spoke:

"These girls are my friends. I studied anatomy and histology with them."

After a long silence he said: "I am a Presbyterian minister. People call me Reverend van Etten, but that's not my real name. I have helped many Jews go into hiding. Because I understand your fear quite well, I'll tell you where I plan to take you. I know a family in Haarlem that I think you'll be comfortable with—a family of four—a father and two teenage children, a boy sixteen and a girl fourteen. The man's wife died a few years ago and his mother lives with them. You can help her with the household chores and make yourself useful in other ways, such as cooking or sewing."

He continued "I don't want to influence you in any way. This is a decision you must make on your own."

"I sense this is the chance I've been waiting for, yet I can't decide immediately. I want some time to think about it."

"I understand and suggest that you think about it for twenty-four hours. I'll return at five o'clock tomorrow afternoon. If you decide to go, you'll need to put on civilian clothes and take off your Star of David. Pack only one suitcase. I'll have it picked up after you leave. I'll tell you tomorrow where to go. It will be just a short walk from here. At least two other student nurses will be waiting there for further instructions as to their destination. After you are fed a warm meal I'll return to take you to the station, where we will catch the train to Haarlem. Somebody will meet us at the station with your suitcase. Okay, I think that's all you have to know for now. I'll see you tomorrow at five p.m."

The tall man who called himself Reverend van Etten walked quietly out the door, his shoulders slightly stooped. I watched him until he was out of sight and then went upstairs to my room. My conversation with the minister forced an enormous decision upon me. In spite of my confusion about what to do, I felt gratitude that during these frightful times, with so much hatred and anger toward the Jews, there were people who were trying to help. First, of course, were my colleagues, who had given my name to Reverend van Etten, and then the minister himself, who had taken a great risk coming to a Jewish hospital. Finally, I felt indebtedness to the family in Haarlem I didn't yet know, who were willing to jeopardize their lives by taking me into their home. These thoughts, for the time being, were enough to restore my faith in mankind.

This was surely the most overwhelming decision I had ever had to make. Although I deliberated over it all evening, I had still not decided what to do when I went to sleep that night. I had twenty-four hours to make up my mind. I thought that some rest might help me to make a reasonable decision, as it had been an extraordinary day and I was tired. It didn't take me long to fall asleep.

* * *

I was awakened from a deep sleep by strange noises and at first I wondered if it was just my imagination. As I turned to lie on my back I saw an image of Reverend van Etten. My heart leaped up to my throat as I remembered the events of the previous day and the minister's offer to help me hide from the Nazis.

"I shouldn't be sleeping; I have an important decision to make," I mouthed the words silently so as not to awaken the other nurses in the ward.

Putting on my robe, I crossed the hall to the women's bathroom. No sooner had I opened the door and stepped into the hall than I saw a German soldier in the hall. He was walking right toward me, with a rifle on his shoulder, and couldn't have been more than ten feet away. I casually acted as though the incident didn't surprise or frighten me and nonchalantly crossed the hall. Once alone in the bathroom, though, my knees began shaking uncontrollably. When I came out a few moments later, the soldier was gone.

The Germans were notorious for conducting round-ups after midnight. They pounded on the front doors of houses and ordered everyone inside out of bed, often not giving them adequate time to dress themselves or their children. It was 2:00 a.m., and I didn't want to think about why Germans might be in the hospital in the middle of the night.

I rushed back to the room, imploring in a hushed but urgent voice: "Girls, wake up; I haven't the faintest notion what's happening but I think the Germans have taken over the hospital." I told the other nurses about my frightening encounter with the German soldier on my way to the bathroom.

Soon, there was complete pandemonium with everyone wide awake and wondering what to do. "Shhhhhh," I pleaded, "be quiet. It'll be bad enough if they discover us on their own, so let's not call attention to ourselves."

Nobody knew what to do or expect. I suggested that we all get dressed and pack in case we should have to leave the hospital in a hurry. The threat of being transported at any moment without warning was never out of my mind. Each nurse busied herself with her own preparations, and the ward soon grew quiet once again.

After having moved into the Joodsche Invalide some six weeks before, we were now all sleeping in one ward, with nineteen nurses and no private bathroom. This was in stark contrast to the hospital, where we had enjoyed the luxury of semiprivate bathrooms connecting every two rooms. In fact, the ward in which we now slept provided only the barest of necessities: a bed, a night stand, a chair at the foot of each bed, and a small closet with some shelving atop. There was a washbasin at one end of the ward.

Now that everybody on the ward had been awake for awhile, and because of the unbearable tension, all the nurses suddenly had to use the toilet at once. Since nobody felt brave enough to chance bumping into a German soldier as I had, it soon became obvious that we would have to improvise.

One of the nurses decided, in desperation, to use the washbasin as a toilet, and all the others got in line behind her to follow suit. The first girl used it successfully. A great sigh of relief could be heard throughout the room. For the second girl in line the experience was not so successful. As she climbed on top of the washbasin, it collapsed under her weight and crashed to the floor. The noise was unbelievably loud and I was certain it would draw the Nazis to us in a hurry. Fortunately, the Germans were not nearby and did not hear the noise our fiasco had caused.

Before long the sound of voices and footsteps began to echo in the distance. All the nurses remained quiet and most of us crawled back into bed. The voices and footsteps sounded increasingly louder, and I wondered if this would be my last night living in freedom. But surprisingly, instead of stopping at our ward as I feared, the unseen individuals continued down the hall. As the noise faded, a general breath of relief could be felt throughout the ward.

Later on, after the Germans left the hospital, I learned that the purpose of their "visit" had been simply to determine the building's dimensions and layout, and to make a list of patients and staff. Our director and chief physician, Dr. Kroonenberg, had guided them through the facility. When they reached our ward they had asked about the occupants. Dr. Kroonenberg had courageously lied: "This ward is for scarlet fever patients." The Germans, fearful of being infected, wanted nothing to do with scarlet fever.

It made me furious that the Nazis were afraid to expose themselves to a contagious disease, but had no fear about hauling innocent people out of bed in the middle of the night and cruelly shoving them into army trucks or burning them while they were worshipping inside their synagogues. Yet, I realized later, reflecting on this incongruity, that it was precisely their fear of infection that had saved me from becoming one of their victims. And so it was that the Germans passed by my ward that fateful night. Dr. Kroonenberg may well have saved me, as well as all the other nurses, from deportation.

After a while, most of the nurses relaxed a little, and some even went back to sleep. For me, however, sleeping was out of the question. My encounter with the German soldier in the hallway had shaken me to the point where I knew unequivocally I must go into hiding.

I had been offered chances to go underground before. But this time it was different. This time, the Nazis had been in the hospital; tonight they were only taking inventory, not humans, but who knew what might happen tomorrow? And this time Dr. Kroonenberg had risked his life to save his nurses. Next time we might not be so lucky. Besides, this time I had written proof from friends that an honest man was sincerely trying to help me. I knew I had to stay out of the Nazis' grip. I also knew that if I didn't do it now, I might not get another chance.

Even though I couldn't have explained why, I felt confident that I could trust Reverend Van Etten. Somehow I knew he would do his best to see me safely to a hiding place. As frightening as it was to put my trust in a complete stranger, I knew that it could not possibly equal the terror I would experience in the hands of the Nazis. I didn't have to think about it anymore. When Reverend Van Etten returned this afternoon, I would go with him. Whatever happened, the matter was now out of my hands.

As I lay in bed waiting for dawn, I secretly began to plan my departure from the hospital by visualizing what I would take. Since I was only permitted one suitcase, I would have to limit myself to my most essential clothes.

Morning came quickly and I realized what luck it was that today was my day off. Had I been on duty I don't know how I could have managed to work all day and still be ready to go by 5:00 p.m.

There were many things to do. One of the first was to rip all the name tags out of my clothes. I knew that forgotten name tags could have fatal consequences. One of my closest friends, Jupie Engelsman, had been caught because the Nazis, during a house search, had discovered that the name on the tag in one article of her clothing was not the same as the name on her identity card. I didn't want to make that mistake.

I packed only the warmest and most practical clothes, and though I didn't know why at the time, I decided to take my nurse's uniforms. I tore up all my letters—even Don's—and tore up all the photographs of Don and of my family. I didn't think twice about scratching my name and Don's inscription out of my two treasured gifts from Don, a book about Madame Curie and the three navy-blue-and-gold embossed dictionaries, French, German, and English.

How odd it was to be so deliberate and calm while destroying my most precious keepsakes. I had always been one to cry easily, being somewhat sentimental. But now I felt relieved to be clearing away any evidence that might endanger my life. I was acutely aware that while my actions took the form of destroying all evidence of my existence, I was actually affirming my desire to continue living. This thought gave me an eerie sense of unreality, just for an instant. But I was too busy to dwell on such thoughts for very long or to let them distress me.

My preparations took hours. I left off packing only briefly to find a bite to eat downstairs. When I finished, in the early afternoon, I had organized all my possessions, and packed my one suitcase. The rest of the afternoon passed slowly since I had nothing further to do but wait and trust that Reverend Van Etten would really come back at five o'clock as he had promised.

Late in the afternoon I changed into civilian clothes. It was perfectly natural for me to be dressed that way, since it was my day off, so I wasn't afraid of drawing attention to myself. I put on my navy-blue pleated skirt and my navy-blue sweater covered with embroidered flowers. This outfit had practically become my off-duty "uniform."

Normally my days off were quite boring and I invariably preferred working to being off-duty. There was really no place for me to go, and I didn't like walking outside the hospital with the Star of David so prominently displayed on my chest. Since I wasn't allowed to be outside without it, I generally found I much preferred to remain inside. But this afternoon would be different. I wouldn't ask anyone's permission when I took off my Jewish Star one last time and walked boldly in public without papers.

I stayed in my room until nearly five o'clock, anxiously waiting for Reverend van Etten to return as he had promised. Suddenly I became distraught: "This could be my last chance. Where else can I go if he doesn't show up? I don't even have any way of contacting him to assure him I want his help."

At a few minutes before five, unable to contain myself any longer, I went downstairs. Descending the stairway I saw him standing in the vestibule. What a relief! I hurried over: "Oh, thank you for coming back. I'm so glad you're here. I could think of nothing else after what happened during the night." The words just came gushing out.

He looked at me, and it seemed an eternity before he spoke: "Yes," he finally said, "I know what happened last night. I know they were in the hospital. They also arrested many people in Amsterdam. Are you ready to go?"

"Yes, my suitcase is packed and upstairs in my room."

"Well, why don't you go get it and I'll tell you where to put it." I was halfway up the stairs before he finished his sentence. I returned quickly with my bag.

"All right, put it down here." He pointed behind him to a corner of the wall. "Somebody will come shortly and pick it up for you. Don't worry about it; you'll see it in Haarlem. Now let's get you out of here."

It was time to give me directions, and his instructions were simple and clear. "You have to walk about three blocks to an artist's studio." He told me the street name and number. "Walk as though you were taking an uneventful stroll. Carry only your purse and pray that you aren't stopped, because you have no papers. I'll pick you up tonight and take you to Haarlem. Good luck." With those words I was on my way.

Luck was with me that day. The streets were deserted and I didn't meet anyone. I soon found the address, and when I rang the bell the door opened almost immediately. As soon as I stepped inside I saw two of my fellow nurses also waiting to go into hiding, just as Reverend Van Etten had promised. The looks on their faces were of intense relief.

My friends welcomed me warmly and I was overwhelmed. We spoke in low voices. But it was the words that were not spoken during those few moments that touched me the most. My friends had gone out of their way to help me by sending Reverend van Etten to the hospital. We were all in it together and we knew we had to succeed. This was such a daring undertaking, filled with immense danger for all of us. My friends' eyes, focusing on me, convinced me that I could do anything expected of me and gave me strength and courage I didn't know I possessed.

I was also moved by the cooperation of those working in the underground, each performing a different function. Their faces glowed with complete devotion to the cause, and their efforts said everything. It was a moment of life and death for all of us. No words were necessary, nor could they have conveyed the intensity of our feelings.

Two women I didn't know served me and my friends a warm meal consisting of *hutspot*, a typical Dutch stew of potatoes, carrots, and onions. Before the war there would have been big pieces of beef and lots of gravy, but no meat was available now. Nevertheless, the *hutspot* tasted good and I ate it with relish. There was a small pudding for dessert. At the time I was not aware that I was actually eating my first non-kosher meal, which under the circumstances was probably normal.

I felt extreme excitement like nothing I had ever before experienced. What I was doing was unbelievably dangerous. Yet I was not afraid—only confident that I would see this experience through to the end, no matter what obstacles came my way.

There was little time for conversation, so I didn't find out where my friends would be going. Even if we could have shared this information, it was best if we didn't know. That way, if one of us was captured and forced to talk, the others would still be safe.

Reverend and Mrs. Ader (alias van Etten)

Photographs from J. A. Ader, *Een Groninger Pastorie in de Storm,*
Franeker: Uitgevery T. Wever B.V., 1981

After an hour, Reverend Van Etten came for me. We walked to the train station. He had already bought our tickets. All we had to do was walk through the gate where the conductor clipped them. The train was waiting at the platform and we boarded quickly. Shortly thereafter we departed.

The other passengers looked innocent enough, but I couldn't help wondering whether the man sitting across from me was a German or whether even now there might be policemen moving through the train to check identity papers.

Twenty minutes later we arrived in Haarlem. From the station we walked to my first hiding place. Reverend van Etten rang the doorbell and we were ushered inside without delay. In the hallway Reverend Van Etten introduced me to my host and hostess, Reverend van der Waal and his mother. Mrs. van der Waal led me to the living room, where she said: "You must be tired. Please sit down." A few minutes later the men joined us. Reverend van Etten said: "Before I leave, Miss Fonteyn, tell me what name to use for your identification papers." After some discussion, with both of us offering suggestions, he ultimately chose my own given name, Chrisje (pronounced Kree-shya), and selected de Boer to be my last name.

Reverend van Etten then gave me one of his long thoughtful looks, to which I had finally begun to grow accustomed. After some time he spoke: "I'm not altogether unfamiliar with the science of physiognomy. Your facial features are not typically Jewish. With your dark hair and brown eyes you could just as well be of Italian descent."

Before I could properly thank him for all his help, he had gone. In retrospect I realize that he must have wanted it that way.

From the day I left the hospital until the end of the war, I would be known as Chrisje de Boer.

12

Chrisje de Boer

Although the trip to Haarlem had not taken long, I was relieved to have safely arrived at my first hiding place. I was also keenly aware that the van der Waals were taking a great risk in hiding me.

My new host, Reverend van de Waal, offered to bring my suitcase upstairs for me. After he returned, his mother escorted me to my room. She gave me directions to the toilet and bathroom in case I should have to get up during the night. My room was a *zijkamertje* (pronounced zee-ka-mertche), a small bedroom next to a larger one at the end of a hallway. Though my bed was narrow, the sheets were bright and clean.

Sleep didn't come easily that night. The excitement of the day had been overwhelming. In just one day I had gone from hospital nursing to domestic work in a private home. I had much to think about as I began my new life in hiding. I pondered my new name, Chrisje de Boer, as I reviewed the events of the last forty-eight hours. "I wonder how I'll like my new home. What kinds of things will I be doing here? And I hope Reverend van Etten has made it safely back to his own home and family, after taking such a great risk to help me."

I was so thankful to Reverend van Etten for seeking me out and helping me. But before I could fully contemplate my gratitude, a wave of panic washed over me as I realized that many would perish as a result of Nazism. I felt safe here—as safe as was possible under the circumstances. But what about Reverend van Etten? What about the countless others like him, who time and time again risked their own lives to help people like me? Would they, too, be safe? These were my last thoughts that night, as I finally fell into a fitful sleep.

The next morning at breakfast I met the van der Waal children: Karel (pronounced Carl), sixteen years old, and Mary, fourteen years old. They were attractive children with blond hair and blue eyes.

The children did not talk much during breakfast. I sensed that they were late for school. They soon finished their breakfast of porridge and a glass of milk. Then they gathered their books and, with a friendly smile, left the house to go to school.

During the day I helped Mrs. van der Waal with the household chores. The time usually passed quickly as I peeled potatoes, washed dishes, dusted, made up beds, and did other routine household chores. Sometimes I simply assisted Mrs. van der Waal in the kitchen. She had me do such things as climb a little stepladder and reach for big pans she needed that were stored on the top shelves.

The children's grandmother was pleasant. She must have been in her seventies and was very proper. I considered myself lucky to have ended up with such decent human beings. I was always happy to make myself useful.

One morning, as I was washing the breakfast dishes in a small dish pan, Mrs. van der Waal entered the kitchen. "Chrisje," she said, "you have such nice sudsy water in your dish pan. You shouldn't throw it out when you are through with the dishes. Why don't you save it to wash Karel's socks. He has such sweaty feet and this will be a good opportunity to get his socks really clean."

I thought of my mother. She would have shuddered at the thought of washing someone's dirty, sweaty socks in her kosher dish pan. Of course Mrs. van der Waal was right. With everything in such short supply, she didn't want to waste a thing and neither did I. I complied with her request and washed Karel's socks in my used dishwater. I got them really clean!

It didn't take me long to settle into my new environment. My duties didn't take very long and my routine was usually uneventful. As I got to know them better, I looked forward to the children coming home from school. Later in the day Reverend van der Waal assembled the family and we all sat down to dinner. In the evening, my daytime duties completed, I felt I could relax a little and spend some time with the van der Waals. I enjoyed feeling part of a family again.

The longer I stayed with the van der Waals, the more I became aware of a vague sense of apprehension whenever I heard cars or people passing in the street. At NIZ, street noises hadn't carried past the thick hospital walls, so I had never really thought about danger while I worked there. But from the van der Waals' house I could hear what was happening in the street. I tried to tell myself that my sense of security at the hospital had been only an illusion, and most of the time I managed to put thoughts of house searches and arrests out of my mind.

Soon enough I discovered that Karel and I shared a common interest in literature. After he came home from school we sometimes had time to talk. One afternoon, Mrs. van der Waal passed by when we were talking in Karel's room. She immediately called me out and sternly told me that she never wanted to find me in his room again.

I wondered if she really thought I had improper intentions. Certainly that had been far from my mind. I decided to make the best of the situation and not let the incident bother me. I was uncomfortable about it but doubted that it caused Mrs. van der Waal not to trust me. These kind people had offered to share their home with me, and my admiration for them conquered any awkwardness I might have felt.

Although she walked with difficulty, Mrs. van der Waal was on her feet much of the day. She worked as hard as I did when she could have let me do most of the work. Watching her walk reminded me of the long hours I had worked in the hospital with nothing to wear on my feet but ill-fitting shoes.

Mrs. Van der Waal was well organized and ran the household despite the terrible wartime conditions. She spent long hours in the kitchen cooking. Due to the severe scarcity of food and the strict rationing, meal-planning took a long time. It must have been difficult for her to produce satisfactory meals, yet she managed to do so commendably.

Because of the rationing, we did without many items one would normally take for granted in the kitchen. If we were lucky we got one egg a month. I specifically remember Easter, when we were each allotted an egg, a departure from traditional Easter dinners, no doubt. There was practically no meat or cheese available. Usually, the bread was very bad and spoiled quickly. It was damp and the color was an unappetizing dark gray. Other choice items, such as sugar and butter, were also severely restricted. Each person in the household was allotted only half a stick of butter for three weeks. In Holland this was barely enough for one decent meal. The Dutch eat great amounts of bread, particularly with breakfast and lunch. Growing up, I had always loved butter and had become accustomed to spreading it in a thick layer on my sandwiches. It took great discipline to make my butter allowance last the three weeks until a new ration was issued.

At the van der Waals', we each had our own butter dish. This practice seemed almost laughable, since the dishes held such paltry portions. I always tried to mete out my butter carefully so that at the end of the three-week period I would have enough left to spread just one piece of bread a little more generously. This seemed a reasonable solution; if I controlled myself carefully I would be able to reward myself with one delicious sandwich at the end of the ration.

Once Mrs. van der Waal noticed that I still had a good-sized piece of butter left when she handed me my new ration.

"Well, Chrisje, don't you like butter?"

I could feel myself blush as she made the remark.

"Of course I like butter. I tried to save some for . . . " She interrupted: "Have you seen Karel's butter dish? The poor boy has been spreading mustard on his bread because he was wasteful the first two weeks. And look at Reverend van der Waal. He uses butter as if there is no tomorrow. He's been spreading bouillon-extract paste on his bread for the last ten days."

Now everyone was laughing. Despite the atmosphere of levity, I knew I would be unable to keep my cherished butter for myself.

"Chrisje, since you have so much butter left, why don't you give it to me so I can use it to season the vegetables tonight." I never considered telling Mrs. van der Waal how much I loved butter and how hard it had been for me to save this much over the last three weeks. I simply handed her my butter dish. My only consolation was that the vegetables were delicious that night and it felt as though we had consumed a feast.

★ ★ ★

I had been with the van der Waal family almost six weeks when Reverend van der Waal began a conversation at dinner that was to have a profound effect on me for the rest of the war. "Many people are in hiding, but often the hiding places where they are staying are not adequate. I've been doing a lot of thinking lately and have come to the conclusion that we will have to build a hiding place. This is not only for your safety, Chrisje, but for the safety of our family. In the meantime I think it would be best if you moved to a safer place."

I felt my knees weaken. What was going to happen to me now? Where would I go?

Before I could ask anything he continued: "I've already made arrangements for you. Tomorrow night Reverend van Etten will pick you up here and take you to your next underground address, which does have an excellent hiding place."

Reverend van der Waal was apologetic: "Chrisje, I hope this doesn't upset you too much."

Soon everyone began talking. "Oh, Chrisje, we'll miss you. You're one of the family now," Mary said.

Mrs. van der Waal added: "I will really miss you, Chrisje. You have been an enormous help to me."

For the first time I realized that the children must have known all along who I was. I felt both sad and nervous about leaving this family. Still, I was confident that I could trust them. I knew that Reverend van Etten and the van der Waals would see to it that I was placed in a decent home.

The following evening after dinner, Reverend van Etten came for me. It had not taken me long to prepare for my departure since I had only one bag.

I said goodbye to Reverend van der Waal and his mother. Mrs. van der Waal put her arms around me: "Chrisje, we'll be thinking about you. Be careful." I thanked them for taking me into their home. It seemed such an empty phrase to utter in light of the risk they had taken by hiding me.

After we said our goodbyes, I became uneasy. I hated to go in the street, where I felt exposed and defenseless. But there was really nothing left to say. I steeled myself to go outside when Reverend van de Waal opened the front door. Reverend van Etten and I were on our way to my new destination.

Once we were under way I realized I had not been outside for six weeks. I hadn't missed it; and again felt anxious and vulnerable. I told myself not to be scared—that if I wasn't careful, my apprehension would show in my facial expression. "Walk briskly, like everybody else, and think positive thoughts," I bolstered myself silently.

Reverend van Etten and I walked without speaking. We both looked around cautiously and kept our eyes open. After catching the streetcar to the station we took the train to Amstelveen, a small community just outside of Amsterdam, close to Schiphol, the site of the Dutch International Airport. The trip was short and uneventful. When we arrived in Amstelveen, we were met at the station by a short, rather stocky man with a big smile and a pleasant, comforting voice. He was dressed in a long, dark wool coat. The man greeted us warmly and welcomed me to Amstelveen. Reverend van Etten left us immediately, neither man saying anything other than hello. I noticed a sense of understanding between them, an almost imperceptible smile during the exchange, implying that this was not their first such encounter. I was aware that no introductions had been made and realized that they must have discussed me privately while arranging our rendezvous. By now, I trusted Reverend van Etten. The matter of introductions, which would normally have been considered a social indiscretion, now simply confirmed my faith in him.

Without delay the heavy-set man and I left the station on foot. As we set off he took my suitcase and said that we would be home in five minutes. The streets were deserted, but we walked silently and quickly. It would have been unwise for us to talk in the street or for him to tell me where we were going. There would be plenty of time to talk later. We were both careful; and luck was with me once again.

13

Vredeveld

M y guide and I soon reached Vredeveld ("Peaceful Field"), a nursing home for the elderly, as I would soon find out. It was a large, stately building. The beautiful green lawn and black wrought-iron fence around the building gave it a private feeling. We walked the stone path to the front door and climbed a few steps into the entrance hall. A small office facing the front door was situated in the middle of one long corridor. I would later learn that someone was always on duty in the front office during the day to watch out for unwelcome outsiders.

Once we were inside Vredeveld, the heavy-set man said: "Let me take you into the office and introduce you to my wife." It wasn't until he opened the office door that he introduced himself: "By the way, my name is Boon" (pronounced Bone).

A woman who was at least six feet tall was looking through some papers in the office. I was struck by her stern appearance as much as by her beautiful hairdo and elegant dress.

"And this is my wife," Mr. Boon said.

"Hello, Chrisje. Welcome to Vredeveld."

After a brief conversation, Mrs. Boon suggested: "Let me take you upstairs and show you to your room."

I said good night to Mr. Boon and thanked him for all his help. "Sleep well, Chrisje, we'll see you in the morning."

Mrs. Boon and I walked up the two flights of stairs to the attic. Mine was the last room on the right side of the hall. It was furnished only with basic furniture, but I thought it was enough to be comfortable—a single bed, a four-drawer chest, a little table, a lamp, and a chair.

"Well, Chrisje, this is your room," Mrs. Boon said. "Let me show you where the showers and washbasins are." After showing me around a bit she continued her instructions: "Breakfast is served at 8:00 a.m. Somebody will knock on your door at 7:00. That should give you plenty of time to be downstairs in time for breakfast. I hope you sleep well your first night at Vredeveld." I thanked Mrs. Boon for her kindness. Though we had only exchanged a few words, her warmth made me feel welcome. Once I was alone in my room I sat on the bed and looked around. Somebody had carried my suitcase upstairs. I felt a sense of gratitude to be in my new hiding place.

★ ★ ★

I was awakened at 7:00 a.m. and was ready to go downstairs by 8:00. Mrs. Boon met me at the foot of the stairs and introduced me to Miss Visser, the cook. Miss Visser was well aware of who I was. She knew I was the third Jewish girl to come to hide in Vredeveld and that I had arrived the day before.

I learned later that Miss Visser was the Boons' confidante and knew everything that happened at Vredeveld. It was important, for safety reasons, that some of the staff at Vredeveld be aware of the underground goings-on. After all, the Nazis often conducted unannounced house searches. In case of an emergency, those in hiding would have to be warned as quickly as possible.

Although it was important that my true identity be kept a secret overall, I felt safe with the knowledge that several trusted staff members would be informed, and I understood the need for them to know. I was always on guard against people I didn't know, but I grew to trust and appreciate Miss Visser.

Mrs. Boon escorted me into the dining room. Some twenty girls were already seated. "Girls, this is Chrisje de Boer from Utrecht. She arrived late last night. Chrisje is a new employee at Vredeveld."

Vredeveld, Amstelveen

At breakfast I learned there were many jobs at Vredeveld. Some girls worked in the kitchen, and others in supplies. Some kept the premises clean or worked in the laundry, and others were involved in direct patient care in Vredeveld's twenty-bed infirmary.

I was quiet at breakfast and concentrated on eating. I was feeling somewhat self-conscious and didn't want to talk. I preferred just listening even though I was pretty sure most of the girls didn't give me a second thought. To them I represented no more than the arrival of a new employee, an event that took place often.

After breakfast, Mrs. Boon caught sight of me in the hall and asked me to come into her office. When I entered, I was greeted by Mr. Boon as well. I was feeling somewhat overwhelmed with my new surroundings when Mrs. Boon asked: "Chrisje, did you sleep well, and do you think you'll be comfortable here?"

"I must be dreaming," I thought to myself in a daze, as though this weren't really happening. Out loud I responded: "Mrs Boon, I am so very happy to be here. I will work hard and try as best I can to make you happy."

"What do you think you can do at Vredeveld to make yourself useful?"

I collected my thoughts: "After I left high school I took a fashion-designing course. Two years ago I worked as a practical nurse at Wertheim House. I started nurse's training a year and a half ago at the NIZ. I like to sew and make most of my own clothes. I also like to knit and do all sorts of other handicrafts, such as crocheting and embroidery. I love to play the piano and sing. I have taken piano lessons from conservatory teachers ever since I was seven years old."

I was pleased with what I had told Mrs. Boon about myself and hoped she would be able to come up with a good way to use my skills. I realized I felt very comfortable around both of them.

Mrs. Boon asked if I would accompany the girls on the organ when they sang their hymns each night.

"I'll be happy to play the organ anytime, Mrs. Boon. But I must confess I have never touched one, although I'm sure I can learn."

Mrs. Boon was silent for a few moments, apparently trying to digest everything I had just told her.

"Chrisje, would you be willing to work downstairs in the linen room?" She explained that the linen room was where the residents' clothing was stored, and where clothes in need of repair were mended. The room also housed all the linen for the entire facility of eighty residents, plus the twenty-bed infirmary.

Clean linen had to be distributed and kept in good condition. Rips or holes had to be repaired. It sounded like a fun job and I responded enthusiastically that I would gladly take it on.

The next question Mrs Boon asked was not that easy. "What will you say to the other girls about family, if the question ever comes up?"

After a moment's thought I suggested: "It would probably be best to say I am an only child and that my parents were killed in a car accident." Mr. and Mrs. Boon both thought this sounded plausible and would not be likely to cause any suspicion.

After we had settled on my job and family background, Mrs. Boon took me downstairs to the linen room and introduced me to the girl who had been working there. She was about to get married and I was her replacement. Working in the linen room, I soon learned, was not hard. I had no trouble learning the job and quickly settled into a routine.

Mrs. Boon didn't waste any time initiating me into Vredeveld's religious activities. She led me to the little organ in the downstairs hall practically as soon as I arrived. It was a small one-manual reed organ. The air was dispensed by bellows worked by the feet. This little pedal organ had its own stops, some of which sounded one or more octaves lower.

The hardest thing about learning to play the organ was concentrating on pushing the foot pedals at a steady rhythm. I felt I was standing on a seesaw, and I must have appeared out of balance. Also, the touch of the keyboard was quite different from the piano. On the piano, I could control the volume by the amount of force with which I depressed the keys, but the keys on the organ felt lifeless under my fingers. Consequently, whatever I played was far from perfect.

Fortunately Mrs. Boon frequently offered encouragement: "Chrisje, you're doing just fine," she'd say.

With a little practice I quickly conquered the organ—pedals and all—and actually learned to play the instrument with some degree of proficiency. Soon it became part of my daily routine to accompany the girls when they sang hymns after dinner. I improvised and embellished the accompaniments to my heart's content and sometimes even transposed them into different keys.

I had never heard any Christian hymns before, and soon I was deriving immense enjoyment from my job as accompanist. Some of the hymns were beautiful, and I grew to love the melodies. How ironic that the only girl at Vredeveld who was able to accompany the singing was an Orthodox Jewish girl who had never before even touched an organ, much less played or sung any hymns. But that didn't stop me from learning to play hymns. I was happy to contribute to the other girls' activities; it made me feel more a part of things.

After the hymns, Mrs. Boon often asked me to sing a solo. Sometimes she accompanied me and sometimes I accompanied myself. I loved being able to play again. Music always found a way into my life.

★ ★ ★

I grew to love Vredeveld. I felt relatively secure and protected being in a institution again, as I had been at NIZ. Even better, I liked my work and was paid twenty guilders a month. I had heard about others in hiding who were forced to live under terrible conditions. Some couldn't move around for fear of being heard by neighbors. Others had to spend the entire day and night lying prone between the rafters in an attic. When I heard accounts such as these, I found them almost unbelievable. How could people live like that? Some did not even have ration cards. Food was scarce enough with a ration card. It must have been unbelievably difficult without one.

Reverend van Etten provided the Boons with ration cards and identification papers for me. He secured these from the underground. The ration cards and papers were specifically made for people in hiding.

Whenever I thought about the conditions others had to face, I was reminded how lucky I was to have been placed at Vredeveld, where I could live among such caring and honest people. At the same time I was confused. I couldn't quite understand how the pieces of this puzzle were supposed to fit together. Why was I lucky enough to be here when my family had been deported?

Mr. Boon was so kind to me, and his presence radiated such confidence and courage. Mrs. Boon often complimented me for

Reverend and Mrs. Dick Boon

playing the organ and occasionally wrote me a thoughtful note. These small acts of kindness made me reflect on my own family. I missed them so. I wondered if they were faring as well as I. Were they properly fed? Were they well? I wanted so desperately to know how they were bearing up. But since there was no way to contact them, there were no answers.

Try as I might to master my fears for my family, my thoughts frequently drifted away from my control. Moreover, I couldn't avoid a chronic awareness of the danger that threatened me. One never knew what to expect. A house search could take place at any moment. Though I felt as well prepared as possible for such an eventuality, that didn't stop me from fearing each new day. And I couldn't stop speculating about my family's whereabouts and condition. These nagging uncertainties cast a gloomy shadow over the relative calm I felt at Vredeveld.

I tried not to dwell on such negative thoughts too long, since I knew they would change nothing except my attitude. I knew that the best therapy was to stay busy, and that's why I worked as hard as I could.

★ ★ ★

I gradually grew accustomed to the routine at Vredeveld. Every morning we had a fifteen-minute coffee break upstairs in the lounge. That was the time I got to know the other girls a little. Usually I listened. The break also gave me a chance to mend my own clothes—mostly socks and underclothes. It seemed I was forever mending. We all needed to patch up everything to make each article of clothing last a little longer. The interaction among the girls was good, and I began to establish solid friendships.

Soon a fourth Jewish girl arrived at Vredeveld. I knew her from the NIZ, where she had worked as a registered nurse. Her name was Henny, and she was put to work in the infirmary.

★ ★ ★

I had been working in the linen room for around six months when Mrs. Boon came downstairs one morning to ask how I would feel about giving up my job there and coming upstairs to work in the Boon family's living quarters. She explained that her daughter and son-in-law and their three children, all under six years old, had just moved in with them. They, too, were in hiding. Piet, her son-in-law, was a minister; he had often preached from the pulpit about the injustices the Germans were inflicting upon the Dutch people, but a friend had tipped him off that his arrest was imminent. Mr. Boon had suggested that they come and live at Vredeveld. As Mrs. Boon put it: "We want someone upstairs we can rely upon in every respect, and we think that you are that person." Now it was my turn to train a new girl in the linen room. I moved upstairs to the Boons' quarters a couple of days later.

★ ★ ★

Don's Diary: *November, 1943*

Because it has been cold and dark in the hut the last few weeks, I wasn't able to write for a while. During the day we worked on our vehicles and were often on exercises, sometimes more than one day long. The last exercise lasted for nine days. In the meantime we moved from Wolverhampton, England, to Barrow. There are always patients who have to be transported to hospitals in Red Cross ambulances. Now we are in Dovercourt Bay. Everything is quite different here. We're under a real roof, and there are tables and chairs to sit on so I can write again. We live in villas now, private houses used by the British to house the military, and they are not bad at all.

Bert and I and the other Jewish soldiers were off a few days for Rosh Hashanah and Yom Kippur. We spent those days in London. For me, as for many others, London is the highlight of England. It is almost as though the London air makes you feel good. I know London quite well and like it a lot. Naturally I always discover new things and have new experiences. Yes, I really love it here, not only because of my English friends but because of the foreigners I know. London also means conviviality to me. I spent a lot of time with the Mirkins and feel very much at home with them.

I haven't heard from Lili in a long while and am not very sad about it because it became too much of an obligation for me to have to take her out. But in place of one lost friend, somebody else showed up. Gerda has moved to London, because she felt she wouldn't be able to get ahead in Wolverhampton. The first time I took her out I felt very depressed. I had just received a Red Cross letter from Kitty. It was obvious that her whole family had been deported and that she was afraid for her own future. Although I always thought this was possible, just the thought hurts me more than I can express.

The week after that I had not even realized how Gerda had changed from the little girl in Wolverhampton to a very good-looking young lady. She was dressed much better and her make-up had improved. It did not take long before I was completely captivated by her charms. It was obvious, also, that she had grown very fond of me. She talked to me with much more openness than in Wolverhampton. Wouldn't any man have been flattered when she confessed that she could talk with her own niece uninhibitedly because she had grown up with her, but that I was the only man she felt she could be open with and completely trust? I had to discourage Gerda's fondness for me, because to do otherwise, I thought, would have been unfair to her.

The next time I saw her I had thought about it all week. I knew it would not be easy but it had to be done. I decided that the best thing was to be as honest as possible and tell her how I felt about her and then listen to her perspective. Gerda talked about her new job, her bout with the flu, her sister's marriage being in trouble, and her own worries this past week. After she finished a quite confused story with all the details, it was my turn to talk.

"Gerda, you know that I'm very fond of you, but because I have my girl in Holland and hope to see her again, you can, at best, only be second on the list. Had I never known Kitty I might have fallen in love with you. It's always difficult to predict what would have happened, so we had best not talk about it. I miss Kitty terribly. These last four years, and especially now, when I see nothing but men around me, I really need to have female company once in a while, but you must understand that at the moment, for me, you can't be anything else but a good friend who has my confidence and to whom I can talk freely when I feel the need for it."

Gerda's reaction was somewhat like the following. "You know that I have always treasured your friendship very much and that I can talk with you as with almost nobody else. I never thought that our relationship would be anything but platonic, not only because your girl in Holland is waiting for you, but also because I don't think we would be right for one another. You and I both need someone who can lift us up once in a while. In the long run we would only depress each other." And as always, after applying some intelligence and common sense, the whole problem was as good as solved.

November, 1943

In connection with having read an interesting book, *Whither Medicine* by Josef Loebel, translated from German, I feel compelled to write something about an idea I had. One of the many abuses in our army is the sick-report. The relationship between doctor and patient is substandard. The doctors are commonly referred to as veterinarians or horse-doctors, although such names are really too flattering. It's impossible to get an accurate diagnosis in the short time they spend with a patient. From the doctors' point of view, I hear that they have many complaints about the way medicine is practiced in the army. The difficulties are twofold. The higher-ups order the doctors to keep as many men as possible on active duty; the higher-ups bear the responsibility for deciding whether the men are given more tests, but they really aren't much interested in the consequences.

Some examples: Dr. Prins's advisors recommended that outdoor gymnastics should be discontinued because of the "average middle age" of our soldiers, and that while on maneuvers, they shouldn't have to sleep outdoors with just one blanket. The higher-ups rejected the recommendation, and as a result, because of their tyrannical ways, several men came down with rheumatism or arthritis.

December, 1943

I talked with Mr. van Dam from Rotterdam. He very recently left Holland and still has contact with Holland through the neutral countries. I asked whether he knew anything of Maurice and Sara Zilversmit. It became clear that there were only nine Jewish families left in Rotterdam and they were not among them. He knew that they were deported some while ago, and he feared for their lives. He promised to try to find out the details. He also said that the situation of the Jews in Holland was worse than terrible; consequently I have little hope that I will ever see anyone again.

About Kitty I may be able to get some news. In a couple of weeks someone by the name of Lobo is coming here from Gibraltar. It is a small chance. Kitty's mother's maiden name was Jessurun Lobo, so you can never tell. I would have little hope, were it not for the fact that she is in nursing. I have heard that the two smaller Jewish hospitals, the CIZ (Centraal Israelietisch Ziekenhuis, i.e. Central Jewish Hospital) and the PIZ (Portugeesch Israelietisch Ziekenhuis, i.e. Portuguese Jewish Hospital), are no longer in existence. About the NIZ he couldn't tell me anything. I can't conceive of anyone daring to do anything to Kitty. That is, of course, childish of me, because there are no limits to what those barbarians are capable of. And to think that I sit here powerless to do anything.

★ ★ ★

Living with the Boons I came to know them quite well and learned a lot about their background.

The Boons were Moravians, often referred to as Hernhutters, named for Hernhut, the place in Saxony where this religious group was formed in 1722. There are approximately 275,000 members scattered through many countries. It was a missionary church with workers sent out to many countries, mainly in tropical regions. After Mr. Boon was ordained as a deacon in Zeist, a town near Utrecht, he left for a post in Surinam, in what was then Dutch Guiana, on the northeastern coast of South America. Surinam already had an established Moravian community, and Mr. and Mrs. Boon were assigned the task of managing a home for orphans and neglected children, called Saron. The Boons' residence was on the premises. They soon adapted themselves to their new life, and their teenage daughter Leni made new friends among her classmates. They settled in nicely, and before long felt happy and useful there. In the meantime, Mr. Boon was given an additional assignment as minister of seven local parishes and supervisor of indigenous ministers. This job often took him away from home, sometimes for long stretches of time. Consequently Mrs. Boon had to manage the children's home, assisted by some of the black parishioners. Mr. Boon's new job required him to travel into the jungle. He served seven communities, working with the native people, teaching them about Christianity.

Work in the tropics was very hard. Many of the settlements Mr. Boon served could be reached only by boat; there was no other means of transportation, not even dirt roads. Extreme heat and mosquitoes were an ever present problem. Traveling in a kind of river boat that the natives called *corjalen*, he visited many faraway places. It sometimes took days on end, over waterfalls, dangerous whirlpools, and rapids, to reach his destination. Although he was always accompanied by two men who were experienced in maneuvering boats through the rivers, it was hard and stressful work.

As much as he liked his work, after seven years in the tropics Mr. Boon had contracted dysentery and was physically and mentally exhausted and hopelessly overworked. He was called back by the church to return to Holland on sick leave.

After one year Mr. Boon had recuperated and was anxious to get back to the work he loved so much. His heart was in the tropics and he wanted to return. Once again, the Boons packed up and went to Surinam, this time leaving Leni in Holland to finish her studies. During the second assignment overseas, Mrs. Boon got to know a young native woman, Marrie Brader, who worked in the children's home. She grew very fond of her and soon discovered that Marrie showed excellent potential for nursing. Mrs. Boon took Marrie under her wing and did everything for her, short of legally adopting her.

But after a year the Boons had to face the inevitable. The tropics had caught up with them again and they had to return to Holland, this time permanently. They took Marrie with them to be trained as a registered nurse in Diaconessen House in Utrecht, a Christian hospital. Marrie graduated after three years and went back to the tropics. As a registered nurse she was now very valuable and much in demand. There were no nurses-training programs in Surinam. Marrie also worked at a leper colony part-time, a totally new experience for her. She stayed on a few more years but then returned to the Netherlands to be close to her "adoptive" parents and took a position at Diaconessen House in Utrecht. Meanwhile, Mr. and Mrs Boon became the directors of a nursing home in Haarlem and later moved to a similar post in a much larger home in Amstelveen, named Vredeveld.

After the German invasion of Holland, Mr. Boon became deeply involved with the underground movement. There was a nucleus of activists in Haarlem who had contact with Reverend van Etten, who was originally from Groningen. The group's main purpose was to save as many Jews as possible from being deported to Germany. They had access to people who made counterfeit but foolproof identification papers and ration cards. Needless to say, the work was very dangerous.

Mr. Boon offered Vredeveld and his private home for people in need of a place to hide. He built some excellent hiding places, under the sloping attic roof, stocked with bottled water, cans of food, crackers, blankets, and so forth. A couple of little doors led into these nooks, but they were concealed so skillfully that a stranger walking through the attic would not have been able to detect them.

14
Life Underground

After six months in the linen room, I moved upstairs. The Boons had rather large quarters. With three small children in addition to everything else, I could see that I would be plenty busy.

When I arrived at their apartment, Mrs. Boon met me in the hall with an apologetic look. "Chrisje, do you think you'll be able to manage everything up here?" She went on with a smile: "And all these children, the house is really full." She showed me around the house. Afterwards she asked: "How will you organize all that work?"

I told her that I wanted to think about it and make a list for the week. "I would like for you to look at it later and make whatever changes or additions seem necessary," I said. Mrs. Boon thought that was a good idea.

I sat down that night and made a detailed list of things I thought would have to be done. This was quite a home I would have to manage by myself, I thought; it had better be an efficient list. When I handed Mrs. Boon the list the next morning, I could see from the expression on her face that she was pleased as she read through it. She remarked about the thoroughness with which I had put it together, and when she handed it back to me, she laughed and said, "Well, Chrisje, all I can say is good luck, you'll be a busy girl."

After I moved upstairs, I realized there was another person in hiding, a law student named Arie, who had been at Vredeveld almost since the beginning of the war, forced to take refuge with the Boons because of his refusal to sign the student declaration.

This is what had happened: In October 1940, the Germans had required university professors, students, and government officials to fill out the *Arier Verklarung*, a questionnaire indicating whether they were of Aryan descent or members of an "inferior" race. Many did not comply. At the University of Leiden, many members of the faculty protested. Nevertheless, on November 4, all the Jewish professors were fired. The next day the students organized a strike, and the following day the German authorities closed the university. It remained closed for the duration of the war.

Arie's parents had met the Boons in Schoonhoven, where they had become the best of friends. Arie's job at Vredeveld was to listen to the BBC on a radio safely tucked away upstairs in the attic, type up the news he heard, arrange it in newsletter form, and stencil it. Copies of the newsletter were then delivered each night to Mr. Raadskeller, the president of the Boerenleenbank, directly across the street from Vredeveld. Mr. Raadskeller was in charge of distributing the paper in the community.

I became aware of the printing of the newspaper shortly after I started to work upstairs. Listening to the BBC was a serious offense against the German occupation laws. The local newspapers which we were allowed to read printed only a bunch of lies. It would have been pretty depressing without any real news from the BBC. That radio upstairs became our connection to the outside world—our lifeline. Mrs. Boon told me later in strictest confidence that the radio in the attic was the reason they wanted me upstairs.

During my first six months at Vredeveld, I had been extremely careful. For example, I knew that if I approached a window that faced onto the street, somebody outside, just by chance, might recognize me. Since that might have put all our lives in danger, I tried to keep away from the windows. The Boons were very much aware of the fact that I was very careful. I didn't mind being inside all the time; that way I would not endanger anybody, I thought.

One of the Jewish girls in hiding, Betty, regularly visited a friend in Amsterdam. She had been born and raised in Amsterdam and knew the city well. I know that the Boons were concerned whenever she left for the weekend; nonetheless they never told her she couldn't go on these outings. I know that I was always relieved to see her come home on Sunday afternoon. If she had been caught by the Germans and had talked, all of us, including the Boons and the senior residents, would immediately have been sent on a transport.

Mr. Boon was a pleasant but quiet man with a wonderful sense of humor. The fact that he voluntarily put himself in so much danger every minute of the day never seemed to bother him. I believe that the whole rescue operation gave him a tremendous sense of satisfaction. Not only was he a wonderfully kind human being, he was a deeply religious man who trusted completely in God. He had faith that we would all survive the war years, and his faith sustained all of us. Of course, he and Mrs. Boon had provided Vredeveld with the best possible hiding places and had taken every possible precautionary measure. At the first sign of danger, such as the arrival of German police for a house search, we were under orders to go up to the attic and crawl into our hiding places, where we were to remain until the Boons let us out. Despite the constant danger, Mr. and Mrs. Boon seemed to live a normal and meaningful life which they both enjoyed to the fullest.

One Monday morning, while I was busily preparing breakfast for our ever growing family, Mr. Boon came in. As usual before breakfast, he was still in his pajamas. "Well, Betty came home early yesterday," Mr. Boon said, "she looked happy, and naturally I was glad to see her." We made more small talk and then, out of the blue, he said: "Chris, you're always home and never even put your head near the window, much less stick it out. You must be getting awfully bored being indoors all the time."

I tried to assure him that it didn't bother me at all. "You know, Mr. Boon, my work keeps me very busy and I'm always surrounded by people. I really never feel lonely, nor do I miss going outside. Being inside makes me feel safe; at least I don't endanger myself or anyone else." Of course, he was glad to hear that, but he continued: "I want you to know that Mrs. Boon and I have been.talking. Of course we'll leave it completely up to you, but if you want to, you could go to church with us on Sunday mornings." I was very surprised by this suggestion. He continued: "Amstelveen is a safe little village; you can go out on Sunday mornings, I think, without provoking any suspicion or creating danger." I felt such great respect for these wonderful people who had offered me their home to live in. Normally it could have been difficult for me to go to church with them, but under the circumstances I happily accepted.

Since my days as a student nurse at the hospital, my religious beliefs had been continually dwindling. Being exposed to so much misery on a daily basis, I had begun to ask many questions. All the useless suffering and killing—when was it going to end? Friends and neighbors being deported, picked up in the streets or even from their homes—I could go on and on with the list of suffering; and then, finally, the deportation of my parents and my brothers and sister. The deportation of my family made something inside of me snap. I had so many questions, but there were no answers. I gradually began to realize that I would have to find my own answers and trust my own instincts. By the time I was living at Vredeveld I had no qualms about joining the Boons on Sunday morning in church.

However, having been brought up in an Orthodox Jewish family, I knew virtually nothing about Christianity. As religious Jews we were not even allowed to have a copy of the New Testament in our home. Now I became interested in the history of Christianity. I decided to turn this unexpected exposure to another religion as an educational experience.

I remember vividly that on Good Friday I felt genuinely sad that such an exceptional person as Jesus had to suffer such a terrible end, but I didn't believe that he would rise on Easter as the Christians did. Nonetheless, I was sad for him and for all the cruelty that was inflicted on him.

I began to feel comfortable on my weekly trips to the Presbyterian church, which became, from that time forward, my regular Sunday morning routine. I actually enjoyed getting ready for church. I got dressed up, like all the other girls who were going to church. I carried my secret deep inside me, enjoying being out with them and being part of this great group of people. When we got home from church, there was always a special Sunday lunch with dessert that Miss Visser had prepared in advance. She knew how to turn sugar beets into something that actually tasted very good.

Naturally, I learned something from my Good Friday and Easter experiences at Vredeveld and my outings to church every Sunday morning. That part of it was really good. But there was another part of me. My thoughts kept going back to when I was together with my family in Utrecht. I often tried to shake such thoughts out of my head, especially now, since I had to be so careful not to draw attention to myself with suspicious emotional outbursts. But during the Easter holiday, these thoughts persisted more than I liked. I vividly remembered the preparations for Passover, with all the children very much involved in doing their share of the work. I always had to be on guard at every moment, taking special care to have my emotions well under control. I was Chris de Boer; Kitty Fonteyn did not exist for the moment. My family had disappeared, our lives cruelly separated. Those like me who had not been taken away would have to carry on and hope that there would still be a future for us.

★ ★ ★

December 7, 1943

December started out cold and wet. There was no heat at Vredeveld, but there was no point in complaining, it was just one more of the inconveniences we all had to bear. I thought about the many children going to school in last year's shoes and clothes they had long outgrown, sitting in unheated classrooms. How much longer would this horrible war drag on?

But at this time of year, in spite of it all, we were thinking about Christmas and how to celebrate it. One had to be quite inventive, improvising little homemade gifts with whatever one could find. The stores were practically empty. In a way that made the choices easier for us. Mrs. Boon talked about baking *stroop wafels* (waffles filled with syrup, an old Dutch delicacy) for Christmas. She would teach me how to do it, she said. She owned a waffle iron, with very long handles.

One day, preoccupied with the preparations for Christmas, I went up to my room after work. It had been a very busy day and I was looking forward to lying down on my bed for just a few minutes before dinner.

When I entered my room, I was surprised to see a Red Cross letter on my dresser. Mrs. Boon must have put it there. It was from Don: "Dearest Kitty, Was extremely happy with your letter. We are all healthy and well. I will never forget you. With kisses, yours always, Donald." It was postmarked August 6, 1943, addressed to the NIZ in Amsterdam, and had reached Chrisje de Boer at Vredeveld four months later. How the letter ever got to me was a complete mystery, but I was ecstatic. Never could I have wished for a more wonderful Christmas present! Because it had been addressed to a Jewish hospital, it could have incriminated all of us at Vredeveld if it had fallen into the wrong hands.

Red Cross letters were really just printed forms available for anyone who wanted to write overseas. There were restrictions, however; one could only write twenty-five words including return address. In this letter Don had actually gone over the limit. Despite its brevity, a little message like that was a priceless gift, the contents so small, but so meaningful. It gave a tremendous boost to my morale in those awful, depressing times.

36557/43

From :

WAR ORGANISATION OF THE BRITISH RED CROSS
AND ORDER OF ST. JOHN

To :
Comité International
de la Croix Rouge
Genève

Foreign Relations
Department.

Expéditeur   SENDER   Absender

Name ...... Z I L V E R S M I T 2.794
Nom
Christian name ...... DONALD
Vorname Prènom
Address ......
Adresse
...... RED CROSS MESSAGE BUREAU, 222,
...... 120. PALL MALL,
...... LONDON, S.W.1.

MESSAGE   Mitteilung
(Not more than 25 words)   (25 mots au maximum)   (Nicht über 25 Worte)

...... L I E F S T E K I T T Y : WAS ERG BLY MET JE BERICHT.

...... WY ZYN ALLEMAAL GEZOND EN WEL. ZAL JE

...... NOOIT VERGETEN. MET ZOENEN VOOR ALTYD DE

...... JOUWE. DONALD.

Date Datum...... 5.8.

Destinataire   ADDRESSEE   Empfänger

Name ...... F O N T E Y N
Nom
Christian name ...... KITTY
Vorname Prènom
Address ...... NED. ISR. ZIEKENHUIS NIEUWE KEIZER-
Adresse   GRACHT 110
6 AUG 1943   LL
...... AMSTERDAM C.
...... HOLLAND.

Reply overleaf (not more than 25 words)
Réponse au verso (25 mots au maximum)
Antwort umseitig (nicht über 25 Worte)

30 AOUT 1943

Red Cross Letter – Don to Kitty

I received only one other letter from Don while at Vredeveld. It was sent to a name and address that Reverend van der Waal had given me to use for correspondence while I was still in Haarlem: Chrisje Franken, Oranje Nassau Laan 84, Overveen, Holland. On the return address Don called himself Walter Jansen, a good non-Jewish name. Of course, I recognized his handwriting. This second letter was mailed February 1, 1944 and received on May 3, 1944. "Dearest Chrisje, Everything fine with me. You are always in my thoughts and I hope to see you soon. Embraced with many kisses, Walter." Don's return address read: Red Cross Message Bureau, 222 Pall Mall, London, S.W. 1. It was always the same return address and didn't give me any clue as to what he was doing in London. I assumed he was working as a chemist in a laboratory doing research in connection with the war, but I couldn't be sure.

I received several such letters from Don during my training at the NIZ. I don't remember just how many, but one time I received two at once. What joy! I was allowed to write one letter a month. Although these were not passionate love letters, they were actually much more than that because every word was testimony of sincerity and deep commitment, which was all we needed to hear. Altogether I may have received as many as fifteen letters.

When I went into hiding I had ripped up all Don's letters, pictures, and personal possessions. Now I missed those wonderful messages I had treasured so much. I used to read them over and over, and when I saw how Don signed his letters, "Yours always, Don," I would invariably think, Will we ever be reunited? Thanks to these short messages, we could communicate the most important things to one another. I wrote back to Don immediately. "Dearest Don, I am alone and help someone with domestic work. Don't forget me. I love you so very much. Embraced with many kisses, Chrisje." Oh, it was so good to hear those few words from Don. I desperately hoped he would receive my Red Cross letter and know that I was safe, at least for now.

★ ★ ★

Don's Diary: *January 4, 1944*

1943 is gone and 1944 here. Everyone is calling it the victory year. It will be the year we have hoped and longed for. Will it be a victory year for everybody? No, that isn't possible. Many of our soldiers will never witness the end of this war. They will lay down their lives in payment for the victory of others. Those who sacrifice the most will never be able to pick the fruits of this victory. And for others the laughter will be less spontaneous than what we now expect it might be.

On New Year's Eve many of the Jewish boys were very quiet. It was almost as though they didn't belong or were not a part of the celebration. For them, last year was not as much of a success as it was for the Red Army and the Anglo-American air forces. Their friends and relatives in Germany and the other occupied countries of Europe have had a terrible life, if they have not already been exterminated by the oppressor. Many of them have lost their enthusiasm for this war.

As for me, I can only say that sometimes I feel great indifference as to how this war will end. I don't have much left and therefore stand to lose little. Next week I go on furlough to London, maybe my last one in England, maybe my last anywhere. In contrast to my most recent furlough, I will try to make it as happy and pleasant as possible. The last time I was in London I spent most of my time buying books and studying. My visits to Suzy and Leslie were the high points because I had some great talks with Leslie; he is such a fine person. I study a lot now, almost every evening, and it gives me the satisfaction I was unable to find in the army before. I also seem to have more time to read, especially when I have ambulance duty, two out of three weeks. It is a quiet life with plenty of time to think about all sorts of questions and problems in addition to how lonely I am.

On my last furlough my friendship with Gerda seemed to have come, more or less, to an abrupt end. I am not quite sure why that happened, but I must confess that I have lost interest in her.

It makes me wonder how Kitty and I will react to each other, that is, if we ever see one another again. Could we have grown apart? Or will we be attracted to each other right at the outset because of the artificial stimulation of sexual desires so long unsatisfied? Or will we be able, after all these years of not seeing each other and only thinking about one another, to overcome the years and continue as if we had never been separated?

It is interesting how I think about Kitty all the time and idolize her. Could she also be thinking about me all the time? Sometimes, when I enter a room, I suddenly "know" that Kitty will be there. I call this a hallucination because I don't have a better word.

On January 1 we moved to Frinton. It is a very small village, without even a movie theater. We live in rich-looking villas. I am sharing a room with a man from Morocco, who speaks only French and Spanish. He is a nice fellow but extremely lazy. The bathrooms are beautiful with hot and cold water. I am afraid that it won't last long, it's too good to be true. The village is very close to an anti-aircraft firing range where I have duty every three weeks. I earn six pounds extra for these duties. Otherwise the extra pay has been discontinued.

January 23, 1944

Another letter from Kitty, after I had not heard from her in such a long time. I gather that she is alive and well and is living under another name and address. She is helping someone with domestic work and is with a strange family. I cannot express my joy in words yet, because I have just found out and am still overwhelmed. Her family has been deported. I was so afraid that she would go the same way someday. Now there is a good chance that she will survive her ordeal. *Ondergedoken*, "in hiding," or as some call it, "underground."

February 10, 1944

I wanted to talk to Leslie about something that is worrying me. Just suppose that I lose my life in the war and Kitty is left alone without family, as the situation undoubtedly already is at present. It would be my greatest wish that my parents help her and take her under their wing. Maybe she would like to come to the United States after the war to study something special. The question I have is how to ask my parents this without worrying them needlessly. At such a distance they may think that something has happened to me.

Leslie suggested that in my letters to my parents, I should prepare them for the reality that they are going to have a daughter in the future. As time goes by, they will accept the fact as something very

Red Cross Letter – Kitty ("Chrisje Franken") to Don

natural and, if necessary, give her all the privileges a daughter deserves. I think that's a good approach: I will try it.

A letter from home. It worked out just as I had hoped. Mother wrote: "How wonderful that you had another letter from Kitty. I have never doubted that she is a very capable young woman, and I hope you will be so lucky as to get her back, and that she will still be the same girl with the qualities you expect in your future wife. I know how *you* have changed in these five years, and undoubtedly she will have changed too, having gone through such trauma. However, she is too young to be alone in the world. You can tell her that she can call our home her home. Rest assured that we will take care of her even if you are not here anymore." So that problem is solved.

★ ★ ★

At Vredeveld only Mr. and Mrs. Boon, Mr. and Mrs. van der Does (the janitor and his wife), and Miss Visser knew there were four Jewish girls in hiding on the premises. The Van der Does had to know, for safety reasons, but they could be trusted completely. We Jewish girls found out for ourselves who our counterparts were. We must have instinctively known each other by recognizing certain mannerisms, perhaps, or some other subtleties.

Mrs. Boon was once visited by a woman friend who also was active in the underground. Mrs. Boon asked her friend to pinch her when she thought she saw a Jewish girl. The friend gave her four pinches, each of them for a girl who was not Jewish. So much for the accuracy of physical stereotypes.

I was allowed to practice piano in the lounge. Taking full advantage of my spare time, I tried to practice as much as I could. Sometimes the girls at Vredeveld wanted to dance. It was so easy for me to accommodate their wishes; it was really a pleasure to play for them. I was only too happy to comply and would switch from Chopin to lighter music.

Mrs. Boon asked me more than once to sing hymns on Sunday mornings as part of a religious service sent out over the speaker system. I never quite liked the way my voice sounded so early in the morning, not having had time to vocalize properly. However, the residents at Vredeveld would stop me often in the hall to say: "Chrisje, you sang beautifully this morning."

Miss Visser, the cook, was everybody's sweetheart. She was like a mother and confidante to the girls, and often smilingly called us "her children." She did little kindnesses for the girls to make them feel at home. Everything was in short supply, including hot water. During the long cold winter nights the girls would congregate in the kitchen, which was the only place at Vredeveld that was comfortably warm, thanks to the big wood-burning stove Miss Visser kept going on certain evenings.

On Saturday nights, as a special luxury for the girls, Miss Visser kept a big kettle and huge pans of water on the old-fashioned wood stove. She had restored a discarded old washtub for us to use as a bathtub and had improvised a little partition in the kitchen to provide us with some privacy. From time to time, when someone was bathing one of the other girls would come up next to the partition and add some hot water from the big kettle to the tub—what luxury and service! We took our baths one after another. I remember Miss Visser saying somewhat impatiently: "Come on, Betty, it's your turn!" This was fabulous compared to standing in the cold attic, taking a sponge bath with ice cold water over a small washbasin. Unsanitary, you say? Well, never mind, one couldn't be too fussy under the circumstances; we all used the same water. The water was deliciously hot, we girls were all healthy; what more did we need?

Rheni, who had been born in Germany, was the first Jewish girl to go into hiding at Vredeveld. Her parents and family had all been deported as well as her boyfriend, Jacques. She often cried out, "Oh, Jacques," when she was talking about him. Rheni made herself useful with whatever Mrs. Boon asked her to do. Her job was to clean and tidy the downstairs residents' rooms. Since she was blonde with gray eyes, I am sure nobody suspected who she really was. She liked to read in her spare time. One book in particular that she raved about and often quoted passages from was *Moses and Monotheism* by Sigmund Freud. Her bedroom in the attic was next to mine.

Betty came to Vredeveld in a somewhat roundabout way. Her parents and sister had been deported in June, 1943. Betty had been working at the Jewish Council as a telephone operator and had gone into hiding, staying briefly in two different places in Amsterdam. One evening, she was told that "somebody" would come to visit her. It was Mr. Boon, who came to look her over to see whether she would be a good choice to work in Vredeveld's kitchen. Betty was accepted and started working in the kitchen in October, 1943. Before she came, she and the person she was staying with made some nurses' aprons out of old sheets for her to wear on the new job. Betty soon became Miss Visser's right hand in the kitchen.

Everybody agreed that Mr. Boon had made an excellent choice in hiring Betty. She could grind up potatoes faster than anybody else. The trick was to finish the grinding before the potatoes had a chance to turn brown, and Betty had mastered the secret! Miss Visser needed an inordinate amount of ground potatoes for porridge in the morning. If medals had been given for grinding up potatoes, Betty would have won one. I often saw her scouring away at Miss Visser's forty-gallon pans trying to get them clean, not always an easy job with the inadequate cleaning agents available to us.

I had a little trouble with Betty in the beginning. Not that I ever discussed it with her, but initially I found her a bit loud and too visible. I often worried about it. My biggest fear was being discovered, and I was always careful not to draw attention to myself. But pretty soon I discovered that she was a good person and I trusted the Boons' choice; Betty and I became friends. On really cold nights we sometimes slept together to keep warm.

Our little rooms in the attic were unheated and terribly cold. During the night ice formed on the windows. Winter had barely started, but already I dreaded the cold and the months to follow. Holland is a damp country under normal circumstances, but now, with temperatures hovering around freezing, even the blankets and sheets felt damp and there was no hot water. I would put my daytime clothes under the blanket at night when I got undressed before going to sleep. In the morning I got dressed "under the blanket." It was one way to save body heat.

One of the other Jewish girls told Mrs. Boon about Betty and me sometimes sleeping together. She must have had an enormous sense of duty. Mrs. Boon never discussed it with me, but told Betty that we had better sleep in our own beds. I wouldn't have cared if any of the other girls had said something to Mrs. Boon, but why did Rheni, who was also Jewish and in hiding, have to do it?

★ ★ ★

I was the third Jewish girl to arrive at Vredeveld, and when Henny (number four) arrived one morning, I recognized a familiar face from the NIZ. I was so very happy. When I met her that day in the hall upstairs, her face was all smiles! I felt that we had something in common, having both worked at the same hospital for so long, but often under sad conditions. She must have been ten, maybe fifteen years my senior, but that didn't make any difference. Her family had also been deported (or perhaps they were in hiding; I'm not sure), and she often spoke about a boyfriend she hoped to see again after the war. No doubt she was as lonely as the rest of us. Henny and I both liked books, and I enjoyed talking with her.

One day we were chatting about our work at Vredeveld. I had already moved upstairs to the Boons' quarters, and in spite of all our sadness, I was often bubbly and enthusiastic. I commented about how fortunate we were to be working in an institution like the NIZ, where we could feel protected. We talked about the Boons and how nice they were to work for. I told her how much

I enjoyed talking with Mr. Boon in the dining room before break-fast, he still in his pajamas. I had long since gotten used to that. Sometimes, I told Henny, he would try to temper my enthusiasm for Don, telling me, in his own sensitive and diplomatic way, not to be so sure that Don would really come back for me after the war. After all, Mr. Boon would warn, Don was in the United States, where there were so many beautiful girls; he might find somebody else and forget me.

I always gave Mr. Boon the same answer: "If Don and I both survive the war, there is no doubt in my mind that we will be reunited, because we have such a strong bond and love one another so much." But as I explained to Henny, I knew deep down that Mr. Boon was worried about me and hoped that yet another of my dreams would not be shattered. And when I told Henny that the Boons were my best friends and Mrs. Boon almost like a mother to me, Henny cautioned: "You had better watch out for Mr. Boon, because last week I saw him with Mary behind the curtain in the infirmary; they didn't know that I was watching them."

Mary was a practical nurse who worked in the infirmary. She was the most unappealing girl I had ever met. She never washed herself, her nails were always dirty, and she covered up body odors with cheap perfume. If Mr. Boon really liked to indulge in such behavior, I was sure that he could have found a more attractive person and somebody in good health. After all, Mary had only recently recovered from tuberculosis.

Was Henny trying to tell me that Mr. Boon was not to be trusted? She might as well have slapped me in the face; I felt instant disgust and didn't believe a word of her story. I tried to dismiss it as jealousy, but the poison had already done its damage.

When Mr. Boon came walking into the dining room the next morning as I was preparing breakfast, I thought of what Henny had told me. Unaware of what was going on in my head, Mr. Boon said as usual: "Good morning, Chrisje," then paused. "What's wrong with you? You look as if you've seen a ghost; you're as white as a sheet."

I mumbled, "It must be your imagination," busily rearranging some dishes on the table because I could not bring myself to look at him. I felt so embarrassed and awkward.

Then, as he so often did, he began talking, this time a touching personal story. First he told me how much he enjoyed his grandchildren and said he felt privileged to have them so nearby. Then he told me that Mrs. Boon was not his daughter Leni's real mother, but was his second wife. He had met his first wife, Finna, in Utrecht, where she had been living with a family named Ketel. Mr. and Mrs. Ketel had taken her in when she was orphaned. The Ketels had four children of their own, the youngest of whom was a girl named Co (short for Coba, a common Dutch name). Co and Finna, being about the same age, had become good friends.

One day, Finna had a visitor, a young man from Schoonhoven who had come all the way on his bicycle. He wanted to talk with Finna about a house she owned, because he was interested in buying it. His name was Dick Boon. He asked if Finna could bike back to Schoonhoven with him to look the house over. Well, Mrs. Ketel had no objections, as long as someone else accompanied them. Finna asked Co to come along.

Many more bicycle trips followed, because they enjoyed each other's company, and who would come along as a chaperon but Co Ketel? Although Co often argued with Dick about this or that, she certainly enjoyed the bike trips. Meanwhile, Finna and Dick became close indeed: they fell in love and soon got married.

About a year later, their first baby, Leni, was born. However, Finna was not in good health; it turned out that she was seriously ill with tuberculoses. The baby, too, was weak and tiny, and seemed to have no appetite. As if that weren't enough, Leni had been born with a persistent dermatitis. Her skin was so sensitive and raw that she couldn't be dressed and diapered like any normal baby. No one seemed to know how to treat her problem and she needed constant attention. In the meantime, Finna was in bed most of the time, and she and the baby were both nursed by Co Ketel.

Barely two years later, Finna died. The baby was only eight months old. Without his wife, and responsible for a baby, Mr. Boon felt like a lost soul, he said. He told me how Co artfully swaddled the baby in very soft cloth and constantly changed her. Miraculously Leni began regaining strength and outgrew her skin problem after struggling for months. In the end she fully recovered, and he felt that Co had been like a mother to her. She seemed the logical person for him to marry. So they married three years later and Co Ketel became Mrs. Boon.

I was so taken by Mr. Boon's story, and felt so sorry for him. It didn't seem fair that such a wonderful human being had been deprived, at such a young age, of sharing his life with the person he loved most. Suddenly I thought of Henny and her gossip and knew that she was a fake and should not be taken seriously.

Needless to say my friendship with Henny cooled considerably, although I was always civil to her. Soon Henny found another victim, Nurse van Teutum, the head nurse of the infirmary. Henny was forever making trouble for her and fighting with her, criticizing everything she did. In the end, Nurse van Teutum left Vredeveld; it was impossible for her to continue there under such circumstances.

★ ★ ★

It was late fall, 1944. I thought that Vredeveld had its quota of "onderduikers," but I was wrong. One day Miss van Vechel (as she called herself, not her real name) arrived at Vredeveld with her daughter Fanny. They had already been in at least eight hiding-places, their lives underground had been very stormy. They often had to change places unexpectedly because of impending danger. One day during a house search, Fanny literally walked down the stairs, passing German soldiers going up the stairs. She fled into the street and escaped. They both were tall and heavy-set women,

Fanny with a friendly smile. Miss van Vechel was a handsome woman but the expression on her face was sad and pensive. They both were doing house-cleaning. Miss van Vechel was very unhappy especially at Vredeveld because she didn't like her job, perhaps because they came so late to Vredeveld, the choice jobs had already been given away. I couldn't be sure what the problem was.

★ ★ ★

There were four elderly Jewish women hiding at Vredeveld. Three of them were usually confined to beds in the infirmary. The fourth, a woman in her eighties, was in good health and very active. Her name, or rather what she called herself, was Aunt Ida. She was a true darling with a very youthful mind. Her room was in the attic next to Rheni's room. All of us were situated close to the Boons' living quarters so that they could alert us at once in case of an emergency, and we could quietly slip into our hiding places.

Aunt Ida and I became great friends. I loved her wonderful sense of humor, her courage, and her constant willingness to help anybody who needed her. At night I would sit on her bed and talk the hours away until it was time to go to sleep. She had been a widow for years and had five children. Her family, including four of her children, had been deported; one daughter was in hiding somewhere in Amsterdam and came to visit her on rare occasions.

Mrs. Boon was forever supplying Aunt Ida with work—a dress to be altered or mending to be done. Aunt Ida had golden hands. She tried to keep her hands and mind busy. She also did a lot of work for the four girls in hiding. She once crocheted the most beautiful vest for me out of leftover yarn. All I had to do was design it and she did the rest. She was a jewel of a lady and a dear friend. Aunt Ida reminded me of my own grandmother, and sometimes I would think about the years before the occupation when grandma lived with us in Utrecht.

Grandmother, Kitty and Sister Susan

My grandmother, my father's stepmother, is very elderly and has a friendly smile, a good complexion, and an enormous double chin. Unlike Aunt Ida, she is always inactive, sitting in her favorite chair in front of the window most of the time. She appears to be heavy, although that could be an illusion caused by the layers of loose clothing she wears. Grandma's waistline has long since disappeared. She is always dressed in black, a sweater over all the layers and a fringed square scarf around her shoulders. She is afraid of drafts and forever reminds us to close the door. Occasionally she will sit outside with us when the weather is warm, and she enjoys the change. She moves with difficulty and I don't remember seeing her do anything in the house except bring a dish or cup into the kitchen.

Grandma gets up late, when most of us have already been up for hours. My mother always brings her breakfast in bed. She does not participate in family outings. She leads a very uneventful life but seems satisfied. I like her very much and often feel the urge to do little favors for her when I have the chance. The only outing she regularly makes is her weekly trip to the drugstore, a couple of blocks from the house. She buys old fashioned babbelaars, *(bull's-eye or a hard globular candy) or other hard candy, special soap, and tons of Vaseline. I can still hear my mother complaining: "How in heaven's name will I ever get grandma's sheets clean?" Even the laundry can't get the excess Vaseline out, and the sheets invariably come back greasy and stiff. Every week grandma asks me to take her on this weekly mission. She holds on to my arm and we walk very slowly to the store. For my assistance, I am often rewarded with a little bag of licorice which I like very much. I remember the old-fashioned drugstore well, with the big glass jars and bottles and the balance with the weights. It is fun to be part of this routine.*

One morning mother brings grandma her regular breakfast tray. After a while she comes back with the tray untouched, all the food still there. She puts the tray on the kitchen counter top and finds a place to sit down. I notice that mother is visibly shaking. I ask why grandma has not eaten her breakfast, and she answers: "Grandmother no longer needs food." Not immediately grasping her meaning, I ask: "But why, mother?"

"Grandmother no longer needs food because she passed away during the night." Mother remains seated, moving her head from left to right, saying: "What a wonderful way to go." She was a registered nurse in her younger years and knows that not everyone dies peacefully. Because father is out of town, mother has to make the funeral arrangements over the telephone. Soon afterwards, Mr. Herschel the shammos *(sexton) comes to the house to talk about the preparations for the funeral, which according to Jewish law has to take place within twenty-four hours.*

Now other people come to the house to wash the body and dress it in a white shroud and put it on the floor. The shades are pulled down and the drapes are drawn. The atmosphere in the house suddenly changes. It is an eerie feeling with grandma's body in the house. Someone comes to watch over her body all through the night. The funeral is only attended by men. Women are not allowed to attend funerals, according to Orthodox Jewish custom in Holland.

My father observes the seven days of mourning. He sits shivah *sitting on the floor on a pillow, eating all of his meals that way and spending all his leisure time sitting on the floor. At night after dinner a* minyan *of ten adult men assembles for prayers. After the week has passed, normalcy takes over and involves us again in our regular daily routine. When we come home from school, there is no grandma sitting in front of the window anymore. In fact the chair has been pushed back into a corner. Her passing leaves a void, and I begin to realize that I have lost a true friend.*

★ ★ ★

Mr. and Mrs. Boon frequently visited the local farmers. They would ride their bikes, sometimes for miles on end in cold and rainy weather, to see what food the farmers could spare for Vrede-veld. On one of these trips, Mrs. Boon was actually able to talk a farmer out of a side of beef, quite an accomplishment in those meager times.

The Boons never bought anything on the black market. Some-times nursing homes were given extra ration cards to enable them to purchase fruit for the elderly residents, but otherwise food was very scarce. Because the Boons were Moravians, they were allowed by the Germans to keep their bikes. They would always return home from their expeditions to the farms with big bags hanging from their bikes. Mrs. Boon would use the handlebars and Mr. Boon the crossbar of his bike and the carrier in the back.

The Boons were not young people anymore, and bicycling all the way to the farms and back was really hard work with a lot of carrying involved. The roads were often in need of repair. Besides, the expeditions were not without danger. If they had ever been caught by the authorities, the food would surely have been confis-cated, at the very least. These episodes brought back memories of how easy life had been before the war and how we had taken for granted all the wonderful goods and services that were available to us.

★ ★ ★

Back in the 1930s, before the advent of the supermarket, there were so many conveniences. Most things were delivered right to the door. Early in the morning the milkman put the bottles of milk on the front porch. The fish man came by the house with fish so fresh they seemed able to jump off the cart. The greengrocer had an array of fresh fruit and vegetables on his cart for you to choose from, and while doing so you had a chance to visit with your neighbors, every-one standing in the middle of the street together, selecting the finest produce right off the cart. The butcher delivered meat to the door and took orders at the same time for next week's delivery. There was also the flower cart, always a pleasure to see with its splendor of colors. Kappie Cohen, the son of the town's kosher baker, deliv-

ered bread daily. He always rode his bike with a gigantic basket attached to the handlebars. The bread smelled wonderful. It was absolutely fresh and came in all varieties, including the best Dutch broodjes, *small round plain buns, raisin bread, dark slices of* roggebrood *(whole wheat bread), all sorts of cookies, Dutch rusk, currant buns, and more. Kappie was often there when we children came home from school for lunch, usually around noon, and we were sometimes allowed to select our own favorite treats. Mother objected only to the napkin Kappie used to pick up the bread. "I wish Kappie would change his napkin more frequently," she'd say. "The one he used today looked rather unappetizing, more like a rag to wipe the floor with."*

Last but not least there was the voddeman *(rag man), who picked up old rags and anything else you wanted to get rid of, and the schillenman who came around to pick up scraps of raw vegetables which were used to feed farm animals. We recognized their familiar voices, and as children knew them all. They were part of our normal life.*

★ ★ ★

The Boons dug several big storage pits in the yard of Vredeveld and filled them with potatoes. This proved an excellent way to store potatoes during the cold Dutch winters. One morning they discovered that one of the pits was empty. Mr. Boon had potatoes removed from the other pits and put in the cellar. "Those potatoes are too precious to let that happen again. The time has come to eat them," Mr. Boon said.

I never ceased to be amazed at what a wonderful cook Miss Visser was. Everything that came out of her kitchen tasted great. However, the food didn't stay with you very long because of the lack of protein. It was not unusual for me to wake up in the middle of the night, hungry, and with nothing to eat. I would get up, drink a glass of water, and hope it would put me back to sleep. By that time, I was usually so wide awake there was no chance I could sleep anymore. I thought about my family—a nightmare—and about Don, wondering when the war would finally be over! Every night I heard squadrons of bombers, monotonously droning high in the sky, flying over Schiphol, the airport just outside of Amsterdam on the way to Germany. (Vredeveld had a big Red Cross painted on the roof to safeguard the building.) Would we live to see the end of this horrible war? During the day, when I was busy, I didn't generally have much time to think, but at times like this, thinking was just about the only thing to do.

★ ★ ★

Mr. Boon often stood in front of Vredeveld making small talk with passersby. He would even occasionally talk with German soldiers. The Boons had put a little round table and two chairs in the hallway near the front door. They also had an easel in the entrance hall with a blackboard which read: "It is forbidden to bring illegal [meaning anti-German] literature into this building." Sometimes Mr. Boon would invite a German soldier inside for a cup of tea. Jopie, who always kept watch in her little office located in the middle of the hall, would get the tea and serve the guest.

While the soldier had his tea, Mr. Boon would pace back and forth proudly in the downstairs hall, hands clasped behind his back, a spring in his step and a smile on his face. I could just imagine what he was thinking: "If you only knew what is going on under this roof!"

★ ★ ★

The turnover in residents at Vredeveld was a normal phenomenon; some would die, others would be admitted and take their places. One day a very old woman died while on her way to make Vredeveld her home. Her body arrived in a carriage pulled by a horse. This sad event gave Mr. Boon an idea. He would try to order some extra caskets. Under normal circumstances that would have been no problem, but caskets had now become scarce and were practically unavailable. With much effort he was able to order a few extra caskets and stored them in a safe place.

★ ★ ★

The Boons tried to think of everything. With all their kindness, they would not be satisfied until they found me a friend outside of Vredeveld. That way I, too, like all the other girls, would be able to go out on the weekend and visit a friend. Mr. Boon called me into his office one day and told me that he and Mrs. Boon were going to put me in touch with a Mrs. Henny Frank. She lived within walking distance of Vredeveld and would expect me to pay her a visit whenever I was lonely.

One Sunday afternoon I set out to visit Mrs. Frank. I knew I didn't have far to walk but did not feel very comfortable being outside by myself. The fear of being stopped by the police was forever with me. I tried to tell myself not to have such morose thoughts, but it was useless. One would have to be completely mindless not to be aware of the danger always surrounding us.

I think I only accepted the Boons' invitation to visit Mrs. Frank because I didn't want to appear ungrateful; I would just as soon have stayed home behind the safe walls of Vredeveld. I was not convinced that it was really so important for me to leave Vredeveld and risk, not just my own safety, but that of Mr. and Mrs. Boon and the other Jews hiding at Vredeveld. Because I was so grateful for everything the Boons had done for me, I went to the Franks, solely to please them.

Despite my fear, in a strange way I felt excited to be outside alone. It was a beautiful day. The sun was out and I told myself to relax and breathe in the healthy outdoor air. It was hard not to feel uneasy, and as I made my way to the Frank house I experienced such a strange mixture of emotions. It was a novelty for me to go visiting. I had not done anything of the sort in a long time.

I was relieved when I arrived at their home. Mrs. Frank had been expecting me and she introduced me to her husband, a kind man with a mop of gray hair. Mrs. Frank must have been in her fifties, I thought. Her hair was thinning and grayish.

The Franks lived in a spacious house, and when I walked into the living room, out of the corner of one eye I spotted a grand piano. I thought: "What a joy it must be to own an instrument like that! I wonder if I'll get to play it."

Mrs. Frank soon got out the ersatz tea and we began to get to know one another. Needless to say, the conversation quickly led to music. She was a graduate of the Amsterdam Conservatory. She had taught there for years, and later, when her children had come along (they had five), she had started to teach privately at home. I told her about my musical background, and before I knew it I was sitting at that gorgeous piano.

Once we discovered how much we had in common, we all relaxed. I felt I had always known these people. It was music, the international language, which had spoken to us loud and clear. Although I was really not in very good practice, I played several of my favorite pieces for her. I could tell that Mrs. Frank was genuinely happy I had come to visit her.

Now it was Mrs. Frank's turn to play. I was nearly knocked out of my seat when she played the Chopin C-major étude for me. Her fingers were strong and steady, spewing out difficult arpeggios, always transposing in accordance with the composer's difficult writing. I knew this étude was a real challenge to play and wondered how many hours she had practiced to learn it. During the war years all ordinary activities, such as shopping for groceries, took a lot of time out of one's day. Mrs. Frank had to have been an organized person to be able to find any time to practice. It was obvious that she was a fine pianist; her playing was first-class.

Our first visit had been a great success. We had really enjoyed playing the piano for one another, and before I went back to Vredeveld, Mrs. Frank offered me a lesson whenever I wanted one.

Back at Vredeveld, Mr. Boon never failed to ask me in the presence of some of the non-Jewish girls whether I'd had a good outing on Sunday. It was very comforting to know that the girls thought of me as just one of them and nothing else. I didn't want to take any chance of being discovered by the non-Jewish girls, even those I worked so closely with. Thus my visits with the Franks were rewarding, not just because I enjoyed them, but because they helped me to blend in.

Although I didn't know it at the time, Henny Frank was active in the underground. Mr. Boon knew that Henny was the safest friend I could have visited.

15
The Invasion

April 14, 1944

Last week I was so happy to get another letter from Kitty. Nevertheless, I am not very hopeful that I will see her again soon. Otherwise it looks as though the longest part of the war is over. The Russians are approaching Germany and the bombing is getting worse every day. You can see that slowly but surely the Allies are beginning to make preparations for the invasion. Maybe it is all fake to mislead the enemy, but something is in the air. I often hear the rumble of the big cannons, and some people claim that the continuous rumbling we hear is the explosion of bombs on the other side. All mail to and from England is now censored. Part of the coast in the east and south of England is closed to all traffic. You must have a special pass to enter or leave the area. All furloughs have been canceled for the time being, and while on the one hand that is unfortunate, it has to start sometime.

April 22, 1944

This week I had duty in our hospital. It was not very busy or interesting. I also had to drive someone to Dartford, approximately 100 miles from here, which was a welcome relief from the monotony.

The next day I started to paint five big red crosses on my ambulance. That was quite a job and it took two days, with two of us, to finish. I also tried to waterproof the canvas roof of the ambulance. I am waiting with great anticipation for rain, to see whether I succeeded. Pre-invasion preparations are proceeding according to plan. This week we all got new gas masks, and berets instead of our caps. There are rumors that we are getting gas-proof battle dress. And that's not all. They say that we are going to move next week to Frinton, Wolverhampton, Stockport, or somewhere else. Our excess baggage is in the process of being shipped to Wolverhampton. And so we continue every day, watching the Russians bring us closer to liberation. Today I received my appointment as a member of the Biochemical Society. I have to send £2 2s. and my thanks for the honor. I wonder what to do with all the journals I will receive regularly, because I have no room to put anything, especially now that I have had to part with my suitcase. The Germans are flying overhead, probably to London because they are not dropping bombs yet, but that could start any moment.

May 31, 1944

A little over three weeks ago I was transferred to Brigade Headquarters, and although that is usually considered the first step on the way to London, in this case it was something quite different. The three ambulances and their drivers were taken out of the fighting units. That means that I am ambulance driver only, responsible for helping and transporting wounded soldiers to hospitals during and after a battle. Sjoert, my hospital driver assistant, and I have to pick up the wounded from the battlefield. That may be very hard at first. But still I feel good about this move, especially because my ties with the Red Cross seemed to be stronger than those to my unit. Not that I want to imply in any way that it wasn't unpleasant to have to leave all my friends and be set down in a relatively strange place. But I was glad that I could continue in my job as an ambulance driver as I have gotten so used to it.

I feel as comfortable with my vehicle as I would with an intimate friend. Therefore I have christened her "Kitty." The work in the Medical Corps and infirmary is of the same nature as it was in the third platoon, except that there is less to do here.

My duties at the hospital and in Walton continue the same as before. Furloughs are now severely restricted: only once a month for twenty-four hours. We have to stay within a 25-mile radius, so there isn't much freedom. In general the boys are really fed up with the war. We're getting all kinds of injections: typhoid, paratyphoid, tetanus, smallpox, etc. First it was optional, but now it is compulsory and sometimes under duress. A few days ago one of the soldiers refused to take his shots. Before he knew what was happening, three men had grabbed him while another pushed a needle into his arm.

The man is now in prison awaiting trial. I am curious to see how the case will end. Most people here think that such treatment goes a little too far even though we are in the army.

★ ★ ★

—— THE INVASION OF NORMANDY ——

Finally, we heard the wonderful news that the second front had been opened. On June 6, 1944, the Allied forces landed on the beaches of Normandy—a complete success.

We had been waiting for good news for a long time. Now we began to hope that it would only be a matter of months until the war was over. The local newspaper didn't report a thing. Needless to say, we blessed that little radio upstairs in the attic.

Once the Allied forces had established a firm foothold, their progress was very fast.

On August 21 Paris fell, luckily without destruction, because it was declared an "open city." By September 4, Americans were pushing beyond Brussels, Belgium's capital; September 8, the Allies were in northern Belgium, 15 miles from the Dutch border.

★ ★ ★

Don's Diary: *June, 1944*

It's my day off and I am on the beach at Dovercourt. The sun is trying to come through the clouds from time to time. It's hard to understand how we can sit here so quiet and lazy while on the other side, a battle for life and death is going on.

The second front started more than a week ago. From here we didn't notice much except that on June 5th we saw a large number of ships pull out of the harbor and heard continuous flying overhead day and night. The only cannons we hear are those of the antiaircraft practice range close by. Sometimes we are shaken up a bit by severe vibrations, probably caused by the big bombs on the other side of the Channel. Otherwise everything is still the same, even the mobilization has been announced today under strict secrecy. The soldiers knew it already, as is usually the case; the secret was out a long time ago. As I said before, it doesn't seem to make much difference.

Everyone is still just as apathetic and cynical concerning the army's leadership. No one is doing anything to improve the situation. The fact that the second front has started brought little enthusiasm to this side of the Channel. Everyone is so fed up with this rotten war; the only thing anyone cares about is when it is going to end. If Germany does not surrender it could still take a long time. This week I received another letter from Kitty, and that's about the only thing I'm still interested in. My purpose is to find her alive and hopefully in reasonable condition. I need her so much as a woman and as somebody to love. My life is empty without her and my work. It has been clear for a long time that neither one could be replaced, not even partially, to compensate for the monotonous and useless existence we lead here. My only good solution is always Kitty. There are so many men here, not nearly as sensitive as I, who regret having fallen for women who really were not worth being with.

I know that both Kitty and I must have changed a lot, but that could be a help as well as a hindrance. Time will tell. It would have been much easier if I had been able to stay in touch with my work, but I must say that this interruption, although unpleasant, has also had its advantages. Maybe I have forgotten a lot of chemistry, but I've also learned a lot. Maybe I have become more of a human being and less of a scientist. After all, the most important thing in life is to live as happily as possible. One almost never learns such things before most of life has already been lived, and by then the knowledge is of little use.

Today we were mobilized. In a couple of weeks we could cross. It could be either a success or a failure, but if we have anything to say about it, it will all be over soon.

July 4, 1944

We're on our way to a different camp to get some rest. God knows that our men don't need any rest. Most of us are very irritable, which is not surprising, since we have nothing to do and are getting no furloughs

The Germans are using the V-1 bomb. For us it is a diversion to see one in the sky; for Londoners it is probably less pleasant. The Allies are doing very well on the battlefield. Dr. Zak, one of the brigade physicians, said today that it will all be over before October, I hope he's right but can't quite believe it. We're all losing our patience. Even Fred Stokvis is nervous and feels terrible. Others are drinking more than usual, and to make matters worse, they're sending us to a tent-camp area, out in the wilderness with nothing to do. I don't think it's funny. In London there is real chaos. The Dutch government is a junta which slips from one crisis into the next. The military force is even worse. People who don't fit into the brigade, for some strange reason, always get promotions. It creates a lot of jealousy, which doesn't help the morale of the troops. Nobody seems to know what is going on, and the stupidities that take place are kept hidden under the guise of military secrecy and necessity.

July 11, 1944

Today is my twenty-fifth birthday, and although it's a day like most others, because of this occasion, I want to write a few words. The seclusion and loneliness have given me ample time to think about these past twenty-five years.

The tents we are living in at the moment give us the illusion of being completely at one with nature as it was in the beginning. We notice relatively little of the war compared to other soldiers. The camp is beautiful, especially when the sun comes out. I haven't left the grounds yet; there is no place to go. Now that we are mobilized we seem to have even less to do than before, and what we do is only causing confusion. Our equipment, which has been ordered, is still arriving in Dovercourt because someone forgot to mention the change of address. In the meantime the mistake has been discovered and someone in charge is trying to correct it. Tomorrow we'll have drill for a couple of hours, but it seems more like a get-together for the staff officers. The crosses for the graves have arrived in the meantime, but we don't need them yet.

July 27, 1944

At the moment we are involved in a mock operation against the Belgian Brigade. We have improvised by using a part of our practice field to accommodate the wounded soldiers. The battle hasn't started yet because the infantry is not quite through digging the trenches in their location. Some of the boys are still playing poker, and I am sitting in my ambulance, alone. Field exercises are usually very boring, but at the same time they provide us with a couple of days' work. I am trying hard to look like a tramp. We have to wear our work uniforms. As part of this mock operation I am wrapped in oil-like cotton to protect my skin. My beard is quite long and I am dirty from top to bottom. My ambulance is in good condition. I have just finished painting the name "Kitty" in white on the hood of my vehicle. Everyone asks "Who's Kitty?"; and then of course I tell them. There are two doctors present for the exercise, but they are a little way up the road in an empty farmhouse that is to be the Regimental Aid Post. Last night we were able to sleep relatively well, but tonight we will probably have to pull back.

An exercise like this is not the worst thing we have to go through. Yesterday I saw a list of Jewish people from Holland who had arrived in Israel. Needless to say, I was surprised when I saw Aunt Sara Zilversmit's name on it. She and Uncle Maurice were deported to Westerbork, the transit camp in Holland. Uncle Maurice died in Westerbork. Aunt Sara was deported to Theresienstadt. Since she had very special papers, she was taken out of the camp and with a very few privileged people sent to Israel. I had little hope of finding Kitty's name on the list. Hopefully she will be able to survive these few last months. It must be a horrifying existence for the people who have gone into hiding; we hear how some live under terrible conditions. If I ever get Kitty back I won't have lost very much during this war. It has always been my plan from the very beginning, when Holland was first occupied, to find her and help her as much as I can. I can hardly imagine how we will react when this happens. Are we still the same people of six years ago? Could we, after such a long time, get married as though nothing had happened? Can she get used to the United States? Would I be a good enough husband to make her happy and make her forget all those terrible years?

What I will do if I don't find her I cannot even imagine. Then I would want to kill all the Germans, but even that would not solve anything. I count so much on sharing the rest of my life with Kitty. If that isn't possible I hope that I will be killed here or somewhere in battle.

★ ★ ★

We heard terrible news about Reverend van Etten. At the end of July, 1944, he was arrested in Haarlem by the German police and put in prison. They found incriminating papers on him. When I heard the shocking news I felt as though the bottom had fallen out. When the news reached Mr. Boon in Vredeveld, he called each Jewish girl into his office separately. He told us that he feared a house search by the police. Reverend van Etten would undoubtedly be interrogated by the Gestapo and subjected to severe torture. One could never be sure whether the victim might not give away vital information. Mr. Boon and the people at Vredeveld would also be in danger of arrest. So he arranged for all the Jewish girls to leave Vredeveld until the situation cooled off a bit. For emergencies he had several addresses where they could temporarily stay. He told me that I could remain in Vredeveld. I don't know what reasoning led to this decision, but I didn't ask any questions.

The next few days nothing unusual happened. When Mr. Boon thought it was safe for them to return home, he picked up the girls himself and brought them back to Vredeveld. I felt quite on edge during these few days. Reverend van Etten had apparently not given the Germans any information, but the thought was ever present, and haunted people in hiding, that someone, somehow, would betray us.

Although Vredeveld was not searched by the police, no one knew what might happen tomorrow. We tried to carry on as normally as possible. A few days after Reverend van Etten's arrest, Mrs. van Etten set out for Vredeveld. After the arrest of her husband the underground urged her to leave home at once because she was no longer safe there. She packed the most necessary things, some clothes for her and Hansje, her two-year-old boy, put her suitcase on the luggage carrier of her bicycle and Hansje up front in a basket on the handlebars. "Where are we going, Mommy?" he asked. "We are going to stay with different friends, and you are going to have a really good time," she said. Hansje had already slept in four different beds the last three days, and he repeatedly said: "Mommy, I want to go home now."

A few days later Mrs. van Etten arrived at Vredeveld. Mrs. Boon had told me in advance that she was coming, so I was prepared. I saw her come down the stairs. She had a faint smile on her face and seemed very much in control of herself. At the sight of her I was overcome with emotions: pity for her and guilt at my own implication in her misery. I had to avert my gaze and go to my room and sort things out in private. I knew that Mrs. van Etten was pregnant with her second child, and I wondered what thoughts were going through her mind.

At the time of his arrest, Reverend van Etten had already helped more than 200 Jews go into hiding. His home in Groningen was filled with people in hiding all through the war. Sometimes with only minutes' notice, people who had no place to go rang the doorbell at night after dark, and were allowed to stay. Life had become so full of risk and insecurity, and yet, like her husband, Mrs. van Etten carried on with her head held high and enormous trust in her religion.

★ ★ ★

Don's Diary: *August 9, 1944*

We landed on French soil a couple of hours ago. It's 2:30 in the afternoon and much has happened in the last week. Almost immediately after the mock exercise against the Belgians, all of our week-end passes were canceled.

The next four days we had to work incredibly hard to get every-thing ready. We could have done all this work during the preceding six weeks. No one believed that we would leave immediately, much less that we would cross the Channel. Thursday morning we left for London to pick up more soldiers in training camp. Friday we drove to Southend harbor and boarded the ship. We stayed on board and Sunday evening we sailed from Southend, which is located east of London on the North Sea.

This evening we arrived north of Bayeux, France, and stayed on board ship overnight at our landing place. In the morning we would be transferred to landing craft: all the cargo, vehicles, and men. The weather had been beautiful the last couple of days during the passage, and I have never seen an ocean so beautiful and smooth.

In the morning there was lots of commotion on board as we prepared to disembark. The cranes to lift the heavy cargo and vehicles were put into place. The landing craft which surrounded the ship during the passage were now lined up to do their jobs. The cargo-nets were fastened atop the deck and thrown over the railing of the ship for the soldiers to lower themselves down to the landing craft. We drivers of the various vehicles had all been instructed in advance

Don's Ambulance "Kitty" at Normandy Landing

to prepare to drive our vehicles off the landing craft and onto the beaches.

I looked over the railing to get a good look at the cargo- nets and the height of the ship. I wondered if the nets were securely fastened, and then I had a novel idea. I asked my officer whether I couldn't just as well sit in my ambulance while the crane lowered it onto the landing craft. He wouldn't hear of it, saying he had never heard of such an unusual request. When it was my turn to go down the net, without a life jacket, I made it safely into the landing craft, where my ambulance was already waiting for me.

I got in quickly, started the engine, and drove off the craft into the water. I got stuck halfway because my engine got wet and conked out. Fortunately I was able to start it up again, free my truck, and drive onto the beach of Normandy. We continued along the beach following the signs "Gold" to our designated meeting place. The "Gold" signs had been put on the Normandy beach by the invasion commandos.

It is terribly dusty here and the roads are in very poor condition. I must stop now. Kitty, we are now finally on our way. Maybe one or two more months.

August 10, 1944

Because of the blackout we drive without lights. Every vehicle has a tiny red light on its rear fender so that the vehicle behind it can find its way by following the little red light. The roads were very dusty last night. Consequently half of our column, including myself, took a wrong turn. Fortunately, a few hours later, the errant part of the column arrived safely at the right destination.

It's quiet in the camp except for the many fighter planes flying over all the time. We clearly hear the artillery in the distance. The food is not bad, but monotonous. We eat mostly hardtack and corned beef. The mood among the men is very good and no one seems nervous. Tomorrow we have to relieve British paratroopers; we'll be much closer to the enemy.

The weather is dry and hot. Water from a deep well comes as a welcome relief. The country is almost completely destroyed, although here and there we notice some cattle and a few ducks and

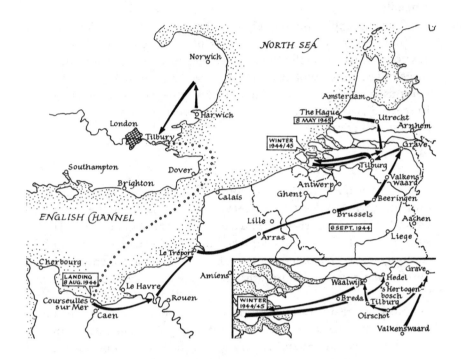

Route of the Princess Irene Brigade

Modified from: *Van Brigade en Garderegiment Prinses Irene,*
Theo de Kort, AD. Donker, Rotterdam

geese. In the village one can buy butter, cheese, and sugar without
ration cards.

Thursday, August 17, 1944

Saturday, August 12, we left for the front line near Breville. The
first two days we worked like dogs, digging shelters, ditches, chop-
ping wood, etc. Between Sjoert and myself, we had to lift the
wounded men onto stretchers and transport them in the ambulance
to the nearest hospital. Didn't get any sleep because of the awful noise
of mortars and artillery. The Germans are throwing lots of hand
grenades and they drop very close to us. This caused more wounded
men, and Sergeant Hammers, our commander, was instantly killed.

A terrible shock for all of us. We escaped death through the eye of a needle.

Tuesday approximately eighty men developed terrible diarrhea and high fevers; it was very busy for us. Wednesday we'll get two days of rest; we are really looking forward to it. Today we'll advance three miles, which will bring us closer to the fighting line. I felt very nervous and jumpy for awhile, but now I feel almost normal again. I received two letters from home. The weather here is good and I hope it will continue.

August 20, 1944

It's very quiet today. We don't even hear the cannons in the distance anymore. Yesterday there were two deaths and eight men wounded because of the mines we encounter here in no-man's land. Everything is full of booby-traps, and most of the boys are not careful enough, I think. I decided not to pick up anything or touch anything. I prefer to pass up souvenirs rather than take a chance at being blown to bits.

Now we're ready to leave in an hour, but of course, no one knows where. I hope that we won't have to go too close to the front line. The news in general is very good: the war cannot last much longer. Everybody feels we'll be going home soon.

August 23, 1944

We moved to Chateau Benauville. The weather is very bad and vehicles sink deep into the mud. We advanced to Dozulé. The people who live here are just now returning, since the Germans left only forty-eight hours ago. Little villages are completely destroyed. The villagers are very friendly. They have plenty of cider and butter but no bread or any other food. Most of the male villagers are still imprisoned by the Germans. One woman told us that her little boy of ten was murdered in front of her eyes by a German soldier because she couldn't offer him anything to drink.

We heard Paris capitulated today and there are rumors about a new landing near Bordeaux. In any case things are going well, the mood among the men, reasonably good. We feel we are going direction "home."

August 24, 1944

We're already five miles past Dozulé. The civilians were very happy with the bread and candy we gave them. Everybody is delighted the Germans are gone. The women and girls came out to greet us with all sorts of souvenirs.

August 25, 1944

Thursday evening we arrived in Pont l'Eveque, and now we have advanced approximately five miles. Everything is quiet and the weather is good.

Monday, August 28, 1944

Saturday the Princess Irene Brigade advanced to Pont Audemer. There was still a lot of shooting and several men were wounded. However, we were rewarded by the civilians, who gave us a tremendous welcome. Up to this point we had not experienced such spontaneity. Some of the boys were so emotionally stirred that they wept freely. At night we pulled back about twelve miles to get some rest, which we really needed.

The predictions are that we'll be in Holland in fourteen days. It can't go fast enough for me. I wonder whether Kitty knows that I am on my way.

Monday, September 4, 1944

We are already above Dieppe. Yesterday we drove 110 miles, it's unbelievable how fast we are moving ahead. The Americans are pushing beyond Brussels. Maybe a few more days and we'll be in Holland.

Today I worked hard on my brakes because they weren't working very well. Now I certainly don't want to stay behind. Now I have to try to get some sleep. I have a hunch that tonight we won't have a chance to get much rest.

Friday, September 8, 1944

Northern Belgium, fifteen miles from the Dutch border. We advanced to Brussels in one day. The welcome and reception by the people in the villages and later when we entered Louvain was tremendous and an emotional experience.

As soon as we had passed Louvain we ran into the Germans. There was fierce fighting. There were quite a few wounded and we lost several vehicles. That same night I drove a wounded man to Brussels. In Brussels I was able to sleep for the first time in several days. Some of our troops are already past Diest, but we are still in Diest. A Dutch S.S. man, who was our prisoner, tried to escape; he was shot by our unit without much ceremony.

September 13, 1944

Now we are in Laak, and have been here for a couple of days. Luckily it is very quiet here. Sjoert and I are living with civilians, a family with seven children. We haven't been spoiled like this for a long time. I think we will have to wait until the road to Holland is somewhat cleaned up; the last few miles have been difficult. However, I don't have to be among the first ones. When the fighting gets very bad, I usually don't feel so well!

There are many dead and wounded civilians, and we are very busy taking care of them. Anyway, it is becoming clearer by the day that the Germans have their backs against the wall. It is impossible to think that the war can last much longer. I hope not; we're all so fed up with it. My last thought always—Kitty.

★ ★ ★

September 17-26, 1944

On September 17 the Allied forces started the great offensive designed to bring the war to a quick end. They had planned to drive to Berlin through Holland. The important part of the operation was to capture the bridges over the Maas and the Rhine with the help of paratroopers.

American paratroopers landed near Nijmegen and British paratroopers landed near Arnhem. Simultaneously, motorized troops advanced from Belgium and drove toward Nijmegen to assist the paratroopers. At that time, the Dutch government-in-exile ordered Dutch railroad workers to go on strike to stop German troop movements. The American paratroopers succeeded in capturing the bridge near Nijmegen and were able to save it from destruction by the Germans. But the British troops failed to establish a firm foothold near Arnhem. During the night of September 25, the British had to be evacuated to the west bank of the Rhine, with heavy losses. Thousands of men lost their lives.

★ ★ ★

Don's Diary: *September 24, 1944*

We advanced from Laak to Eindhoven in Holland. The reception we received from the people here was not very exuberant because a couple of days before the city had been bombed by the Germans.

We have now been in Grave, southwest of Nijmegen on the Maas, for a couple of days. Sjoert and I are staying with a young couple who really take good care of us. Yesterday we went to a neighborhood farmer who gave us plenty of milk and eggs. I met one of the daughters, Siska, who went back with us to Grave. We walked arm in arm. She asked me whether I was Catholic because she was not allowed to go out with Protestant boys; any diversion is welcome at this point.

Prospects for peace in the near future do not seem so promising now due to the failure of the attack on Arnhem. I am getting more fearful every day about the prospect of going to Amsterdam. The Germans are so cruel and destructive that my chances of finding Kitty alive are getting slimmer by the day.

I am still hopeful, but it is rapidly vanishing with the end of the war not yet in sight. We aren't making as much progress now as we did in Belgium just a few days ago. Still, I don't believe that the Germans can last much longer. I don't feel much like writing these days. It seems as though the rest of my life will depend on the next step, whether or not I find Kitty.

★ ★ ★

The disaster of the Allied enterprise at Arnhem wiped out all hopes for the speedy liberation of the rest of Holland. Although by the middle of November most of Zeeland, North Brabant, and most of Limburg had been liberated, the Allied forces had to change their strategy. The next objective was to open the port of Antwerp on the Scheldt, to establish a solid front along the Maas and the Rhine. By the middle of November, most of the fighting in Holland had ceased.

Now Holland became strategically unimportant because the battles to be fought had shifted to the south. The Allies had succeeded in reaching the lower Rhine and the Remagen bridgehead. There the fighting continued.

★ ★ ★

Don's Diary: *October 24, 1944*

In reality not much has happened since I wrote last month. We have little to do; peel potatoes in the morning and that's about all. Yesterday we were in Eindhoven and had time to visit a friend. It was nice to be in a different setting for a change and to sit in a comfortable chair. For the first time since we left England we saw a movie.

The best news is that I received three letters from Kitty. The last was dated May 22. I hope that she'll be able to hang on these last few weeks. From what I hear, it must be terrible in the big cities at the moment. I know it doesn't help to worry about it, but still I can hardly sleep at night any more. After all these terrible years, to have to endure the disappointment of losing Kitty would be too cruel. If I don't find her, the war, for me, will be lost. At the moment I don't want to think about it.

October 30, 1944

We are at a farm between Tilburg and Breda. The stove is warm and the lights are on. It's very quiet both inside and outside. The sound of the German artillery no longer reaches us. Since yesterday we have only heard snipers, still hidden in the forest. Germans soldiers are taken prisoner regularly; here, the war is over. The last few days, fortunately, there have been few wounded soldiers. When we were in Tilburg there were many wounded; the brigade suffered severe losses but also experienced success. We went through some anxious hours. The situation in Brabant and Zeeland is now much better, but in the big cities it's getting worse by the day. When I think about the future, which I do often, it is never in terms of whether I will be killed or wounded. I don't even think about that. It is always whether or not I'll find Kitty.

★ ★ ★

November 15, 1944

At Vredeveld, toward the end of the year, we were warned that the Germans would be making a house-to-house search of Amstelveen. Although all the Jewish girls at Vredeveld were thoroughly prepared and knew what to do in case the Germans searched the building, I felt butterflies in my stomach. This would be the test; how brave was I going to be? But truth is sometimes stranger than fiction; the Nazis bypassed Vredeveld. What could they possibly have expected to find in a nursing home other than a group of old people! I felt such a tremendous sense of relief when the town's search was over; through the eye of a needle once again!

★ ★ ★

Terrible news reached us on November 20, 1944. Reverend van Etten had been shot by the Germans.[1] It was incomprehensible. I felt chilled with shock. My first thought was about Mrs. van Etten; how would she get through the trauma? Her second baby had just been born. A new baby, overwhelming joy for a couple when there is love and devotion. But this terrible and cruel murder turned great joy into unspeakable sorrow.

★ ★ ★

1. After the war I learned that Reverend van Etten's real name was Bastiaan J. Ader. Mordecai Paltiel, *The Path of the Righteous: Gentile Rescuers of Jews During the Holocaust* (Hoboken, N.J.: Ktav, 1993), has an account of his and his wife's activities on pp. 141-42. See below, pp. 276-85, for the statement about him written by his widow soon after his death.

Hunger—*Winter, 1944*[2]

Because of the railroad strike now in full force, which the Germans had been unable to break, an embargo on foodstuffs had been imposed from the eastern to the western part of Holland.

Throughout Holland the food situation became very serious. People were dying of hunger. In the big cities, Amsterdam, Rotterdam, and The Hague, the suffering was terrible. Food rations were reduced to starvation levels, 1,300 calories daily; later that fell to 900 calories. Because of the strike, it was hard to find out what was really happening in the war. Most channels of communications had been cut off. There was almost no mail coming through, and only a few telephone lines were still in operation. Everyone was preoccupied with getting food. No one had time for friends anymore because every bit of energy had to go into obtaining and planning for the family's food. Sugar beets replaced potatoes; tulip bulbs were declared safe for human consumption. Bulbs have virtually no food value and were almost certain to cause indigestion, but at least they were something to fill the stomach. Housewives were desperate, they had the hardest job of all. Lots of time was needed to prepare the meager meals and especially to find food for the children. Women in Amsterdam, shabbily dressed and worn out, took to the streets to demonstrate, crying over and over: "We want food for our children."

Many husbands were either in hiding or in work camps in Germany; the women had to do everything, from cutting wood to standing in line for food, sometimes for hours on end. Frequently, by the time it was their turn, the food supply had been exhausted.

Housewives had to do without the most basic necessities. There was no heat, electricity, or hot water. The authorities turned on the gas for only a couple of hours each afternoon, in time to prepare a scanty meal. At night park benches and trees disappeared. In Amsterdam alone, 1,500 houses were robbed of every piece of wood; doors, windows, even staircases were pulled apart. Houses sometimes collapsed, killing people in the process, because all their supports had been removed.

Schools were open only half-days now, but later in the year they had to be closed altogether. The children had no warm clothes to wear and no shoes to put on their feet. The schools were unheated, and by now most buildings had been confiscated by the Germans. The food situation became worse by the day, and north of the Rhine people were literally starving to death. In Rotterdam alone almost 3,000 died of starvation.

Hospitals stopped functioning as well. Doctors couldn't cope anymore. Not only were they underfed, they were discouraged, because they lacked the most basic equipment and medicine. They had to operate in unheated

2. H. A. van der Zee, *The Hunger Winter*, London: J. Norman & Hobhouse, 1982, passim.

operating rooms and had virtually no bandages, soap, or hot water. A little scratch could easily turn into a serious infection. The many skin diseases that developed during this time erupted because people had no soap and hot water to wash themselves with.

Another common ailment doctors had to deal with was hunger edema, pain and swelling in the limbs and increased apathy. When Holland was liberated, it was found that 5,500 people were suffering from hunger edema. Scabies was also quite prevalent. Women stopped menstruating and men became impotent. When people were sick and had to go to the hospital, they were put on a stretcher or a cart pulled by a horse and sometimes even by other people. There was no public transportation. Because there was no electricity, elevators no longer operated, a calamity for hospitals, nursing homes, and laundry facilities. Some hospitals had their own generators to provide electricity.

The Zuiderkerk (South Church) in Amsterdam was temporarily turned into a morgue. There was no wood available for caskets and the bodies were just piled up until such time as they could get a decent burial. Improvised caskets were made out of cardboard boxes with removable wooden bottoms that could be used over and over again. Needless to say, the sanitary conditions and the stench at the makeshift morgue were unbearable for families and undertakers, not to mention a dangerous source of infection.

During the course of the occupation it often happened that a Jew in hiding died. That was a different story altogether and caused great consternation, because the body had to be disposed of secretly, since it was a capital crime to hide a Jew. How could one get rid of a body without being caught by the Germans? Fortunately the Dutch underground had an extensive "back-up system" for emergency situations. In a worst-case scenario, when someone in hiding passed away, whether or not Jewish, the underground took care of it.[3] In cases of illness and toothache, the underground had connections with reliable doctors and dentists. The underground also helped to resolve tensions or friction between hosts and people in hiding, shortages of food, and lack of ration cards.

★ ★ ★

November, 1944

Christmas was approaching rapidly, and although no one had any illusions that it would be a great Christmas, most of the girls at Vredeveld were talking about starting some projects for family and

3. For further details, see Louis L. de Jong, *Het Koninkrijk der Nederlanden in de tweede wereldoorlog* (Rijksinstituut voor oorlogsdocumentatie).

friends as Christmas gifts. One had to be very inventive these days because there was nothing to buy in the stores. The shelves were completely bare, and in the windows only empty boxes were on display. We gathered scraps of fabric, yarn, or anything else we could find to see what we could create. Actually it was not so different from what we would have done at home under normal circumstances. It was interesting to see what one could make out of nothing. We surprised ourselves and discovered talents we didn't even know we had.

The food supply was dangerously low. We didn't know how long this situation would continue. Many people in the big cities were already starving, and we wondered what the winter would bring. We had no difficulty deciding what to bake for Christmas, because there wouldn't be any baking this year.

Under the circumstances it was impossible to suppress all thoughts of Hanukkah around this time of year. I couldn't help but think about what we would have done at home under normal conditions. Home seemed so far away. Could life ever be normal for me and my family again? Best not to dwell on a situation I could do nothing about.

Here I was in my room at Vredeveld telling myself there was no harm in indulging in some fond memories. In fact, I thought, it was probably healthier than suppressing all happy thoughts. Why not lose myself in the past for a little while and relive some of the highlights of life with my family when things were normal? I couldn't prevent my eyes from getting teary. In my imagination I saw four lit-up menorahs, one for each male in our family—and then there was a knock at my door. "May I come in?" a voice said. It was Aunt Ida, who wanted to show me what she had just invented. She had found some scraps of yarn and had artistically twisted the threads into a colorful lovely corsage. "How do you think the girls would like these for Christmas? Don't you think they will brighten up some of those dreary sweaters they should have been able to discard a long time ago?"

She was so excited about her invention that she didn't even notice that I was not in the happiest of moods. When my answer didn't come quickly enough to satisfy her, she looked at me and said: "What's wrong Chris? You can tell me, please." I told her how I had been thinking of Hanukkah at home this time of year when things were happy and normal. It had made me sad and teary to let myself go like that.

She immediately had an answer. "You know as well as I do that things cannot get worse, so don't forget, the future can only get better. We should try to be optimistic, and who knows what next Hanukkah will bring." She was so courageous and so strong that I suddenly felt embarrassed for showing my weakness to her. She was past eighty years old, and four of her five children had been deported. She'd had more than her share and yet . . . she was so brave!

Don's Diary: *April 1945*

We are driving the ambulance between southern Holland and Belgium to transport wounded soldiers. In the middle of November the Brigade moves to Zeeland where we move around some. During December our battalion settles in Middelburg (Zeeland) and I am housing with a family there. The basement of their house is flooded one day as the result of the bombing of dykes by the British. So our living space is severely compromised. We stayed in Zeeland till the middle of April. During that time we did not engage in much military effort except an occasional trip to bring a patient to a hospital in Belgium or liberated Holland.

I detested being idle so much, because it inevitably led to worries about Kitty: If I find Kitty nothing can hurt us. Money or no money, job or no job, America or no America, everything will be all right as long as Kitty is with me. If I don't find her, I can't think of anything worse. Then I wouldn't care what I do. I would probably go back to the States and devote my life to scientific work. Maybe, in the future, I'd travel to sparsely populated parts of the world to help by working for the education of the underprivileged and the mentally ill.

I would work only to exist and struggle to forget how, because of cruel forces, my most precious possession had been taken away from me. In the end I would just have to wait until time eventually eroded my memory. Then a busy time begins with many transports to hospitals when our ambulance crew joins the rest of the Headquarters of the Dutch army near Herpt[4] in northern Brabant at the edge of the river Maas. The Dutch infantry crossed the river and engaged the Germans in a four-day battle. No time to do anything except drive the Dutch, British and German wounded, who had been shipped southward across the river, to a small military hospital in Vught, some six miles southward.

May 1945[5]

Now there were clear signs that peace was right around the corner. There were rumors of negotiations. The Red Cross dropped food parcels from the air for the starving population. The Germans began to repair the Hedel bridge and clean up the mine fields. During the day no one was allowed to fire anymore.

---

4. A village close to s'Hertogenbosch.

5. Don stopped making regular entries in his diary on April 21, 1945. The following remarks were written on a separate sheet on June 11th and cover events in May and early June.

16
Free at Last!

May 5, 1945

At 8:00 a.m. on May 5, 1945, the BBC announced the German surrender. Holland had finally been liberated by the Allies. It was Arie, who had brought us the news from the BBC throughout the war, who picked up this wonderful bit of information. He quickly turned off the radio, slipped out of the hiding place in the attic for the last time, and closed the little door behind him. He stormed into the Boons' living quarters and conveyed the news to us.

My immediate reaction was that of immense relief. What wonderful news! Then came thoughts of doubt. Was it really true? But moments later I took a deep, deep breath and realized that it must be true. It was just yesterday when the girls at Vredeveld had watched the most spectacular sight: Allied planes dropping food parcels over Schiphol airfield. It was a breathtaking sight, and already then we knew that peace was at hand.

I felt that an overwhelming pressure had suddenly been lifted from me; of course it is true, I thought.

The Boons had just finished serving refreshments downstairs. They were jubilant. Their glowing faces expressed the whole story. They had won the war for us; had entered the world of the underground at great risk to themselves, never faltering, pushing ahead to do their job. It was something their consciences had told them they had to do, and they did it with great pride and faith.

Someone pulled me by the hand, I don't remember who it was, to go outside to dance and sing in the street. The girls at Vredeveld seemed wild with joy. They were pushing and screaming: "We are free, let's go and dance." It was so exciting, one couldn't help being pulled in by this jubilant bunch of girls.

Soon afterward I broke loose from the circle of dancing girls and rushed to my room. I had to be by myself and think. There were too many unanswered and frightening questions to be asked. Where was my family? I had not heard one word from them since their deportation in June, 1943. It was an unsettling thought that chilled me to the bone. Of course I realized that Europe was now in total chaos and it might be a long time before we would know anything. It could take months or longer to sort everything out. It would be a nerve-wracking time!

And there was Don, always on my mind. Was he still thinking about me?

Don's Diary:

The announcement of the capitulation over the BBC on May 5th was no surprise for those who knew what was going on but nevertheless everyone went absolutely crazy. This was the moment we had been waiting for, for five years. For us the war was over, but for many the joy was not really as great as the surface exuberance seemed to indicate.

At that time the Princess Irene Brigade was still south of the great rivers. On the 6th of May, we went to Wageningen by way of Nijmegen. The city was totally destroyed. In Wageningen we had to polish and check our vehicles once more, which annoyed everyone terribly. Officers of both sides came together to negotiate, apparently because of fear that the good news announced over the BBC might not be true after all.

I began to doubt more and more that I would find Kitty. I would catch myself daydreaming of her. Then suddenly, like a thunderbolt, I was jolted back to reality. Our departure for The Hague was suddenly announced. I was pleased but also disappointed. Pleased that at long last I would now see what Holland looked like, but disappointed that we were not immediately going to Amsterdam.

The journey to The Hague was overwhelming. For hours on end we were at the mercy of the enthusiastic, liberated people. They stood screaming and laughing along the roadside for miles on end. There were festivities everywhere. In The Hague, where we were the first liberators, the enthusiasm was boundless. Our trucks were overloaded with people who just jumped on board. The distribution of cigarettes and cookies was quickly stopped because of the danger that people might be killed—trampled to death as they tried to grab some of the souvenirs handed out by the soldiers. It looked like a ridiculous scene played by an hysterical crowd. We were all relieved when we finally reached our cantonment, civilians were not admitted.

May 8, 1945

The next morning I got up early to see how I could get to Amsterdam. Luckily Dr. Boerma wanted to go to Amsterdam also, so we went together in my ambulance. I took him to his destination and then set out to find Kitty. I made my first attempt with a heavy heart; the decisive moment had finally arrived. I went to the last return address Kitty had sent me on one of her Red Cross letters. I drove to Roelof Hartstraat 76–2, Amsterdam, South. I found the address without too much trouble. I could see the number I was looking for; it was across the street. I parked my ambulance and got out. I was very nervous and felt somewhat unstable on my feet. A young man came out of the house just as I reached the front door. I quickly approached him and asked whether he could find out for me if there was a young woman there by the name of Puck Veen. The young man was only too happy to help me and said: "Wait here. I'll be right back!" He disappeared briefly and returned a few moments later. He told me that there was, indeed, a Puck Veen living there, but that she had lived here for thirty years. I sat down on the steps at the entrance of the house; a wave of nausea swept over me. I felt very upset and disillusioned. After a while I went back to the ambulance. I decided to try another of the return addresses Kitty had used. That too didn't pan out. Returning to my ambulance I had to sit down to get hold of myself. As I tried to collect my thoughts I suddenly had an idea. It was too much of a coincidence that Kitty would have sent letters to me with the name and address of someone who had been living here in Amsterdam all these years. Kitty must have had good reason to do that. Instantly I knew I had to go back to the same address and talk to the real Puck Veen; I had nothing to lose.

I returned to the Roelof Hartstraat. I stepped on the brake when I saw the house, got out of the ambulance, slammed the door shut, and rang the doorbell. A lady opened the front door by pulling on a heavy piece of rope. She was standing at the top of the stairs; I couldn't see her face, but when she saw me, she immediately asked if I was the fiance of Chrisje de Boer.

It was a miracle; I knew that I had made contact. I sat down on the bottom step, my head swimming; I was afraid I would faint. I stayed there until I had regained my composure enough to get up. Then Puck Veen asked me to come upstairs. Not only did she know who Kitty was but she also knew where she had been hiding. She told me that she herself had been involved with the underground during the war. She knew Mr. Boon and had given him her name and address for Kitty to use for her correspondence. Then she gave me directions to Vredeveld in Amstelveen. Now the puzzle was beginning to fit together, I thought, as I walked back to the ambulance.

When I reached the 1 Amstelveen Road, I rang the doorbell. It was already early afternoon. A young woman opened the door. Her name was Betty. She was very surprised to see a Canadian soldier on the porch asking whether there was a girl employed there by the name of Chrisje. Betty just stood there staring at me as though she barely believed what she had just heard. She said she was afraid to let me see Kitty so she called Mr. Boon, who came downstairs and took me to Kitty's room. Then Mr. Boon set out to find Kitty.

★ ★ ★

Vredeveld, *May 8, 1945*

The last three days had been disastrous for me. All during the war, I was always dressed immaculately in my white nurse's uniform. My hair was always combed and neat, but now it felt as if there were no reason to do any of these things. I felt numb inside, as if nothing mattered. I did my daily duties routinely with my thoughts miles away. I was totally drained and emotionally exhausted, walking around in a daze. For the first time in my life I had trouble sleeping. Here I had been so courageous all these years, but now, when I needed to think and plan for my future, there was nothing to plan for. I felt immobilized. Usually the perpetual optimist, I had lost all my stamina.

I met Mr. Boon upstairs in the hall. He told me he had been looking for me. "Chris," he said, "I've heard from Don!" I looked at him in disbelief and said, "I don't believe it." We heard such things throughout the war and there was never any truth to it.

"Besides," I said, "if you've heard from Don, why haven't I heard from him?"

"Well, Chris," Mr. Boon continued, "Don is in Holland." Speechless, I stared at him. Finally I repeated, "but why haven't I heard from him?" Then, in a flash, I knew that Mr. Boon was trying to tell me something.

"Have you seen him?" I asked. Mr. Boon smiled. "Chris, he's in your room; come on, I'll take you there." Suddenly I realized that I looked terribly untidy and I said: "I can't face Don looking like this; I look just awful. My apron is wrinkled and dirty, and my hair isn't combed. I can't face Don looking like this!"

Mr. Boon put his arm around my shoulder. "Come on, Chris, you look just fine." We walked toward my room, and when we got to the door, I simply couldn't open it. Reassuring me again, Mr. Boon said, "Come on Chris," and gently pushed the door open.

There was Don sitting on my bed. He looked just wonderful! We stared at each other silently. He had put on quite a bit of weight, which was very becoming to him. He looked at me, his eyes sparkling; I felt bewildered and ecstatic at the unexpected wonder of seeing Don. I wanted to put my arms around him and squeeze him, but instead I walked up to him, took both his hands in mine, and said, "I always hoped this would happen, but was afraid to believe it!" Then I let go of his hands and took a few steps backwards so I could get a better look at him. I looked at his face, nodding my head in astonishment.

Don stared at me, almost in shock.

"It's unbelievable that you're here," I said. "I like you in your uniform! I was puzzled when your first Red Cross letters came from England and not from California. I decided to wait and see whether your next return address would shed some light on what you were doing there—but it didn't."

Now it was Don's turn. "I can't believe how well you look," he said. "I expected the worst, but to look at you, you look just as I remember you. You haven't changed at all."

"You can thank Mr. and Mrs. Boon for that; they're the most exceptional and caring people I have ever met. They have helped to save many people's lives. How was I ever so lucky to end up in such a place? But how did you find me?"

"I'll tell you everything," Don replied, "but first, can't we slip away somewhere for a few hours? I have to be back at the base in The Hague at 6:00 p.m."

I thought for a moment, then said: "Let's take a walk, and talk, and see whether we're still the same people we were six year ago." Don had his ambulance downstairs. We could drive to Schiphol and walk on the quiet country roads. There were so many questions I had to ask him, and so many things to tell him. I wanted to tell him about my mother and father and the children, about all the friends and relatives who had been deported to Germany. I wanted to tell him about Aunt Sara and Uncle Maurice. But first, we each had a confession to make. It took only a few moments to clear it out of the way. "There's something more important I must ask you," Don said. "Are you still religious?" It took me by surprise that he would ask that question now, in the midst of our reunion. I answered somewhat apologetically and said: "No, I'm not. I couldn't be, after all that has happened." Don was relieved by my answer, because he too had lost his religion a long time ago.

Now that the most important thing had been cleared out of the way, we went downstairs. It looked as if everyone at Vredeveld had assembled on the lawn. Some were standing around the ambulance, to welcome the first soldier to liberate Amstelveen. Cameras

Don's Return to Vredeveld

and film, which people had saved all through the war for long-awaited events like this one, suddenly appeared. I approached the ambulance and Don proudly presented it to me.

When I saw the name "Kitty" painted on the hood of the ambulance, I looked at Don and said: "What a coincidence."

Don took me in his arms once again and said laughingly: "Who do you think put it there?"

We drove the short distance to Schiphol. It was already a beautiful day, and Don's being with me increased the beauty tenfold. There was so much to tell.

"Where shall I begin?" Don asked as he parked the ambulance. "I want to hear it all; please begin at the beginning, but let me tell you something first," I replied. "You may not be aware that I have only just now realized that you were actually in the army all along. I thought you were probably working in England as a chemist, maybe in connection with the war. I decided not to draw any conclusions and to wait and see whether your next letter would shed any light on my questions. It's a good thing I didn't know the truth, I would have been worried sick!"

Don said: "It's amazing, with the censorship on, how much we could actually convey to one another."

"Yes," I said, "it's wonderful how well we were able to communicate with those few words on our Red Cross letters."

We were both silent for a moment, and then I asked Don to tell me about the last six years. And then I found myself listening to all the extraordinary things he had been through.

"Well, after the attack on Pearl Harbor, I felt I had to be a part of the action. I couldn't stay behind and watch people murdering one another. Bert said right away, 'if you join, I'll do the same!'

"The American Army didn't want us because Bert and I were not American citizens. The Dutch Army didn't want us either, because we had filed our first papers for naturalization shortly after we had entered the United States. We decided to join the Princess Irene Brigade under the command of Prince Bernhard as part of the Canadian Army. We joined immediately."

"Are you trying to tell me that you gave up graduate school and joined the army voluntarily?" I asked. Don looked at me and said: "It was worth it. Bert had already left a few weeks earlier to get his training in Canada. I had some work to finish up at the university and left two months later to start my training in Toronto. You can imagine what that must have meant to mother and father, having both sons go off to war."

"After our training we were shipped to England. I was in England for three long years, so close to you yet so far away. I went through the whole campaign, landing in Normandy, going through France, Belgium, Holland, and now I'm with you." He squeezed my shoulder. "I've actually been on Dutch soil now since last September, when we moved up from Laak, in Belgium, to Eindhoven."

"Did you receive many of my Red Cross letters?" I asked. "Oh, your letters were a godsend," he answered. "I thought your idea to go into nurses' training was an excellent one and might even save your life. As a matter of fact, when I received the letter in which you wrote: 'I am alone and help someone with domestic work. Don't forget me, I love you,' I was overwhelmed with joy. I knew it meant that you had gone into hiding. It seemed from your previous letter that your family had been deported, and I was very afraid that you would suffer the same fate someday. I could only hope there was a chance that you would survive the ordeal, and each of your letters renewed my hope."

"I can't believe how well we communicated our thoughts to one another," I replied. "Imagine, just twenty-five words per letter. I think it really is because we were so well in tune with one another before the war, don't you?"

"I'm sorry that I had to write the terrible news to you about my parents, dreadful as it was. It was important to me for you to know. That was the worst thing that has ever happened to me. Luckily I could visit them often, because they lived close to the Hospital. Mother would fix a cup of ersatz tea. My parents were always very interested in my course work; you know that my mother was a nurse when she was young. Eddy was with them, of course, and sometimes we had a good laugh. He was only fourteen years old and the poor boy was cooped up in the house. The little visits I had with my parents meant a break in the day's routine for them. However, I didn't go outside anymore unless it was absolutely necessary. I never felt safe outside with the Star of David displayed on my chest. When I visited my parents, I never did so without first asking at the front desk whether it was safe outside.

"But on that terrible day, when I entered their living room, the expression on their faces told the whole story. Mother said that they had to report for transport in the morning. They left for Westerbork the next day. I haven't heard a word from them since. I have no idea what has become of them, and I wouldn't even know where to start to find out. With the deportation of my parents, my religion went out of the window. I could no longer believe in a benevolent God."

"Their departure left a real void in my life. It was a good thing that I was very busy at the hospital and kept my mind occupied. At first, especially, it was very difficult not to think about them. My routine seemed shot."

We were silent a while. Then Don said: "I can't believe what you've been through. It must have been a nightmare. You must be very strong and healthy, and how lucky you are that in spite of all the misery, you ended up with these wonderful people, the Boons! How will we ever be able to repay them?" We walked without speaking for awhile.

Don continued; "Of course, the Allied forces made phenomenal gains right after the invasion. We advanced very quickly. We practically zipped through France, Belgium, and Holland, but when the Battle of Arnhem turned into a disaster it prolonged the war by another eight months.

"We knew how much the Dutch people were suffering and how cruel and destructive the Germans were. We knew that the hunger in the big cities was terrible and the food situation deteriorating daily. The chances that I would ever get you back became slimmer every day. I felt that my happiness for the rest of my life would depend on whether or not I found you. But then I received three more letters from you, the last one dated May, 1944, in which you wrote: 'I am healthy and well. Don't worry about me. Give Bert my love. Will love you forever, Kitty.' I was delirious with joy. But the end of the war was still not in sight, and I couldn't bear the thought of not getting you back so close to the end.

"I've been stationed in Middelburg for several months now, and from there I carried out my ambulance duties. The situation in Brabant and Zeeland had improved, but we knew that people in the big cities were dying of hunger. It was very depressing."

Don took a deep breath and was quiet for awhile. I welcomed the silent interlude, and we continued to walk slowly.

I was so touched by his account. The revelation of his feelings for me was so pure and so sincere, it was almost sacred. But no, it wasn't; it was the way Don had always been. I had always known that no matter what happened I could count on him under any circumstances. Suddenly I was overcome with emotion. I began to comprehend how much he had suffered because of me, not knowing from day to day whether I was still alive, while being in imminent danger himself every minute. How could he have lived through all that anxiety, waiting, always waiting, not knowing whether I would survive my ordeal?

We sat down at the side of the road. I looked at his face; his expression was all devotion and honesty. His courage and perseverance had never left him. As I looked at him tears just started to run down my face and kept coming and flowing freely. It felt so good to cry. They were tears of joy and relief. Don assured me that it was perfectly all right to cry. We sat close together, his arms around me. I felt so comfortable and so at peace with myself, I didn't want the moment to end.

Don gave me plenty of time to regain my composure; and when the tears stopped, he whispered in my ear: "Time is slipping away from us. I'm afraid we have to go back to Vredeveld now." His voice brought me back to reality and I responded "I almost forgot, you're still in the army."

As we drove back in the ambulance, it occurred to me that we had picked up almost exactly where we had left off six years before. The possibility of our drifting apart, which we had both been so afraid of, didn't seem to have happened at all. We continued to drive home, and when Don brought me back to my room he said: "Wait here, I have something in the ambulance for you." A few minutes later, he returned to my room with several helpers he had picked up along the way. They carried some large wooden crates, four to be exact, into my room. The space was not big to start with, and with all those crates there was hardly any room to turn around. Don had been saving his rations and the packages his parents had sent him during the war—all for me! Don asked whether there was anything I needed, because he could get me whatever I wanted. Still in a daze, I thought for a moment but couldn't really think of anything. Don couldn't believe it. "That's impossible! Everyone I've spoken to needs everything under the sun." I explained that I had been wearing my nurse's uniform almost all the time over the past few years and consequently had saved my clothes very carefully. In addition, I had done a lot of mending and made new out of old. Don looked at me in disbelief.

He kept insisting that there must be something I needed. Overwhelmed as I still was and not able to comprehend all the enormous joy I was feeling, I couldn't imagine that I would need or want anything ever again!

With Don insisting, I all of a sudden knew what I could use. I needed a new pair of shoes. I remembered night duty in the hospital. The long hours on my feet, working short-staffed, wearing wooden sandals with synthetic straps had given me blisters and sore feet. A new pair of shoes would seem like a blessing from heaven.

My wish was easily granted. "Well," said Don, "that's simple. Among other things, you have cigarettes—plenty of them." He pointed at the crates. "People are paying seven guilders for one cigarette. Go to the nearest shoe store. Most stores have saved some good merchandise, and I'm sure you can find what you want."

[230]

Time passed too quickly and soon Don had to leave. He was due back at the base at 6:00 p.m. and he was late already. "Don't worry," he assured me, "I'll see you on your birthday," which was May 17. Once again those wonderful strong arms were around me. I walked him down the stairs and outside to his ambulance.

A lot of the Vredeveld residents as well as people from the village were standing around the ambulance talking about the first Allied soldier in Amstelveen and how he had come there to find his fiancée after six years.

It was not as easy for Don to leave as he had thought. Many of the villagers had questions for him: How did you do it? How did you find her? Why do you have to leave so soon? "I'll be back on May 17th." He pointed at me and smiled. "I promise to answer all your questions then," and then he drove off.

When I went inside, I saw Mr. and Mrs. Boon in the hall. They had been watching us and knew that Don had just left. They looked at me with eyes that expressed everything they felt in their souls. Kitty's dearest wish had come true. I had been talking about it all those years. Mr. Boon had often urged me to see things more realistically, trying to prepare me for the possibility that Don might forget me after so many years, but he had indeed come back. Their happiness radiated from their faces.

Mrs. Boon put her arms around me and said: "*Ach, kind*" (Oh, child). I think that was probably all she could say at that moment. Mr. Boon just stood there, watching us. What could anyone have said after such a miraculous occurrence? Now it was time for me to go to my room and try to unwind and be alone with my thoughts. Of course that was just wishful thinking. When I opened the door, I was barely able to squeeze into the room because of all those crates blocking the way to my bed. I went downstairs to get some tools to open the crates. They would have to be opened with hands stronger than mine.

I knocked at Mr. Boon's office. Yes, he had the right tools and would pull out the nails for me. I went back to my room while

Mr. Boon got his tools. A few minutes later he came upstairs, pulled out the nails, and left immediately afterwards. He told me to get some rest in one of the other girls' rooms. I sat on a crate, half numb and still overwhelmed by it all, trying to clear my thoughts, when I was suddenly struck with great curiosity. What in heaven's name was in these boxes? I knew I had to unpack them right now. I opened the first one. Never had I seen anything like it. The boxes were filled with all the things we had done without during the war. There was jam, peanut butter, chocolate and candy galore, soap, toothpaste, shoe polish, 4,000 cigarettes (I counted them), dried fruit, shoelaces, needles, thread; everything anyone could have wanted was packed in these boxes.

I had no place to put it all. At first I put the things on my bed, so that I could get rid of the crates. I don't remember which bed I slept in that night, but I surely must have found a place where I could stretch out and dream about the fulfillment of my hopes.

Early the next morning I got up and continued to try to organize my room. The dining room seated seventy people. By noontime, I had managed to place a surprise on everyone's plate; a pack of cigarettes for the men and a chocolate bar for the women. I went back to my room, fashioned some baskets out of newspaper, and filled them with a variety of things: one each for the Boons, Miss Visser, Mr. and Mrs. van der Does, and all the girls at Vredeveld. I divided the remainder among everyone else. Best of all, as far as I was concerned, my bed was just about empty.

Next I went to a shoe store which Mrs. Boon had recommended to me. There I found a wonderful pair of leather shoes that felt like gloves on my feet. After years of poorly fitting wooden sandals, this was sheer heaven. I paid the man 500 cigarettes—in other words, 3,500 guilders. He was overwhelmed, and so was I. The atmosphere at Vredeveld had noticeably changed. The war was over, certainly the most important thing, but I was the news event of the day! People who had never noticed me before now stopped me in the hall or outside to congratulate me. It was a celebration for all of us.

The week that followed seemed to last as long as the war. Only yesterday on our walk at Schiphol Don had told me that his unit was still surrounded by German soldiers who had surrendered but had not yet been disarmed and moved to prisoner-of-war camps. It was practically like living in an armed camp. "Why did I have to think about that now?" I thought to myself. "Why couldn't I just think about the wonder of our reunion?" But the thought kept coming back into my head, and I was unable to concentrate on anything until Don arrived on my birthday.

Of course, Don wouldn't think of coming empty-handed. He had brought an enormous can of olive oil for Miss Visser, our cook. He walked into the kitchen, handed it to her, and said: "I brought you a can of oil. Maybe you can use it in the kitchen." Miss Visser let out a scream: "My God, where did you find that wonderful stuff? How did you know there's nothing left in the pantry?" Almost at the same time, she leaped forward and kissed him on both cheeks.

For me, Don brought a radio he had picked up somewhere along the way and a bouquet of flowers. Don didn't have to be back at the base for three days, and the Boons invited him to stay at Vredeveld as their guest. There was an empty bedroom in the attic which he could use. We spent three wonderful days of pure happiness together.

Don made the Boons laugh; he was so funny and so happy, his demeanor made them feel as if they had known him all their lives. He introduced us all to boogie-woogie, something new to us in Holland. Don asked the Boons to put on a record, then gave us a demonstration of what boogie-woogie was like. We danced to the music and had a wonderful time. The Boons invited us to have our meals with them. It was very special. That weekend, Don and I became lovers. After the weekend we set the date for our wedding, which we planned for June 28.

Pretty soon, it was time for him to leave again. As I did the preceding time, I walked him downstairs to his ambulance. He stuck his head out of the window once again, saying, "I'll be back as soon as I can," and then turned the corner and was gone.

On my way upstairs to my room, I thought about something Mrs. Boon had told me just a few days before. After taking Don to my room that first day, Mr. Boon had returned to his apartment. Mrs. Boon was in the living room when he entered. She took one look at him and said: "Dick, what's wrong with you; you're as white as a sheet!" He had answered in a choked-up voice: "Don is here!"

It was good to be alone with my thoughts. I needed to get some rest, but I had so much to do and it was hard to know what to do first. We had set our wedding date. The wonderful days we had spent together had been genuine, undiluted happiness, pure luxury. I really didn't want to think about anything else, but one persistent thought kept nagging at me like a bad dream. Where was my family? I hadn't heard a word about them. Could they possibly be in Russia, unable to contact me? They couldn't just have disappeared from the face of the earth. I realized, of course, that the war had only ended three weeks ago, and that wasn't a very long time. Besides, I thought, most of Europe was still in an uproar. Communications were still chaotic, if not totally impossible. It might be a long time before we knew anything.

Since I had not yet heard one way or the other, I still had hope. On the other hand, I knew perfectly well that I was blocking all thoughts of the worst eventualities. I knew about the work camps. I didn't want to think about death camps. I simply couldn't believe they really existed. No one would have allowed such things to happen, it was inconceivable.

When Don returned a few days later, we discussed how we ought to approach this nagging nightmare of mine and where we should begin in order to get some information. Don thought that the best thing to do would be to contact the Red Cross, and he offered to take care of it. I gave him a list of my family's dates and places of birth, their full names, and other details he needed. I placed an advertisement in the newspaper, asking for information about my family.

We found out that the Red Cross was going to start collecting the names of missing persons who had been deported. At yet no one could predict how long it would take to sort everything out.

In the meantime, I decided to write to one of our neighbors in Utrecht, where we had lived for years, and let them know that I, at least, had survived the war. The next day I wrote a letter to the Nebbeling family. I knew that if any member of my family came back, they would go to the Oosterstraat first. I don't remember what else I wrote to the Nebbelings, but I was convinced that through them we would make contact if anyone returned. It was a logical beginning. Of course my parents would stop at the Nebbeling house; where else would they go? I also told them that Don had returned and was still in the army.

17

Marriage

It was less than four weeks before the date set for our wedding, June 28. I didn't have much planning to do, since Mrs. Boon had offered to do most of it for me, but I did have to try to find something relatively decent to wear for the occasion. Don told me that he could get whatever I needed from England. He had good friends in London, Suzy and Leslie Mirkin, and they could order any dress or fabric I asked for. All I had to do was tell him what I wanted. "It's as simple as that," Don said.

I was touched by his thoughtfulness and generosity, but in the end, I declined his offer. It just wasn't a practical idea, primarily because there was so little time left. I didn't want to deal with the anxiety of waiting for the order to arrive on time. Besides, I had more important things to worry about—my parents and siblings and their whereabouts. What I was going to wear at my wedding was actually the least of my problems. The stores were virtually empty, and finding the right dress would be a miracle. Besides, I really didn't want to spend my time shopping. I decided to try to be resourceful and do the best I could under the circumstances.

Suddenly I had a brainstorm! I had an old navy blue summer coat I had worn for many years, that was still in very good condition. The coat was fairly long, an advantage under the circumstances. I began toying with the idea of making a suit out of it. I had to do a lot of mental designing and planning before I dared using scissors. But I knew it would work—this was it! The skirt would have a yoke from hip to waist to give it the right length, and the hem would get a facing; I knew it would work. I had saved a pair of silk stockings and had a pair of alligator shoes I hadn't worn very much. All I needed was a hat. I discussed my plan with Aunt Ida. She thought it was a fabulous idea. She even offered to do all the sewing for me, if I would design the suit and cut it out.

I was so excited that I ran out of her room. In the hall I met Mrs. Boon. I immediately told her all about my plan. I could see by the serious expression on her face that she was with me every step of the way. As a matter of fact she said: "Chrisje, I have a white silk nightgown from way back. If you can make a blouse out of it, the nightgown is yours." She said she would go through her chest of drawers and find it as soon as she had a minute.

Before very long I had the coat all ripped apart and decided to turn the fabric inside out (a typical Dutch procedure). This meant that I would use the inside of the coat for the outside of the suit. The wrong side had something of a sheen, but I thought it would enhance the suit's appearance. With the pattern drafted and the suit cut out, it was important to save every extra inch of fabric. I was careful to brush out the seams and remove the dust.

★★★

That night, after I was already in bed, I heard a knock at the door. It was Mrs. Boon. She had just found the white silk nightgown. "What do you think, Chrisje?" she asked, anxiously awaiting my answer. I examined the garment and it didn't take me long to see that it would work. "Mrs. Boon," I said, "it will make a magnificent blouse." Then she sat down on the bed and put her arms around me. "Chrisje," she said, "I am so happy for you and Don, but we're going to miss you terribly." She was not a sentimental woman. As a matter of fact, she was usually quite businesslike, but that night, as she sat on my bed, she had tears in her eyes. I reflected on the many evenings she had knocked at my door to bring me a warm glass of milk. Mrs. Boon had indeed been like a second mother to me.

A couple of days later, the white silk nightgown was cut out and ready to be put together. Aunt Ida, it seemed, was sewing all the time. What a wonderful disposition she had. She wanted to make herself useful, in the process forgetting her own worries for awhile. With her work shaping up so nicely, I felt I would not lose a night's sleep over the wedding outfit. My suit and blouse would be finished in time!

★ ★ ★

News of Leo: *June 15, 1945*

I had caught an awful cold. I tried to throw it off, but I was so congested and uncomfortable that I had to give in and take it easy. Mrs. Boon suggested that I stay in bed at least a couple of days, resting and drinking lots of liquids. Had I forgotten that the wedding was right around the corner? I thought: "She's right; I should give in and rest." The excitement of the last few weeks had been overwhelming, and it was a relief to give in to my cold. Now at least I could do some thinking, something I had not had time for those last exciting weeks. Little did I know that at this moment a member of my family was desperately trying to find out whether the rest of us were still alive and where we were.

My brother Leo, then twenty-three years old, had been held in Buchenwald as a political prisoner for over one year. The Sunday after Easter in April, 1945, Allied planes had attacked an area close to the camp. He escaped during the bombing and hid in a haystack for seven days. After Buchenwald was liberated, Leo, a mere skeleton at six feet and only eighty pounds, spent six weeks with German farmers who fed him well. He got back some of his strength and started to gain weight. When he felt strong enough to leave the farm and venture out on his own, he got in touch with the authorities, who provided him with transport to Holland.

This is how he finally got to Utrecht, where we had lived all our lives, and how he found me.

Leo's Account: *June, 1945*

The truck stopped in downtown Utrecht. For the first time in five years I could put my feet on Dutch soil without having to be afraid of what would happen next. But I was nervous and felt unsure; I didn't know what to expect. I wanted to go home. I started walking through the streets. I had forgotten most of the names. I walked to Cohen's Bakery. There was no one, the place deserted. Straus's, another Jewish bakery, was open; one of the boys, Bobby, was there. The rest of the family of five had perished.

I walked over the Oude Gracht (Old Canal) carrying a pillow-case-like bag over my shoulder with my belongings, more bag than belongings. I passed people in the street who greeted me as if I were from Mars, probably because I was still wearing my striped pants from the concentration camp. "We're glad you're back. Where were you?" A tall man, over six feet and skinny as a bean-stalk, said: "Why don't you come with me. I have an extra room and you can stay as long as you want. I'll give you a hot meal, the house isn't far from here."

"That's very nice of you, thank you very much, but I'm trying to find my family," I said.

I continued walking down the Smeestraat to the store where father always had scissors sharpened and his glasses repaired. As I looked in the window of the store, someone screamed my name from the second floor across the street. I couldn't make out who it was until she came running down the stairs. It was a school friend, Dora Houser.

"You must come in; my mother wants to see you." After mutual greetings and expressions of happiness that I had survived the ordeal, they offered to let me stay with them. I declined their invitation, explaining that I was trying to talk to as many people as I could in the hopes that someone would know whether my family was still alive. I promised to be in touch later. I walked in the direction of the Kromme Gracht, past the orphanage. It too was deserted.

Next I headed straight for the Oosterstraat, the street on which we had lived for years. I passed Oosterstraat No. 7, the house of Riet Danner, my sister Sue's friend. I passed Mr. Grasmayer's house; he had provided me with my first forged identification papers. I passed the Zijderveld family, the parents of my best friend Jan, who had been killed in a concentration camp; they also lost another son during the war. During the war the Zijderveld house had been my hiding place while I was active in the underground, before I was caught. I could come and go whenever I wanted. Finally, Oosterstraat No. 8, our house.

There was no life, the house was empty and deserted. It looked totally dead. Even the walls looked dead. I went across the street to our friends, the Nebbeling family. Mrs. Nebbeling greeted me like a lost son. She told me that she thought she had seen Donald driving an ambulance and that he was in the Princes Irene Brigade. I spent the night at their house and left in the morning.

I discovered that the Princess Irene Brigade was stationed in The Hague, so that was to be my next destination. Military vehicles were the only means of transportation. My hair had started to grow back, but still looked ridiculous. To most of the people I passed on the road it was a sign that I had returned from a concentration camp. Therefore, it was not hard to pick up a ride. I arrived in The Hague that afternoon and found the barracks. The sign said "Military property, no admittance." I went over to the guard in the little sentrybox and told him that I was an ex–political prisoner, trying to find D. B. Zilversmit. I showed him a card I carried stating that I had been in Buchenwald. They let me go in, but I had no luck—there were no records of D. B. Zilversmit. I walked around and saw a sign, "Staff." That was what I'd been looking for. I went inside and asked someone at the desk whether he had heard of D. B. Zilversmit. Yes, he was in the Medical Corps. Again, I had to go to a different building.

The first man I bumped into was a mechanic. I asked him where I could find D. B. Zilversmit. "Never heard of him," was his reply.

Terribly disappointed, I sat down on the bottom step of the stairs leading into the building. Before long a corporal started coming down the stairs. "Corporal, could you please tell me where I can find D. B. Zilversmit?" "No, I have no idea where he is, he's off for a couple of days." Now I knew I had made contact. "Did he leave an address?"

"No," he said. I asked what kind of army unit this was, if a corporal didn't even know where his men were. I was really getting mad now.

"The war is over and we're all on furlough."

"Don't you have any idea where he went?"

"As far as I know he went to his fiancée because they're getting married." I thanked the corporal for his help and hoped that the wedding would be delayed until I got there.

I can't remember what I did the rest of the day. At least I now knew that my sister was alive, that is, if Don was still engaged to the same girl. I went back to Utrecht the next day, just to walk around and talk to more people. I saw Miep de Vries and her brother, but their parents had perished. I saw Clarie Leefsma, but not Ella, her sister, who had been Kitty's girlfriend for years. Clarie was the only one left of the family. I asked everyone whether they knew where Kitty was living. At least I knew that she had probably survived the war. I was very tired and had to get some rest.

The next day I went to the Information Center for missing persons. Then back again to the Oosterstraat. I don't know where I got the energy. My legs seemed to be walking automatically; I didn't even feel them anymore. I made another stop at Mrs. Nebbeling's; a sixth sense had told me to try again. She was delighted to see me because she had just received a letter from Chrisje de Boer. She gave the letter to me to read and there was Kitty's familiar handwriting and all the details I needed to know: return address, Huize Vredeveld, Amstelveensche Weg, No. 1, Amstelveen.

Then I went to Mr. and Mrs. Zijderveld, and when I told them the good news, they burst into tears. I felt that I was making progress.

The next morning, having slept like a log, I came downstairs. Mrs. Zijderveld had breakfast ready on the table. After breakfast I left and hitched a ride with an English major in a jeep. I told the major where I wanted to go. He was very helpful. As far as I could remember, the Amstelveensche Weg started at the Berlage Bridge. I asked the major to drop me off at the bridge. Little did I know that this was the wrong end of the Amstelveensche Weg, since I had to be at No. 1. But after that good night's sleep and hearty breakfast I was able to tackle the last bit of walking. I don't remember how long it took me to walk to the end of the road, but when I finally saw Vredeveld, I knew that I would never forget that impressive-looking building.

I was terribly nervous as I rang the doorbell. After a few seconds the door opened and a very shy nurse, Leni, asked me what I wanted. "I'd like to speak to Chrisje de Boer," I said.

"Could you please wait a minute?" Another nurse appeared; her name was Henny. She asked me some questions and I answered them all. "Are you family?" she asked. "Yes," I responded, "something like it." She opened the door all the way. "Please come in and wait here." Then Leni came back and asked me to follow her. We went upstairs and stopped in front of a door; she knocked, opened it, and pushed me inside. A young woman was lying in bed with the blankets pulled up under her chin. Here was the face I remembered so well.

"Hello, Kitty."

"Who are you? I don't think I know you!"

"Oh, you know me very well"

"You? Oh, you're Bert, Don's brother."

"No, I'm your brother Leo."

"No, you don't look at all like Leo—where have you been?"

"Concentration camp, Buchenwald." There was a long silence. "Kitty, it's me, don't you recognize me anymore? Look at this," as he pointed to a spot on his forehead and said: "Don't you remember this?"

★★★

Kitty's Story:

I saw that it was a scar the chicken pox had left on the side of his face when he was a child. I remembered that pockmark so well, because Leo was the only one of the five of us to be left with a scar after we all had chicken pox. Leo sat down in a chair next to my bed. All of a sudden I recognized him: "Yes, I remember, that's the way you used to sit down." He didn't look at all like the Leo I had known. He had grown at least a foot since I last saw him. He had changed into a man despite a terrible ordeal. His eyes had a strange expression, he had trouble sitting still, and he constantly fidgeted. Now it was Leo's turn to talk.

He went on for three hours without stopping. He told me about all the horrors he had experienced in the camp, the hunger and cold he had suffered. The cruelty of the S.S., the constant fear, never knowing what misery would come next. Buchenwald was a death camp. It housed 4,000 prisoners when he was first brought there after his arrest in Nice, France. He had been classified as a political prisoner and the Germans never found out that he was Jewish. When he escaped in April 1945 there were 400 prisoners left. The heat in summer, the extreme cold in winter, sanitary facilities nonexistent, constant humiliation and fear, trying to break the prisoner's spirit in every possible way. But worst of all, the prisoners were forced to watch the hangings of other prisoners and threatened that they would be next. Even Leo could not describe everything or give an accurate account of the horrors that went on in the camps. Never can it be put into words or comprehended, he said.

I understood that I had to let him continue. I was the only one he could talk to. It was important for him to unload his anger and misery on someone, and that happened to be me. Here I was lying in bed, sometimes gasping for air, not knowing how much more I could take. I felt so sorry for him and didn't know how to help. Just letting him talk was the best I could do at the moment. Releasing some of this terrible tension and hate was what he needed most. How he found the strength to live through all the suffering, I will never know. Then the door opened and Don walked in. He seemed bewildered at the sight of a strange man sitting at his fiancée's bedside.

"Who are you?"

"Leo has come back," I said.

"From where?"

"Buchenwald."

Don tried to say something friendly, but shocked as he was, it didn't come off very well. Then the three of us sat together and talked for awhile. Don must have noticed that I was at the end of my rope and couldn't take anymore. He asked Leo to go downstairs and find himself something to eat or drink so that I could get some rest.

In the meantime, Leni and Henny had informed Mr. and Mrs. Boon that my brother Leo had tracked me down. They invited him to stay at Vredeveld. Although I had heard rumors about the death camps, Leo's account was the first I heard from someone who had been in a camp.

Don put an advertisement in the Amsterdam newspaper shortly after the Red Cross began to collect the names of people who had been deported to Germany and never been heard from again. The advertisement read:

Wie kan **INLICHTINGEN** verstrekken over:
Leopold Lehman Fonteijn,
geb. 17-12-1876;
Gracia Fonteijn-Jesserun Lobo,
geb. 30-8-1885;
Eduard Fonteijn,
geb. 28-12-1928. Vertrokken uit Westerbork 1 Juni 1943;
Jack Fonteijn,
geb. 28-5-1924. Vertrokken uit Westerbork ongeveer 1 Augustus 1943;
Suze de Leeuw-Fonteijn,
geb. 6-6-1917;
Herman de Leeuw,
ca. 32 jaar. Vertrokken uit Westerbork, ongeveer April 1943.

Wie heeft hen in Polen of elders gesproken ?

Brieven aan: Kitty Zilversmit-Fonteijn, v. Hoogenhoucklaan 54, Den Haag.

275

Can anyone give me information about the following persons, deported to Westerbork, June, 1943:

Leopold Lehman Fonteyn, born December 17, 1876.
Gracia Fonteyn, née Jessurun Lobo, born August 30, 1885.
Eduard Fonteyn, born December 28, 1928.
Jack Fonteyn, born May 28, 1924.
Suze de Leeuw, née Fonteyn, born June 6, 1917.
Herman de Leeuw, approx. 32 years old.

Has anyone seen them in Poland or talked with them anywhere else? Please contact Kitty Zilversmit, née Fonteyn, Van Hoogenbroucklaan 54, The Hague.

With this advertisement in the Amsterdam paper, I had at least made a beginning. This nightmare had to be dealt with no matter how hard it was to face the truth, no matter what the outcome might be. It was so close to our wedding, and this terrible "not knowing" was always present and cast a gloom over everything I did.

★ ★ ★

Our Wedding Day: *June 28, 1945*

I was waiting in my room at Vredeveld for Don, who would become my husband within the next couple of hours. He was always so punctual; why was he late today? He was driving the ambulance from The Hague to Amsterdam. Perhaps he'd had a flat tire or, worse, mechanical trouble.

I was all dressed up in my wedding outfit, the navy blue suit and white blouse that Aunt Ida had so lovingly made, waiting for him to arrive. I forced myself to be calm, telling myself: "He'll be here." Pretty soon, I began to reminisce about everything that had happened since Don had found me, just four days after the war ended. We had each gone through so much. Yet it was nothing compared to what others had suffered in the camps. We had been separated for six long years—an eternity; and the miracle of Don finding me so soon after the war was over had barely sunk in. And now I was to marry the man I loved so much.

I couldn't help but be amused by the memory of what had happened just a couple of weeks before, when Don, on his way to Vredeveld to visit me, had stopped at the courthouse to obtain a marriage license. It wouldn't take long, he thought. Well, life is full of surprises. The official at the courthouse couldn't issue a license without the consent of my parents. An archaic law in Holland, still in effect in 1945, required written permission to get married for children up to the age of thirty-one. Don tried to explain to the man that my parents had been deported to Germany in 1943. There was no way we could get their permission. The clerk was adamant. "Well, that's the law," he said, "there's nothing

I can do." No matter what Don said or how hard he tried to convince the man that he was asking for the impossible, the clerk wouldn't bend. Don, always resourceful, had an idea: "Do you smoke?"

The clerk looked him straight in the eye and said: "Yes sir!"

"So, you like cigarettes?"

"Of course I do, but I haven't had any in a long time."

"Well, do you think," Don said hesitantly, "that if I could get you some cigarettes, maybe two hundred or so, you would then be able to give me that piece of paper?"

"Wait here," the clerk said, already halfway out of his office.

My wedding ring was a simple gold band. The jeweler also preferred cigarettes over money, and the ring was purchased for 200 cigarettes, value 1,400 guilders. Don and I often laughed about my "bride price" of 400 cigarettes.

I looked at the clock. It was 11:10 a.m. The ceremony was scheduled for noon. I jumped up and walked downstairs. I couldn't stay in my room any longer. When I went outside, the first person I saw was Harry Davidson, Don's buddy, also a soldier in the brigade, who had been invited to the wedding. He teased me for worrying about Don's failure to arrive. I should relax, he said, and hope that in the end Don would not change his mind. After all, this was Don's last chance to stay a bachelor.

But before I knew it I heard the familiar sound of the ambulance and there was Don. He slammed on the brakes and jumped out, dressed in a new uniform. He turned back briefly to take something out of the rear of the ambulance. It was my wedding bouquet, white carnations and lilies of the valley.

Don looked radiant, his face beaming with pride and confidence. Before anyone could say a word, Harry's voice was loud and clear: "It's about time you got here. You're late for your wedding."

We walked to the courthouse. It would be a civil ceremony only. They were all there: Mr. and Mrs. Boon, my brother Leo, Miss Visser, Mr. and Mrs. Hooykaas, Harry Davidson, Dr. Boerma,

Kitty and Don at Courthouse Wedding
Left to right, front: *Leo, Kitty, Don*
Rear: *Mrs. Boon (partially in picture), Dr. Boerma, Mr. and Mrs. Hooykaas, Mr. Boon*

a physician in the brigade, Mr. and Mrs. van der Does, and all the girls who worked at Vredeveld.

The walk took no more than five minutes, as the courthouse was just a little way up the road. When we arrived at the door we were directed to the room where the ceremony was to take place.

The members of the wedding party were sitting and talking with one another when suddenly the door flew open and a tiny man, who appeared very nervous, walked quickly into the room. In the process, he slipped on a piece of carpet, and fell flat on his face. He seemed shaken for a second but pulled himself up and stepped over to the lectern to start the ceremony. His voice was high-pitched and agitated. Luckily the ceremony was brief, and I barely heard most of what he said in his short speech. Then there were lots of kisses and embraces and congratulations from everyone. It was a jolly crowd of wonderful people, who sincerely joined with us in our happiness. Afterwards we all went back to Vredeveld.

An early dinner was served upstairs in the lounge. Mrs. Boon had been able to get the most wonderful food for this very special occasion.

MENU

Hors d'Oeuvre
Tomatensoep
Biefstuk, Bloemkool, Aardappelen
Konÿn, Gebakken Aardappelen, en Appelmoes
Chocoladepudding met Vanillesaus
Fruit — Koffie — Gebak
Dessert

Amstelveen, 28 Juni 1945
Ter gelegenheid van het Huwelÿk van
Kitty Fonteyn en Donald Zilversmit
Amstelveen, June 28, 1945

Kitty and Don, Wedding Photo

Arie Van Mazyk designed and put together the two-page menu. On the first page he had drawn an ambulance and a road sign, "San Francisco": He drew a winding road, with an arrow pointed to "Amstelveen" leading to Vredeveld. The menu was signed by everyone present at the dinner.

Miss Visser, as always, had prepared everything just perfectly. There were numerous toasts and speeches, and in the end Don's words of thanks were very much in character with this whole beautiful affair.

We left shortly thereafter on our honeymoon. A couple of weeks before the wedding, one of the residents at Vredeveld had offered us his cottage for fourteen days. It was located on a lake near Amsterdam. He assured us that no one would be using it and insisted that we accept his offer and enjoy our privacy. He gave us the name of the farmers next door, who would provide us with fresh milk and eggs, and then gave us the key. Mrs. Boon had packed us a cardboard box of food. I didn't know what was in it, nor did I care. Dr. Boerma was going to drive us to the cottage in the ambulance to the lake, and would return for us in two weeks!

After Dr. Boerma left us at the cottage, we didn't need anything but one another. The small lake was picturesque, sprinkled with little islands covered in low shrubbery and trees. We even had the use of two canoes and a rowboat.

One day we took a canoe trip on the lake. Although I was not a good swimmer and we didn't have a life-jacket, it seemed safe enough to take a little trip on the water. Before we knew it a storm came up. The wind was strong and I felt very frightened and alone in my canoe, even though Don was right next to me in his own canoe. I've always been afraid of water and a morose thought entered my head: "Could this be the end of our happiness?" Don steered me back and pushed my canoe against one of the little islands. "You stay here," he said, "I'll get the rowboat, I'll try to be back as soon as I can." Then he was gone and I was all alone on the stormy lake.

My fear of water dated back many years. I remembered a scary experience I had when in my early teens. I was waiting in a pool to take my swimming test when someone pushed me under. I almost panicked again, recalling the trouble I'd had getting up and out of the pool. When I finally succeeded in climbing out, I couldn't get any air, because I had swallowed a lot of water. All the fear came back to me, reliving this frightening episode. After some anxious moments, I saw Don, my hero, appear in the rowboat. My relief cannot be described. Don rescued me and rowed me back to safety. The storm on the lake was an experience I could have done without.

My somewhat irrational fear during the storm, in contrast to having been so courageous all through the war, even in times of great danger, I can ascribe only to the fact that Don was all I had left. The thought that anything could happen to him and that I might lose him filled me with immeasurable anguish. Many years later when Don was out of town, I would get very scared when I heard noises at night. I called the police once when I was all alone one evening, because I thought someone was knocking lightly against the kitchen window. After the police searched all around the house, they assured me that there was no one in the yard and that the ticking on the window was only caused by flying insects.

★ ★ ★

On our honeymoon we had plenty of time to enjoy each other and our privacy. It was a gift to be together again, and we were grateful beyond words. We also had plenty of time to talk about the future and to make several important decisions. Don was going to be discharged from the army in August. The University of California would start classes in mid-September. Don had lost four years at the university to the army. He had two more years of study before he would get his Ph.D. and was really anxious to get back and finish up his work. Besides, he was now a married man and the sole breadwinner.

It was a hard decision to make. We had pledged never to be separated again; and having been apart for so long, was it wise to think about parting again? But Don's parents had already started the process of getting me an affidavit of support. Don's uncle had a friend with "connections" at the State Department. He was sure that he could get me a preference visa, which would guarantee my early passage to the United States. With all these positive factors at work for us, we decided that Don would go back to the United States ahead of me to return to school in September. We were so happy and yet so sad, and wondered how many people in our situation would have made such a sensible decision. Surely our separation this time would not be so protracted.

During the triumphant liberation of The Hague by the Princess Irene Brigade, Don had met a lovely couple, Mr. and Mrs. Hooykaas. Mr. Hooykaas was a lawyer and an industrialist. Don had told them that he was on his way to Amsterdam to try to find his fiancée of six years. They had been enthralled with his story, and before they parted, they made Don promise to stay in touch and keep them posted on the progress of his quest.

A couple of weeks after our reunification, Don took me to The Hague to meet the Hooykaas family. We had a very nice visit, and before we left them that afternoon, they offered us a room in their home after we were married, for as long as Don was stationed in The Hague. We accepted their offer.

★ ★ ★

July, 1945

After our honeymoon we went back to Vredeveld. It was terribly difficult to leave the Boons. The thought of saying goodbye to them left butterflies in my stomach. We had shared so much the last year and a half that it seemed almost like betrayal to leave them now. Through those dreadful times they had provided me with a safe haven at great risk to their own lives, always full of optimism and reassurance that we would survive this nightmare. How could I ever thank them for what they had given me? Where would I have been without the Boons? Don and I promised to visit them soon. Then we packed up my belongings and left for The Hague.

★ ★ ★

The Hooykaas family had a lovely, spacious house. Our room was very comfortable and even had a piano. We had our own private

Leo Fonteyn in Dutch Army Uniform

bathroom. Don was allowed to spend his evenings and nights with me, away from the army base, as long as he reported back in the morning for duty.

Mr. and Mrs. Hooykaas had three children. I was not very busy at their house. They employed a couple to do the cooking and a young girl came in every day to do the cleaning and chores. I helped out wherever I was needed, primarily with the children.

Leo, in the meantime, had recovered from his ordeal in the concentration camp, physically at least, and had made up his mind about what he wanted to do. He had decided to join the Dutch Army. When he first returned from the camp, it seemed as if he had lost his bearings. Who would not have been terribly affected by what he had gone through? I knew just by talking with him that it would take a long time and hard work on his part to break loose from the past. He told me he wanted to go back to Germany, "so I can take revenge," he had said. Although he had told me at length about the camp, to the point that I had become physically sick, I still had no inkling of how much he had really suffered and how deprived he had been. I had no right to criticize him because I could see that he was terribly bruised. However, I pointed out that going back to Germany would only exacerbate the problem. Now I could only trust and hope that he would make the right choice.

In the interim Leo had been spending a lot of time with friends who were war veterans. They had fought in Holland after the German invasion in 1940. When Leo was with them, he felt that he was among friends who really understood him. In the end they persuaded him to join the army. This decision, at least for now, would give his life structure and direction, the most important thing under the circumstances. In the summer of 1945 he left for the Dutch East Indies. This colony had been conquered by the Japanese during World War II after the attack on Pearl Harbor. However, the Indonesians were tired of being a colony and in 1948 they won their independence from Holland. They changed the name from Netherlands East Indies to Indonesia.

★ ★ ★

It was wonderful to have Don so close by. Sometimes, during the day, the ambulance would unexpectedly stop in front of the house. Don would invited me to come with him as he went about some army business. I loved to go on these little trips and be with him. Being in The Hague I was also closer to Rotterdam, where the American consulate was located. I was prepared to make as many trips to the consulate as necessary to get my papers in order. But September came too soon and Don left for the States. No sense in dwelling on the loneliness and my empty room, I told myself. Instead I focused on the future. It was a different world now, and there were worse things than loneliness. I decided to keep as busy as possible. Besides my few chores, I immersed myself in music and practiced as much as I could. Bach partitas and the Chopin G-minor ballad provided the best therapy for me.

★ ★ ★

A couple of months after Don left, a big envelope was delivered to the Hooykaas house. It was my affidavit of support. Now things were beginning to shape up. Not wasting any time, I hurried off to the American consul in Rotterdam to have my affidavit checked; everything was in order.

Soon I received a notice from the consulate to come to Rotterdam for my physical examination. I passed the physical and at the same time received my visa. I would be given transport on the first vessel available. As it turned out, it was a small navy ship which was to leave Holland on December 17.

★ ★ ★

Before I left for the United States I had to go to Utrecht to take care of some family business. I had been postponing the trip as long as I could because I dreaded to go. But worst of all, I have no clear recollection of when or how I received the official notice that my parents, my sister, and two brothers had died in Sobibor. I must have gotten the information from a reliable source, otherwise I could never have left Holland.

I have a vague recollection of removing two trunks from the attic of our house. When I arrived at the house and looked in from the street, the downstairs rooms were completely empty. The Germans had taken everything.

I don't remember how I got the trunks down two flights of stairs; someone must have helped me. I also don't know how I got the key for the house. My parents must have left it with our next-door neighbors, the Postmas, when they gave them some of their possessions to be stored.

Our piano was at the Postma's house, as was a big hand-hooked woolen rug; both had been put to use, giving them a normal appearance just in case of an emergency, such as a search by the Germans. I remember selling both items to the Postmas at their request. They had also saved lots of our family pictures. I removed them from the frames because it would be easiest to pack them. Many of our paintings were also at the Postmas'; I just couldn't manage it and left them there.

I filled two trunks with breakables, like dishes and two big Chinese vases and some ornamental silver items. For years, I was under the impression that I had also found my mother's gold jewelry at the Postmas', but several years later Leo told me that he had given the jewelry to me; Mr. Sabel had saved it for mother.

I have absolutely no recollection of Leo giving me the jewelry. My amnesia about these events gives me an eerie feeling and makes me feel very uncomfortable. I clearly suppressed it all as if this tragedy had never happened.

★ ★ ★

During this time, I was staying with the Hooykaas family. Mrs. Hooykaas had not been well. The doctor had found two lumps in her breast and she was scheduled for surgery. She discussed the diagnosis with me, but I was sure she was getting the best of medical care. She was eager to hear something that might boost her morale. "After all Kitty," she said, "you're a nurse." What could I have told her that she had not heard already many times before? I encouraged her as much as I could and hoped that it would do her some good.

Soon everyone was busily preparing for the surgery. The household had to go on without her. The shopping had to be done, the children readied for school in the morning, and a host of other little chores performed. I visited her at the hospital after the surgery was over. Several days later she was helping to manage the household from her hospital bed, an excellent activity to keep her mind busy. Shortly thereafter, she came home.

In the weeks before I was to leave for the United States I still had much to do. On the day Mrs. Hooykaas came home from the hospital I had to go to Rotterdam to finalize arrangements at the American consulate. I felt awful about leaving her that day but I had no choice; I had to take care of my papers. Mrs. Hooykaas assured me that she understood perfectly well that my papers had to be my first priority.

★ ★ ★

Finally it was December 17, the day of my departure for the United States. Mrs. Hooykaas made a special effort to spend some time with me downstairs that morning, and over coffee and cake, we had our last get-together. It was a sad moment. I had such mixed emotions about leaving her in her present condition. On the other hand, I was elated to think that I would soon be with Don again. I felt relieved when my taxi arrived, because our goodbyes could be quick and therefore less painful. Mrs. Hooykaas and I stayed in touch by mail after I arrived in the States. I sent her several packages with items she could not get in Holland. It would be a long time before the stores would be as well stocked with merchandise as before the war. She asked me for stockings and specially requested a piece of royal blue wool for a dress. In California I found a perfect piece of fabric and mailed it to her. Don and I were very sad when we learned a few years later that she had passed away, leaving her husband and the three children.

★ ★ ★

I arrived in Amsterdam and went directly to the port area called Het Y, named after the river Y. This area was used only for small freighters. The ship that would take me to the States was small, old, and very unimpressive. "As long as it gets me across," I thought, "that's all I'm interested in." It was scheduled to leave early that afternoon. After I had boarded the ship, I learned that its capacity was only 10,000 tons. A Navy ship en route to Charleston, South Carolina, its mission was to return war equipment to the United States and, later, to the Pacific.

In addition to the captain and crew, there were ten or twelve civilians on board. I was on deck as the ship pulled out of the harbor. She was by no means a breathtaking sight, but to me this modest little vessel looked glorious. I stayed on deck a little longer until the harbor began to fade. It was getting cold and windy, so I decided to go inside to look around. At that point I noticed that the ship felt quite unstable, and I found out soon thereafter that she didn't have any stabilizers, as the bigger ocean liners do.

Before long I began to feel nauseated. The ship was now rolling on the high seas and a sick feeling overcame me. I decided to go to my cabin and lie down until the nausea passed. On the way to my cabin, a couple of decks below, I felt as though my feet were being lifted off the floor. I found my cabin, took off some of my clothes, and lay down on my bed, hoping that I would be used to the ship by the following day. The duration of the voyage was twelve days, an eternity for someone in my condition. I felt worse and worse every minute, and was glad to be lying down.

I couldn't have been in bed much more than an hour when there was a knock at my door. I answered by saying "Come in," too sick to care who was there. A tall man wearing a black uniform with braid walked toward my bed.

"Hello," he said, "Are you Mrs. Zilversmit?"

"Yes, I am."

"What are you doing in bed?"

"I am so nauseated, I thought I'd better lie down until it passes."

"Well, Mrs. Zilversmit, that's exactly what you shouldn't do. If you don't get up immediately, you'll be in bed for the whole voyage."

I looked at him and said: "That's impossible. I'm too sick, I can't get up."

His reply was businesslike. "I am the captain. I'm going to leave you now, but I'll be back in fifteen minutes to take you on deck. You need fresh air and a good hearty dinner, with a good piece of lard in it. That'll fix you up in no time flat."

The thought of food made me gag and I became aware of how sick I was. I couldn't lift my head off the pillow.

The captain continued: "You get up now and get dressed. I'll be back soon to take you for a walk on deck. After the walk we'll go down to the dining room. You'll be seated at the captain's table, next to me." I gagged again. "I'll see to it that you eat, and then your sea-sickness will get better," he said. Then he turned around and left my cabin.

As sick as I was, I somehow got up and got myself dressed. A little later there was a knock at the door; the captain was punctual. "Are you ready?" was all he said.

He supported me through the narrow hallway and up the winding staircase. He guided me onto the deck. The wind played through my hair, and, miraculous as it may sound, the nausea began to subside. We walked around on deck, drinking in the wonderfully healing fresh air. After a while, the captain thought it would be safe to go down to the lower level, to the dining room. He warned that I would feel the rocking motion more as we went below because of the water hitting against the ship's hull. Just as he said, the unstable feeling in my stomach returned as we made our way down the stairs.

My seat was right next to the captain's. The sea was quite rough, and while we waited for dinner to be served, the dishes started sliding across the table. The little hinged flaps at the end of the table were fastened in an upright position to prevent food from spilling and dishes from crashing to the floor. The nausea came back, and I wondered whether I would really be able to eat. However, I didn't have much time to ponder, since almost immediately dinner was brought in. The captain dished up a plate for me. I protested that he was giving me too much, but he firmly replied: "Even if you have to force the food down, you must eat."

I tried not to think about what I was eating, but just swallowed a little bit at a time. I ate, forcing it down, and it was difficult. I had to be careful not to gag. The food was fatty and repulsive, but I had no choice; the captain was watching me. I managed to finish a good part of the food on my plate. The captain was satisfied that I had eaten enough, and in the process I had miraculously cured myself. The next morning I felt fine; eating a meal would no longer be a problem.

During the voyage I became acquainted with some of the other passengers. One of them was Isabelle Failing, a woman from the province of North Brabant, in the southern part of Holland. After the liberation, she had married an American soldier, and she was now on her way to the United States to be with him. We enjoyed talking to one another. Life on board ship was very good, with no pressure and nothing to do. The food was delicious and plentiful. There was time for reading, talking, or just relaxing.

The next eleven days were uneventful, and each one brought me closer to Don. Soon we would land in Charleston. The last evening on board, a terrible storm came up with severe rain and wind accompanied by thunder and lightning. We had been told in advance that bad weather was coming our way, and apparently we sailed right into it. I found it very frightening. The ship was squeaking and rolling, the wind was howling, and I felt like praying: "Please, don't let this be the end!" I wondered where the captain was, but he was nowhere to be seen. Now, when I really needed him, he wasn't there. After a moment, however, I realized that he was on the bridge where he belonged, trying to safely navigate us out of this mess! I grabbed the first sailor I could get hold of and asked: "Isn't this a terrible storm?" "Oh," he said, "it's not really that bad. We tried to sail around it but are just catching its tail end. It will pass in a couple of hours, I'm sure." Well, that put my mind somewhat at ease, and after a couple of hours, the storm did start to subside—and eventually, all the passengers were able to turn in and go to bed.

The next morning, when I woke up and looked out of my porthole, I could see land. It looked like a sandy island in the distance, but it was actually the coast of South Carolina. Now there were seagulls flying around the ship, feeding on scraps of food. What a glorious sight! As I looked out the porthole, I experienced a sense of wonder and deep gratitude that I would soon be on American soil. In another couple of hours I would be safely ashore.

Don had written that someone from Travelers' Aid would meet me at the pier in Charleston. He had given them all the details about me: what I looked like, what color coat I'd be wearing, and other things that would help to identify me.

As I walked down the gangplank I looked around. Not seeing anyone at first, I simply followed the crowd, uncertain where to go. Just then two women standing off to the right stepped forward and asked whether I was Kitty Zilversmit! "What wonderful service," I thought. "Don, man of the world, can do anything!" It was the next best thing to having Don there himself. But he had to stay in Berkeley, where he was running Dr. Chaikoff's laboratory.

The women from the Travelers' Aid Society were really wonderful, so helpful and comforting. They took me to a restaurant for sandwiches and orange juice. Then, since it was Sunday and the banks were closed, they took me to someone's home where I was able to get a check cashed. Finally, they gave me my train ticket, took me to the station and put me on the train, and showed me my berth. Such service I had never experienced. Even though it came straight from the heart, I'm not sure my English was adequate enough to convey my gratitude.

The train ride across the country took a long five days. I had much time to think and dream in happy anticipation. We arrived in New Orleans on January 1, 1946. There was a long layover, and quite a few passengers, including myself, took a bus tour at night to see Canal Street, all lit up with giant Christmas trees in the middle of the street. It was a beautiful sight. It was actually the first lit-up street I had seen since the end of the war.

Later during the train trip, at a station somewhere in Texas, I was horrified to discover that the restrooms were marked "black" and "white." This was my first encounter with segregation. Wherever I went I saw Coca-Cola signs and wondered what they meant. We passed through Oklahoma, New Mexico, Nevada. To someone from Holland, the size of the United States was overwhelming. Los Angeles, and then finally San Francisco. The train came to a squeaking stop.

I saw Don standing on the platform. I didn't think he had seen me inside the train but suddenly he broke into a run, probably to be in front of the door of my compartment. Before I realized it those wonderful arms were around me. I could feel his heart throbbing against my body.

I don't remember whether there was any conversation, but I do remember Don relieving me of my luggage. It was four months since we'd seen each other. We drove home in my father-in-law's blue Buick. I saw the San Francisco Bay Bridge, but most of all, I saw Don's face. Before I knew it we were turning right on McArthur Boulevard and onto Adams Street. "What a funny street this is," I said to Don, "it keeps winding and going uphill." Don said; "I'm very sorry, but it's the street we live on."

As we pulled into the driveway, Don blew the horn. The car came to a stop in front of the garage. My in-laws hugged and kissed me. We hadn't seen each other in more than six years, and they were genuinely happy to have me home. They showed me our room, a lovely big room with a private bathroom and french doors going out into the yard. It seemed to have all we needed, even a big desk for Don. I would check it out later. My in-laws slipped out of the bedroom, closing the door behind them. Finally we were alone. I looked at Don and said: "There's no lock on the door." "I know," Don said, "we won't be disturbed by anyone; don't worry about it."

It was a phenomenal homecoming. The next day, my in-laws and Don drove me around to show me the sights. The following evening they took me to see the musical "Oklahoma!" Everything seemed somewhat unreal and strange, except Don. He was very real, and it was fantastic to be with him again. The same week, my in-laws took me shopping to pick out our wedding gift. They bought me a brand-new piano, a Kimball, studio type. They had left an open space on one of the walls next to the terrace, where it fit perfectly.

EPILOGUE

Postwar Developments

After receiving his Ph.D., Don became a professor of physiology first at the University of Tennessee Medical College at Memphis and then at Cornell University. In 1959 he was granted a Career Investigatorship by the American Heart Association.

Kitty continued her study of the piano and became a teacher in her own right as well as an active member of the National Council of Jewish Women and eventually became president of the local chapter of Hadassah. She and Don have three children—Lee-Ann, born 1947; Susan, born 1950; and Jo, born 1957. They have four grandchildren—Katie, David, Laura and Evan.

Kitty's brother Leo was discharged from the Dutch Army in 1948. He remained in Indonesia, where he married. He and his wife later settled in Sydney, Australia.

Reverend Bastiaan Ader, the man Kitty knew as Reverend van Etten, was executed by the Nazis on November 22, 1944 after several months in prison. He and his wife, Johanna, who was also imprisoned for a short time, were later designated Righteous Among the Nations in a memorial ceremony at Yad Vashem, the Holocaust documentation center in Jerusalem. Mrs. Ader died on July 31, 1994. An open letter she published about her husband a year after his death is reproduced below in the appendix. Peter and Leni de Bres (formerly Boon) went to New Zealand after the war to work among the Maori. Mr. and Mrs. Boon joined them, but returned to Holland when they retired. Mrs. Boon died in 1982, Mr. Boon a few years earlier. Like the Aders, they were both designated Righteous Among the Nations and memorialized at Yad Vashem.

בזכירה
סוד
הגאולה
(הבעש"ט)

DANS LE SOUVENIR
RÉSIDE LE SECRET
DE LA RÉDEMPTION
(BAAL CHEM TOV)

תעודת כבוד
ATTESTATION

Le présent Diplôme atteste qu'en
sa séance du 20 octobre 1977
la Commission des Justes près
l'Institut Commémoratif des
Martyrs et des Héros Yad Vashem
a décidé, sur foi de témoignages
recueillis par elle, de rendre
hommage à **DIRK et JACOBA
C. BOON KETEL**
qui au péril de leur vie ont
sauvé des Juifs pendant
l'époque d'extermination,
de leur décerner la
Médaille des Justes
et de les autoriser à planter
un arbre en leur nom
dans l'Allée des Justes
sur le Mont du Souvenir
à Jérusalem.

Fait à Jérusalem, Israël,
le 5 juin 1978

בשם רשות הזכרון יד־ושם
POUR L'INSTITUT YAD VASHEM

בשם הועדק לציון חסידי אומות העולם
POUR LA COMMISSION DES JUSTES

Certificate of Honor for Reverend and Mrs. Boon

CERTIFICATE OF HONOR

This is to certify that during its session of October 20, 1977 the Commission to commemorate the Righteous of Nations of the Institute for Commemoration of the Yad Vashem has decided, on the basis of testimony received by it, to render homage to JACOBA C. BOON KETEL and DIRK BOON, who, at the risk of their lives, have saved Jews from their persecutors during the years of the Holocaust in Europe, and to award them the Medal of the Righteous of the Nations and to authorize the planting of a tree in their name in the Avenue of the Righteous of the Nations on the Mount of Remembrance in Jerusalem.

Made in Jerusalem, Israel
June 5, 1978

AFTERWORD
Why I Wrote This Book

Since this is the last part of my story, I want to write down a few more things. In spite of the many years that have passed, I am reminded daily of the Holocaust by all sorts of things. One would think that memories would gradually cease to be painful, but that is only partly true. I abhor that so much cruelty is still being inflicted on millions of innocent people.

It would be less painful if one could forget and suppress the past. It was years before I could read about the Holocaust or watch movies of Holocaust scenes. Once, years ago, I walked into our living room while Don was watching a movie. On the screen I saw a middle-aged man desperately trying to push a wheelbarrow loaded with big rocks, and a guard brutally whipping him with a leather strap. I had to leave the room, I couldn't go on watching. I still can see the scene; although it was years ago, it will never leave my mind.

Don and I were once visiting some friends when Professor Gerd Korman, who was writing a book on the Holocaust, asked whether he could talk with me sometime about my war experiences. I felt myself tighten with fear and almost lost control of my emotions.

Yet there comes a time in everybody's life when one has to come to terms with the past. I made up my mind, and slowly I began to read about the Holocaust and to watch certain television programs. Fortunately, I had much to choose from since there have been many books written on the subject.

When our children began to grow up they knew that something terrible had happened to my family. As they grew into adolescents and eventually mature adults, it became easier for me to talk with them. Much later, when they were all home, visiting us in Ithaca, New York, I shared my family pictures with them for the first time. It had always been too painful for me to look at the pictures, seeing the happy faces and realizing how everything had been destroyed.

That morning our children asked many questions about my parents, the grandparents they had never met, and about my brothers and sister. They also wanted to know about my life in hiding during the war and when I was a student nurse in the Jewish hospital. We talked for hours, and for the children the pieces began to fit together. That day was quite an emotional experience for all of us, but it brought us even closer together. Our children have been instrumental in convincing me that the story had to be written down. They thought it was a tragic story, but also a very romantic one, with Don miraculously finding me just four days after the war ended.

I think that my writing has helped me to work through this terrible trauma, and in the end it became a kind of healing for me. The writing was never easy, and I did a lot of crying in the process. I remember hearing Don talking to our daughters on the phone, saying, "Can't you make your mother stop writing?" Now I am glad I persisted in finishing the job.

I will never get over my past, it will always be with me. Nevertheless I forced myself to think about the horrors my parents and their children, my brothers and sister, went through when they were taken by the Germans. I forced myself for the first time to think about the cattle car on the long ride to Sobibor, three days, two nights. The unspeakable situation that played itself out on the train ride: no sanitary facilities, at best a bucket; no water or food except what they themselves brought along; were they allowed to keep it—I'll never know. The cattle car so crowded, with barely room to stand or breathe; I think of mothers holding babies; was there room to change diapers? Could mothers nurse or feed their infants? I think about my mother, who was overweight, standing up for three days and nights with swollen sore feet; the heat during the summer with barely any ventilation—how many of them were able to endure such unbearable hardship, treated worse than animals! Who would take care of those who succumbed, or were they the lucky ones?

I think about my father, who felt such intense hate for the Germans. Was he able to control his furious temper? What would have happened to him during that dreadful train ride—their children, my sister and brothers who were too young to have found out what life was all about—and in the end . . .

I don't remember how long after the war it was when the Red Cross notified me that my parents, my sister Susan, and my brothers Jack and Eddy had perished in Sobibor in June of 1943.

I was finally able to start writing, it had to be done.

June, 1988.

Thoughts by Jo Zilversmit:

It's a scene that remains in my mind, even now—1 year later. Who knows why? Maybe it was because it was more and more rare that my sisters and I converged at my parents' home at the same time. We were all living these days on opposite coasts with our own lives and varying commitments. So, to pick a mutually agreeable time for a family reunion with the "familie" sometimes required months of planning.

But it was more than that I guess. It was special in a unique kind of way. I was seeing a side of my Mom for the first time; a side I had not given a lot of thought to in the past; a side that none of us had the opportunity to see before. It was her own private battlefield which she had known so personally and today, we were about to be let into that world. It's funny—I had always thought of my Mom as my best friend in so many ways. I thought I knew her well. But sitting with her in the sewing room on that morning, it became apparent to me that I only knew selected pieces of her life in Holland and, for the first time, I had a genuine understanding of the impact it must have had on her life and, in turn, on all of us.

I was the first to wake up that morning except for my parents, who always arose before everyone. Being home always brings out the little girl in me, and I learned quickly that if you want any individual attention in that house, you have to be up early, especially when there are grandchildren to compete with!

As for my regular routine, I met Mom in her bathroom while she was getting dressed. If Dad was there I'm sure he made a quick excuse to leave, as he was only too familiar with the idle chatter that would take place over the next twenty minutes or so. We would share our excitement about having the whole family together again and catch up on any important news in our lives. Mom would somehow always express to me, as only she could do, how much she loved me just by what she would say to me. The words were different almost all the time, but she would always boost my confidence by telling me that she was proud of me and would reinforce how important it is to be able to rely on oneself. I remember feeling how comfortable it was to be home again.

Sometimes we would not talk at all. I would just watch her get dressed and she would comment to me how her breasts were not as firm as they used to be or that her middle needed to lose a few inches. Almost every time, she would remind me of how old she was, "I'm nearly 69 years old you know," she would say and we would both just smile at each other. "69," I thought—it's really amazing to me.

My niece and nephew arrived in the bathroom shortly thereafter for their morning hugs, inquiries into the breakfast menu and then would hurry downstairs to watch Sesame Street. By that time, the house was undoubtedly pretty noisy. My Dad would be listening to B.B. King on the stereo downstairs, (without the earphones) which was everyone's cue that it was time to get up and start the day.

Soon, Lee and Sue were both in the bathroom as well. Sue never stayed too long. She was the more subdued sister who enjoyed the peace and quiet in the morning and, predictably, after her "good mornings" she would go downstairs for her morning coffee and to snuggle with the kids. I remember how she used to play with me when I was young and thought to myself what a good Mom she would make.

Lee, on the other hand, enjoyed her time away from the kids and, much like me, enjoyed being "gezellig" in the bathroom, and there we would stay, until the temperature of the electric heater became unbearable, when we would all retreat downstairs.

But this morning was different, as we did not all end up downstairs. Mom has been talking about the book she was writing and all the memories it stirred up in her. It was at that moment that I remember seeing a look on her face I had never seen before. Her eyes looked pained, yet also optimistic. Was that a look of hope or contentment? I really couldn't be sure. I only know that it made me realize that there was much more about my Mom that I didn't know and I became aware of this incredible hunger inside of me to understand her better.

And that is how it all began. There in the sewing room, where all of her writing had been taking place, my Mom slowly began to tell us about her childhood in Holland—her family and her life once the Nazis invaded her country. Of course I know that she had a family, everyone does, but I knew very little about my mother than the fact that she lost all but one brother to the Germans when she was 23 years old. It was a subject that was not discussed much at home. I guess no one knew how to bring it up.

But there I was, still dressed in a flannel nightgown, cozy on the floor, hugging a yellow pillow with my two older sisters, listening as my Mom began to speak about living in hiding. We sat in complete and utter awe. It was as if Anne Frank was speaking to us, except this was my mother. No one dared to interrupt to ask questions, as this might surely change the subject, and it was such a dear and treasured subject to her, all we could do was soak it all in as if we were a sponge.

The tears hit each of us at different times. To see my Mom cry always had a special impact on all of us and I am sure that only enhanced what we all were feeling. In our own ways, I think we were finally being given permission to look into her dark past and learn about her childhood.

I saw letters to Dad which she had written years ago. As her voice cracked, I could see that the love she felt for him back then was still as strong and committed as it was on that day. I heard my Dad's diary read to me; perhaps the most personal thoughts he ever had were being shared with me and I knew then that I was indeed privileged to hear my Dad's words of love and concern for his girl-friend, then thousands of miles away.

She pulled out pictures of her family—her mother, father, sister and three brothers and, at last, I could see my heritage. It was an emotional, indescribable experience. I saw the similarities between my oldest sister and my mother's mother—my grandmother. There was a striking resemblance. The silence in the room was frightening. Although downstairs we could hear B.B. King singing the blues, upstairs we were somewhere in a dark attic with my Mom as she hid from the Germans.

"Now what is going on here?" It was the voice of my Dad echoing in the hallway as he approached the sewing room. It was the voice which brought us out of hiding and back to reality—back to our house in upstate New York. "What is the possibility of getting some lunch around here?" he asked in his candid but hungry tone of voice.

"What time is it?" Sue wondered. It was well after 1:00 p.m. "Gosje mijne!" Mom got up in a frenzy and began gather up the various pictures and Red Cross letters strewn around the newly laid carpet. They all had taken on a new meaning to me. The once strangers in the photographs held so dearly by my Mom now had names, personalities, idiosyncrasies. They were indeed my family though I had never known them.

"Where did the time go?," my Mom asked, half apologizing for having neglected her husband for several hours. "I was just sharing some stories with the girls and showing them some pictures of my family. I had no idea it was so late!"

But late it was. The sun was shining brightly in the back yard now, and Katie and David were outside running back and forth through the sprinkler, screaming out in joy as they passed through the water. We had progressed from B. B. King to the Swingle Singers who were harmonizing a Bach fugue in A minor. Dad did love his jazz, I thought to myself, in whatever form it came.

As she gathered up the last precious photographs of her mother and father and laid them neatly back in their box, I wondered why so many of the stories she shared with us about her family sounded familiar to me. Indeed, her story-telling had been captivating—very detailed and descriptive—so it was easy to envision, but no; it was something else.

The description of her father sitting on the couch—one arm around his wife and the other hand busily conducting an imaginary orchestra was a scene with which I too was familiar. And uncle Maurice—systematically throwing sea shells out of the train window to question the validity of man's scientific theories—there was an eerie familiarity to that as well.

"But of course!" I thought to myself, "questions and problems." It was a game my Dad invented to play with me while we were on one of our family walks on Sundays. He would ask me questions, mathematical equations to solve, words to spell and define or the like and I would have to solve them. I remember being on our walks and begging him to challenge me further. "Just one more!" I would say, "please!" until he couldn't think of anymore to ask. "I'm sorry," he would say—"But I am completely drained! I guess you must just be the smartest little girl in the world now." We would all have a laugh and continue on our walk.

Throughout my mother's story, I found myself continually being struck by the strong family ties she expressed in her stories. I must say that I too have experienced and continue to experience that same sense of family and commitment. There is a bond in our family that cannot easily be put into words—yet, even unspoken of, it exists and prevails in my sisters and me resoundingly everyday. Is this our Jewish heritage? Perhaps—I really don't know. I was not raised religiously. As with my parents today, it is difficult for me to accept the possibility that God indeed exists. So, clearly it is not the religious aspect of Judaism that has kept our family so centered. But it was clearer to me on that morning, more so than ever, that my parents' experiences during World War II have had much more of an impact on who I am than I was ever led to believe.

On that morning, I was given an incredible gift—my mother's story as she remembers it. I felt as though a dark void which had lived inside of me had been given light. It was as if I was obsessed to know other first generation children of survivors and hear their stories. I was exhausted yet exhilarated; incredibly proud of my heritage and for reasons still unknown to me, I have a better understanding of what suffering and injustice truly is. If any good has come from this story, perhaps this is the greatest.

Kitty, Don, Jo, Susan and Lee-Ann

APPENDIX

An Open Letter by Mrs. Johanna Ader

In 1935 my husband gave his inaugural sermon at the Pieterskerk in Utrecht, beginning with the text from Matthew 5:16, "Let your light so shine before men, that they may see your good works, and glorify your Father which is in heaven." These are the words of Jesus, and perhaps it is good for us Protestants, who are so afraid to voluntarily commit ourselves to the service of God, to be reminded once again that it was Jesus who really spoke these words. My husband's use of these words in his sermons was his trademark throughout his career, and since that brief period has now expired, I can say with confidence that these words, in a true sense, represented his attitude toward real life.

But the light which radiated, and still radiates, from his short, rich, eventful, and very agitated life was borrowed light. It was drawn from Christ, who was its source. My husband's sermons were delivered in language everyone could understand, and in that respect too he followed his Master. He did not believe in complicated formulations. His message was for the people, simple and adapted to daily life. He had tremendous influence on the young.

How great the demands of Christianity are, and how risky being Christian becomes when we decide to be serious about it, became evident during the war years. In every profession, building a career is a temptation. This is true as well for ministers and especially for a gifted minister. In the far northeastern tip of Holland, in Groningen, there was a rather small but diverse community of churchgoers. They had almost forgotten that the church still existed. This situation had developed for a variety of reasons: because of Reverend Niewenhuis, who came and preached, and opened their eyes to the theory and practice of Christianity; and because of the contrast between workers and farmers, which created hostility; but most of all, because of lack of devotion among the servants of the church themselves. The church had lost the respect of the people.

And now, in this far northeastern part of our land, the church's unpaid bill came due. No one wanted to serve as minister there. The work was hard and thankless, and not much could be expected. The church remained closed for years. A big empty space with 400 seats. Eighty years ago it had been rebuilt because of the lack of space. Then the period of rationalism came, with liberal ministers leaning toward humanism.

They knew nothing about how to give an Easter sermon except to talk about such things as the importance of getting up early on Easter so that the women could go to the cemetery, which was very useful. The service turned into a session in humanism but above all a bad service. "We won't go anymore," the people said, and they were right. After a lesson in Bible history the minister would put on his coat and say laughingly: "Do you believe it? I don't." True wolves in sheep's clothing. These liberal ministers did more to break the work of the church than to bring it together, and the people became discouraged.

My husband was called to that community. Very few people attended the services: who cared about words! They had listened to so many hollow messages that no longer touched them. But they paid attention to his deeds.

He knew how to reach the young, and he had a talent for speaking to them in words everyone could understand. Something of the light of Christ, from the other world we all long for, began to shine through. "This minister isn't doing it for the money," people said, "because he gets involved in so many things he isn't paid for." (They spoke in their beautiful Groningen dialect.) They saw his devotion, his boundless energy, his many new initiatives and plans. "Just wait," the skeptics said, "we won't be able to keep him here:

he'll get a pulpit at a more important church and then we'll lose him." And indeed he received an offer elsewhere. It was a real temptation not to have to preach to benches and chairs any longer, but instead in a beautiful new church full of people, with a beautiful pipe-organ, on which he could improvise to his heart's content as he had done during his time as organist in Lochem. And besides, he would be paid a thousand guilders more as honorarium.

It was New Year's Eve, 1942. The service was held in his study because of the fuel shortage. At the end of the service Domie, as the people called him,[1] told the people his decision. "We're going to stay," he said.

It was a sacrifice, and no one knows better than I how hard it was for him to make this decision. A sigh of relief was heard in his study when Domie made his announcement. One of the younger girls who was present in his study later said: "I don't know whether Domie was aware of it." But I too was there that night, and I witnessed an intense tension that could be felt, and a sigh of relief that could be heard in every part of the study when Domie shared his decision with the members of the church that night. His rare sense of duty won out over every other consideration.

During the terrible war years, which are now behind us, there were many people in deep distress who needed help badly. Hundreds, thousands, perhaps even your best friend was a Jew. Maybe you had been students together at the university. In this time of need, your friend reached his hand out to you. You could have clasped it but you didn't. Undoubtedly self-preservation was your reason. But your friend was looking to you for help because he thought you were a Christian. At least that's what you had always said. Now he feels cheated by your Christianity. His last hope has gone up in smoke, because now he sees that in the end, all those beautiful words don't mean a thing, and he jumps into

---

1. Short for Dominee ("Pastor").

the water and drowns himself because he doesn't want to be gassed. He wishes to die with dignity.

Now the war is over and the struggle for the main chance starts all over again. Who bothers to think now about the Jew who drowned himself? You didn't have to play God for him. You shed this unpleasant thought, which could impede you in your work—in your Christian work, in the church perhaps. You go on with life, which keeps you very busy. "The war had many victims," you say. You don't have to think about the ones who died. Luckily you weren't one of them. You might have become a victim if you had helped the Jewish friend. But because you were clever you didn't end up in a concentration camp. You live and the world sees how well you are doing—but of the higher light which is God, you see nothing. Nothing of the works that glorify God, which will endure forever, even when you are no longer of this earth.

When I had just begun to write this "open letter" as one might call it, I received a photograph of my husband's face in sublime rest, bearing a semblance of a smile which was not of this world but a glow that came from heaven. There was a big hole in his forehead where the bullet had entered. Last week, in the prison in Utrecht, I talked to the man who fired the bullet. It is a sacrifice to have to die when one has lived only a short life.

But my husband attained that joyful state of mind. I have seen the contentment on his quiet face, I have heard fellow prisoners tell me about it.

After he had saved as many as two hundred or more people from the claws of the *Grüne Polizei*,[2] he was arrested in the street and thrown into prison. In his unfinished papers, now assembled in a book, he talks in detail about the desperation that took hold of the prisoners, and how he, with searching compassion, tried to help his fellow inmates. I received letters and poems from him,

2. "Green Police," the German security police in occupied Holland, so named because of the color of their uniforms.

smuggled out of prison. The poems give an image of what played itself out in those days. I don't have all of them, four never reached me. He wrote me letters, many letters, with a small stub of pencil which he concealed inside the lining of his vest, but many of them he had to tear up because he could not get them out of prison. He wrote his sermons for his fellow prisoners the same way so that they could have Sunday too, and he secretly handed them out when they were exercising in the prison yard. He talked for hours one night to a man sentenced to death whose cell was beneath his own cell. He would stand on his bunk just below the little barred window, and the prisoner on the lower floor would stand on his bunk in front of his little window. They would talk that way in whispers. And that's how, using bits and pieces of string tied together with elastic from their clothing, they lowered a small Bible into the other prisoner's cell. In that way, slowly but surely, light and comfort entered a dark cell and a dark heart full of despair, because "death is life."

During the hours before this sentenced prisoner was picked up from his cell, all the other prisoners in the cells around his were on their knees, religious and nonreligious men alike, while Domie talked to him through an air duct. "My husband became a religious man while he was in prison, because of the minister who had the cell next to his," a woman told me. It is not difficult to be optimistic when everything goes well, but to continue to be strong of mind when one is treated like an animal is altogether different.

My husband shared a cell with two other men. Every night around eleven o'clock a car would stop in front of the prison with a *houtvergasser*.[3] They called it the *hakkepoffer* because of the strange noise it made. Then they would stand on top of their bunks or sit on their straw mattresses listening intently, because this is when it started. Cell doors were thrown open. Ours too? No, it stayed shut. This evening it would remain shut. "*Heraus*" [out of your

3. A motor driven by steam produced by burning wood.

cell], they would shout. Now there were footsteps in the corridor. The prisoners had to remove all the things they would no longer need from their cells, including their enamel drinking cups. The cups would make a clicking noise on the granite floor as the prisoners put them down. They listened and counted. "Seven," they said to one another. Tonight there are seven. They didn't have to say anything else. Everyone knew what it meant. These people were going to be murdered in the dunes tonight.

"*Sani, es ist zeit,*" a voice would say. *Sani,* short for *Sanitator* [hospital attendant]; he was the prison doctor. In his private life he was a German truck driver. Sani had to establish whether the men were actually dead after they were shot. A little later they heard the *hakkepoffer* drive away from the prison yard. Sani provided my husband with "medical treatment." During his interrogation he had been so mistreated that his eardrum was torn to pieces. The ulcerated wound continued to fester throughout his four months in prison, in spite of, or thanks to, Sani's care. The interrogations were the worst part of prison life. One night, because the Germans preferred to do these things at night, my husband was awakened and taken to the hearing room for interrogation. Six Germans sat around him and kept moving their chairs closer to him. They looked like evil reincarnated, with their grinning faces. My husband had better provide them with the names of twelve Jews, and quickly, because if he didn't, he would be tortured! They explained what they were going to do to him. They would tie his arms under his knees and throw him down the stairs.

But, he wrote me, God never deserted him at those critical moments when he counted on Him, and He helped him get through. He would perspire profusely but, he wrote me, "God never let it become too much, the tension never became unbearable," and afterwards he convinced his fellow prisoners of this fact.

He was thankful that he had company in his cell. The loneliness, when he was first put in prison, began to depress him. One evening around nine o'clock he got company. It was already autumn and dark by nine at night. There was no light in the cell, so he lay down on his bunk. Then the cell door opened and someone was pushed inside, another prisoner. The door closed again. The new arrival saw a tall figure with long hair rise from his bunk (in prison they don't bother much about cutting hair or shaving). "He must be an artist," was his first impression, and he was surprised when the stranger introduced himself as Reverend Ader.

"Please, I hope you don't mind," my husband said, "but I haven't had anyone to talk with; I have a tremendous need for that now, because I've been sitting here alone for weeks. Would you permit me to start a long conversation with you, and would you tell me everything about the outside world?" He always needed people around him. As a small boy he used to run after his mother from room to room like a puppy, telling her everything and asking innumerable questions because he wanted to know everything, and later he did the same with me. It was his insatiable curiosity. He wanted many people around him as in an orchestra, with many instruments, an organ with many voices. The organ in the church in Lochem was restored and extended under his supervision with room left for more voices, he told me. Yes, there always had to be more possibilities; his mind always searching for expansion. And now he was sitting there, day after day, week after week, even month after month, locked in this prison, and walking in his cell, back and forth, like a caged animal. "I calculate that I have already walked home and back twice." Oh, how he longed for it. "As long as I can be with you the middle of November," he always wrote.

But through those thick prison walls, rumors from the outside world reached them about Mad Tuesday on September 5, 1944, when the members of the National Socialist Party left in a rush for Germany. Radio Orange announced that British troops had reached Breda, and everyone expected that the liberation was imminent. But there was only disillusionment and disappointment when the rumors seemed not to be true. They so fervently wanted to be liberated, and it did not materialize, because of failure and betrayal.

And after that things steadily got worse, the Germans becoming more cruel by the day. Shots were heard in the inner yard of the prison. A boy in the next cell was so afraid that he felt as if he were choking all the time. Domie took him under his wing, and helped him over his fear of death. This last enemy had to be done away with. The boy was still very young. He was taken from his cell, and later they heard the shot reverberate in the Gratsmanpark downstairs. Reverend Ader had *"une passion des âmes,"* said Professor Berkelbach van der Sprenkel, when he heard his inaugural sermon. This passion for souls and his shepherd like traits made him a perfect candidate for a minister and a wonderful tool in God's hand; and rather than weakening, his faith in God became stronger during his life in prison. He knew, because of his own unbroken willpower, how to keep others from losing their courage. Soon after the second cell mate, a third joined them. The worst cancer in prison is boredom. They took turns telling about their lives. One prisoner had been a policeman in Utrecht. He had lots of stories to tell, sometimes humorous ones, about the lives of the people. Then they all had a good laugh. And my husband told about his life in the community, his bicycle trip to Palestine, a serial, with a follow-up chapter every day. One afternoon around one o'clock, just after they had eaten a meal, my husband said: "We crossed the Bosporus yesterday and today we will enter Asia Minor."

Then the cell door opened abruptly. "Ader?" a voice asked. *"Ja?"* *"Alles mitnehmen"* [Take everything with you]. That meant he was being transferred either to another prison or to a camp, freedom or death. Who could predict which it would be? But whether it was life or death, he was in God's hand. Thus he was very calm; he shook hands with his fellow prisoners and wished them the best. The door was closed again, and they looked at this as a bad omen. If he was to be set free, they would have left the cell door open to make sure that he didn't smuggle out any pieces of paper or messages.

[283]

"I am a prisoner of human beings," he wrote to me, "but also of God, and that is very comforting." He had complete faith in God.

That morning a letter for him, telling of the birth of his second son, had been delivered to the prison. He never received the message. I see God's mercy in this. It would otherwise have been so very hard to part from this life.

Then the guard returned all his papers. That meant he was free. But no, it was a mistake, he had to give them back. It had been no mistake. It was the last torment, a game of cat and mouse to make him feel he was defenseless prey in their hands. "We are playing with your life, a devil's delight of power. You thought you were free, little man, and that you were going home, but we are going to kill you!" Then he had to get into a car with two other men. In Utrecht three more prisoners joined them. I had the man who shot him tell me everything. Afterwards I traveled the same road. I gladly would have gone the same way with him. There were three cars. Right before Veenendaal they made another stop. Armed soldiers jumped on board. They drove through a blocked area and stopped at a spot under some tall, thick trees, on top of a hill, looking out over the Geldersche Valley. He knew our country so well!

He often roamed about on his bicycle, sometimes for days, over the Veluwe, the Utrechtsche hilltops. If there had been any doubt in his mind, now he knew for sure what his fate would be.

It was raining softly on the twentieth of November of last year [1944]. There, under the trees, the firing squad of marines stood ready with their rifles. He thought of his little boy, of all he loved so much, he thought of me. "If I don't see you again here on earth, be convinced that till my last breath, I will think of you in love," he wrote to me.

It's not for me that I would push these walls away
I gasp for room and scream for justice
I know I am caught in a merciless claw
And know the purpose that awaits me.

It's not for me, I have fought fierce and tough
By day or night I never asked for rest;
I have shared in suffering for the doomed
And now I sail for a faraway and brighter coast.

But I still have to say so many deep things
To her who always waits for me
I have to put the little baby in its bed
And kiss it a soft good night.

Enige aankondiging

✝

Na een leven vol strijd, verenigd met de dierbaren die haar voorgingen

JOHANNA A. ADER-APPELS
emeritus predikante
1906-1994
Draagster van het Verzetsherinneringskruis
Onderscheiden door Yad Vashem
Ridder in de Orde van Oranje-Nassau

31 juli 1994

Hanoi/Den Haag: D. A. V. E. Ader
D. M. Ader-Thomas Ellam

Redlands,
California: M. S. Andersen
Groningen: J. A. G. Froma-Ader

neven en nichten

Uitvaartdienst op vrijdag 5 augustus om 13.30 uur in de Nederlands Hervormde kerk te Nieuw Beerta. Begrafenis om 14.00 uur op de begraafplaats.

De overledene zal vrijdag vanaf 10.00 uur opgebaard zijn in het gebouw van de Ds. Ader Stichting, Ds. Aderstraat, Drieborg.

Gelegenheid tot afscheid nemen in Drieborg of vanaf 12.45 uur in de kerk te Nieuw Beerta.

Bezorgadres voor bloemen: Uitvaartcentrum, Acacialaan te Winschoten.

Correspondentieadres:
Prins Mauritslaan 54
2582 LT Den Haag

Obituary of Johanna A. Ader-Appels

Index